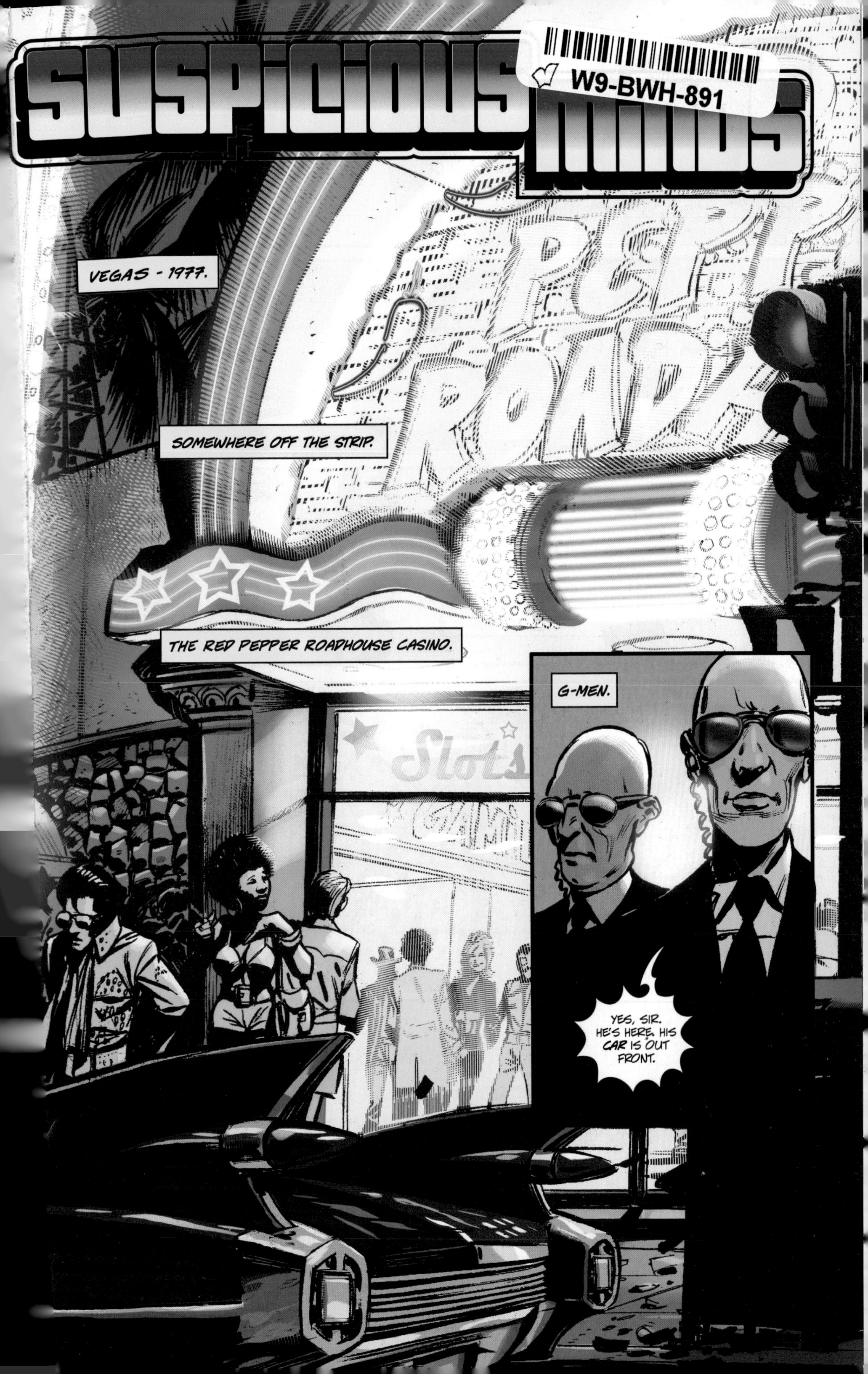
SUSPICIOUS MINDS
VEGAS - 1977.
SOMEWHERE OFF THE STRIP.
THE RED PEPPER ROADHOUSE CASINO.
Slots
G-MEN.
YES, SIR. HE'S HERE. HIS CAR IS OUT FRONT.

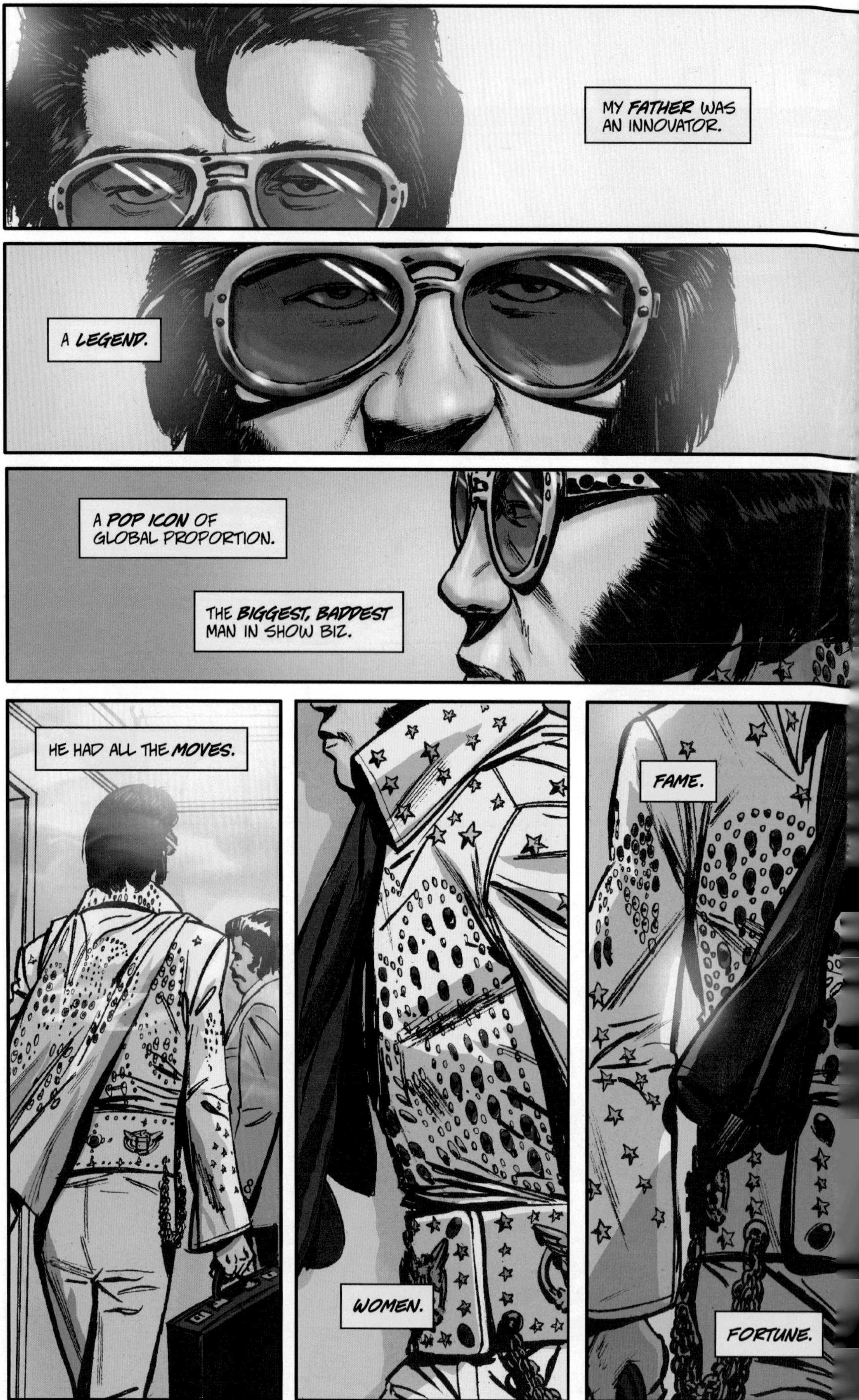
MY FATHER WAS AN INNOVATOR.
A LEGEND.
A POP ICON OF GLOBAL PROPORTION.
THE BIGGEST, BADDEST MAN IN SHOW BIZ.
HE HAD ALL THE MOVES.
WOMEN.
FAME.
FORTUNE.

POP STAR
ASSASSIN
in SUSPICIOUS MINDS

CRASH COMICS GROUP IN ASSOCIATION WITH ALL HAIL ENTERTAINMENT GROUP PRESENTS A FILM BY EDWARD LAVALLEE "POP STAR ASSASSIN"

WRITTEN AND DIRECTED BY EDWARD LAVALLEE VISUAL EFFECTS BY MARCELO BASILE CO-DIRECTED BY MATT CASHEL EDITED BY TARA CLOUD CLARK

ASSOCIATE PRODUCER NATHAN YOCUM PRODUCED BY RYAN SWANSON PRODUCED BY BEHEMOTH ENTERTAINMENT

BEHEMOTH

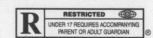RESTRICTED
UNDER 17 REQUIRES ACCOMPANYING
PARENT OR ADULT GUARDIAN

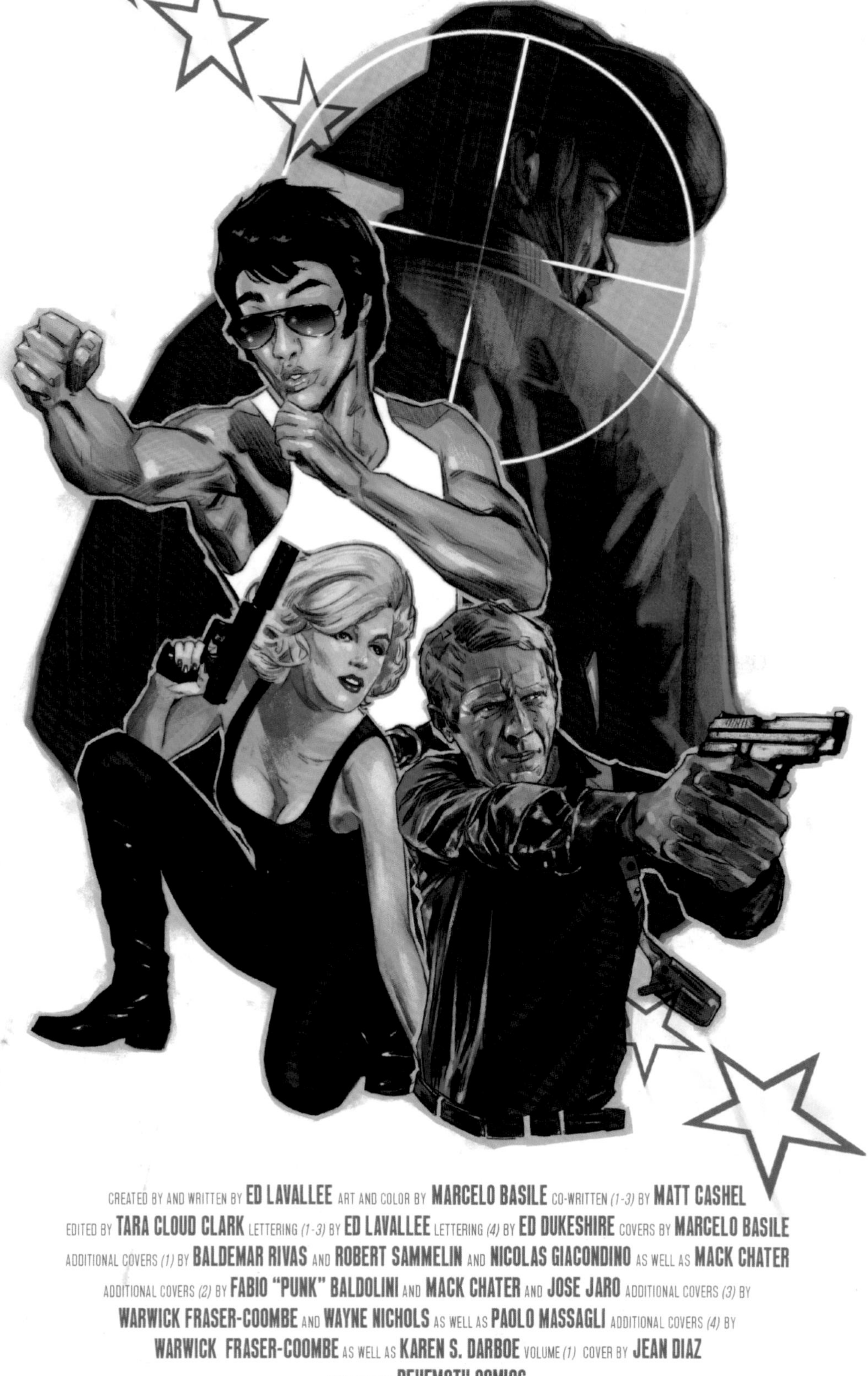

CREATED BY AND WRITTEN BY **ED LAVALLEE** ART AND COLOR BY **MARCELO BASILE** CO-WRITTEN *(1-3)* BY **MATT CASHEL**
EDITED BY **TARA CLOUD CLARK** LETTERING *(1-3)* BY **ED LAVALLEE** LETTERING *(4)* BY **ED DUKESHIRE** COVERS BY **MARCELO BASILE**
ADDITIONAL COVERS *(1)* BY **BALDEMAR RIVAS** AND **ROBERT SAMMELIN** AND **NICOLAS GIACONDINO** AS WELL AS **MACK CHATER**
ADDITIONAL COVERS *(2)* BY **FABIO "PUNK" BALDOLINI** AND **MACK CHATER** AND **JOSE JARO** ADDITIONAL COVERS *(3)* BY
WARWICK FRASER-COOMBE AND **WAYNE NICHOLS** AS WELL AS **PAOLO MASSAGLI** ADDITIONAL COVERS *(4)* BY
WARWICK FRASER-COOMBE AS WELL AS **KAREN S. DARBOE** VOLUME *(1)* COVER BY **JEAN DIAZ**
PUBLISHED BY **BEHEMOTH COMICS**
BEHEMOTH

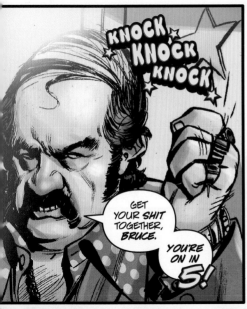

KNOCK KNOCK KNOCK

GET YOUR SHIT TOGETHER, BRUCE.

YOU'RE ON IN 5!

FUCK YOU VERY MUCH, RON!

LITTLE WEASEL.

NOW WHERE WAS I?

OH, YEAH...

WOMEN, FAME, FORTUNE...

HE HAD IT ALL...

AND A PAIR OF BLUE SUEDE SHOES...

WHICH I FIND HIGHLY SUSPECT!

OH!

HE WAS A JUNKIE, TOO.

FUCK IT!

LIKE FATHER, LIKE SON!

SNIFFFFFFFFFFF

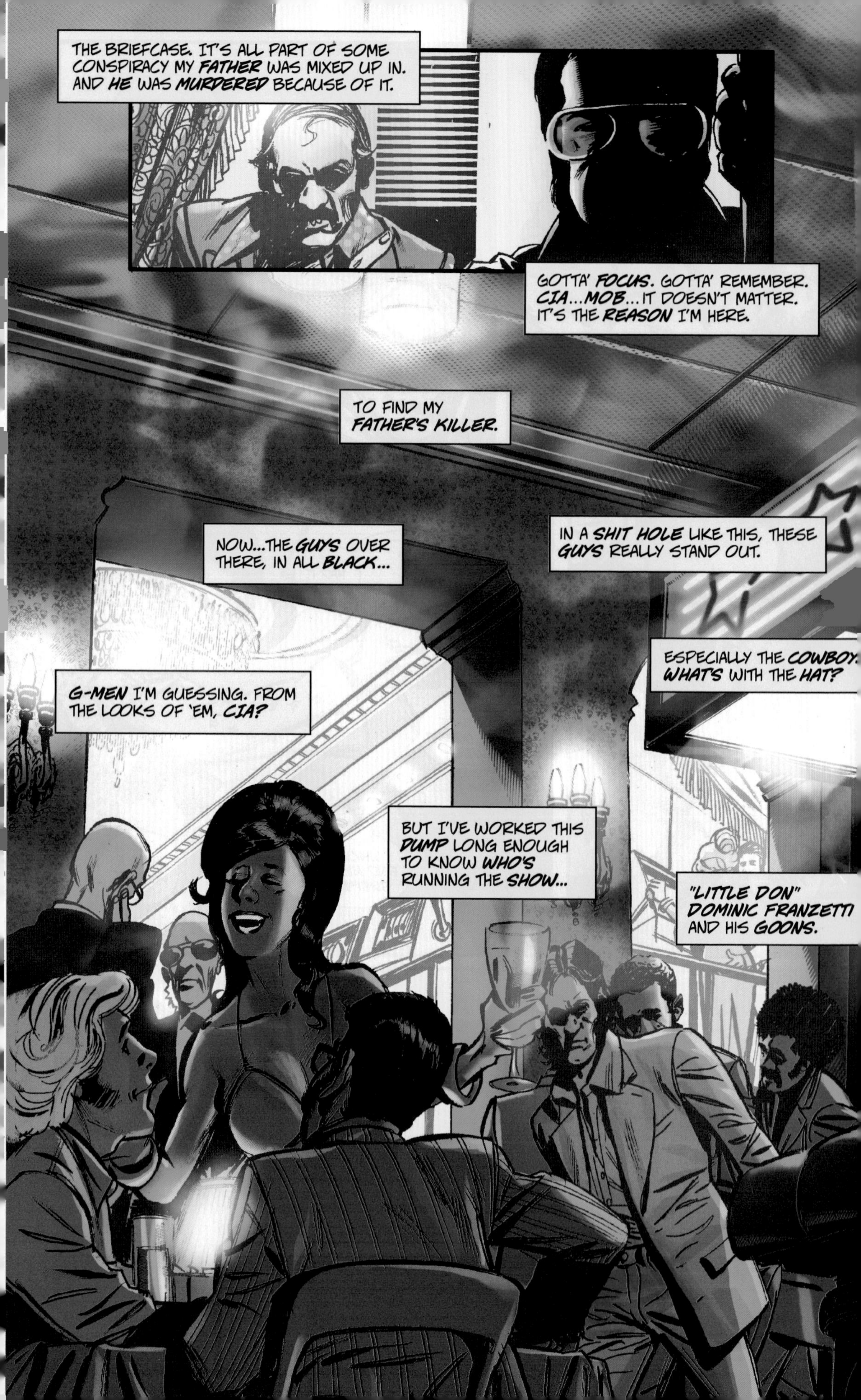
THE BRIEFCASE. IT'S ALL PART OF SOME CONSPIRACY MY FATHER WAS MIXED UP IN. AND HE WAS MURDERED BECAUSE OF IT.
GOTTA' FOCUS. GOTTA' REMEMBER. CIA…MOB… IT DOESN'T MATTER. IT'S THE REASON I'M HERE.
TO FIND MY FATHER'S KILLER.
NOW...THE GUYS OVER THERE, IN ALL BLACK...
IN A SHIT HOLE LIKE THIS, THESE GUYS REALLY STAND OUT.
G-MEN I'M GUESSING. FROM THE LOOKS OF 'EM, CIA?
ESPECIALLY THE COWBOY. WHAT'S WITH THE HAT?
BUT I'VE WORKED THIS DUMP LONG ENOUGH TO KNOW WHO'S RUNNING THE SHOW...
"LITTLE DON" DOMINIC FRANZETTI AND HIS GOONS.

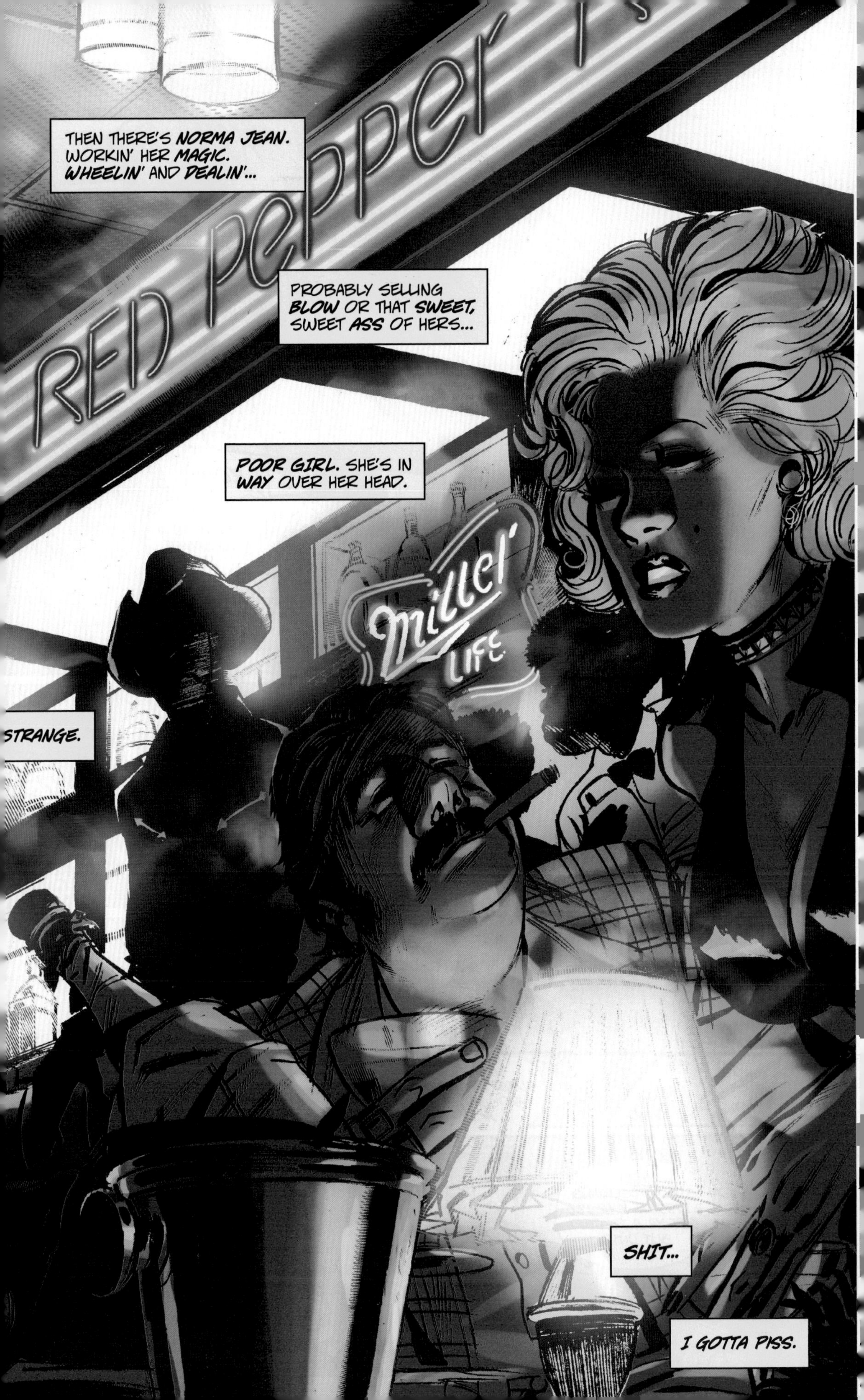
RED PEPPER'S
THEN THERE'S NORMA JEAN. WORKIN' HER MAGIC. WHEELIN' AND DEALIN'...
PROBABLY SELLING BLOW OR THAT SWEET, SWEET ASS OF HERS...
POOR GIRL. SHE'S IN WAY OVER HER HEAD.
Miller LITE
STRANGE.
SHIT...
I GOTTA PISS.

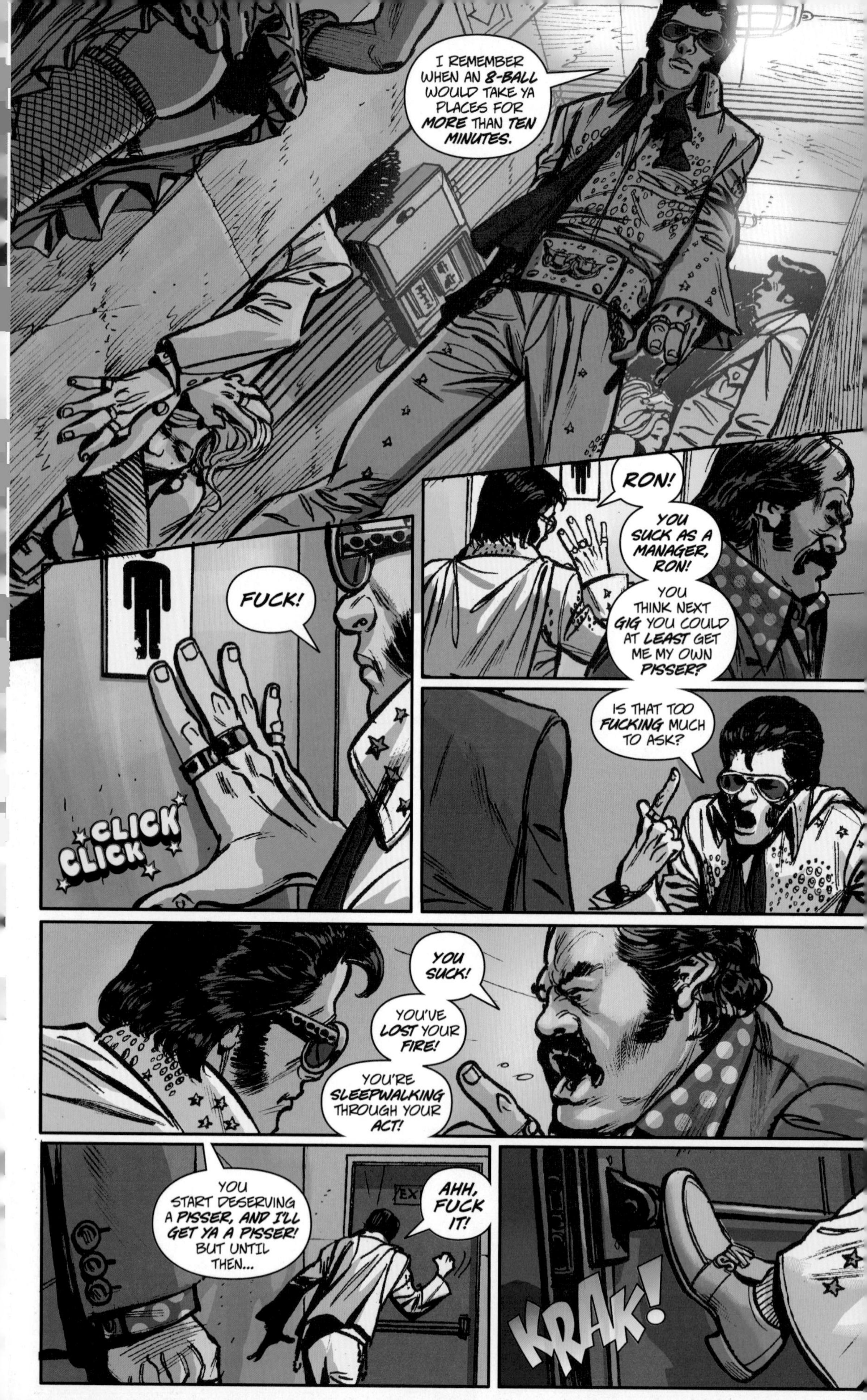
I REMEMBER WHEN AN 8-BALL WOULD TAKE YA PLACES FOR MORE THAN TEN MINUTES.
RON!
YOU SUCK AS A MANAGER, RON!
YOU THINK NEXT GIG YOU COULD AT LEAST GET ME MY OWN PISSER?
FUCK!
CLICK CLICK
IS THAT TOO FUCKING MUCH TO ASK?
YOU SUCK!
YOU'VE LOST YOUR FIRE!
YOU'RE SLEEPWALKING THROUGH YOUR ACT!
YOU START DESERVING A PISSER, AND I'LL GET YA A PISSER! BUT UNTIL THEN...
AHH, FUCK IT!
KRAK!

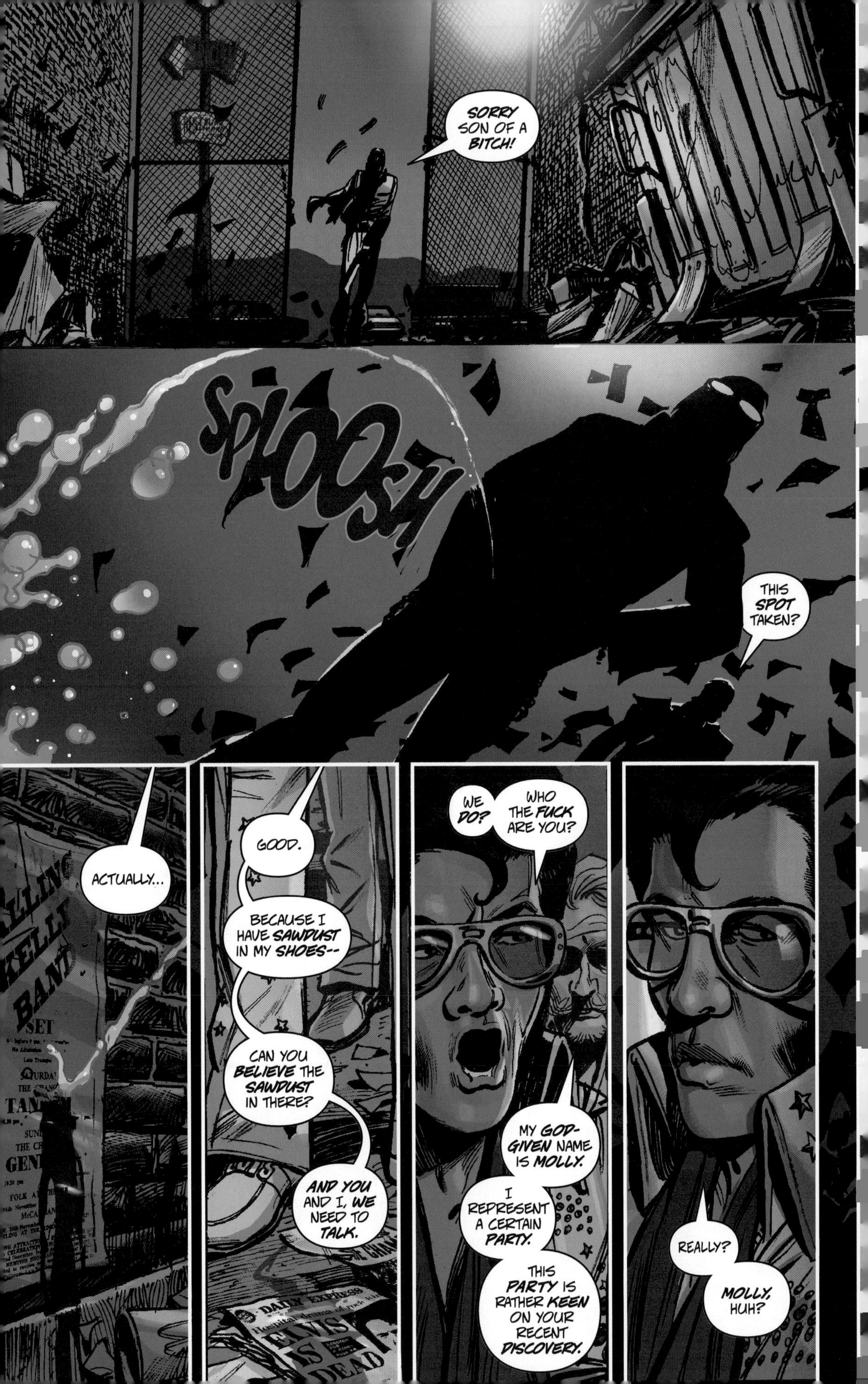
SORRY SON OF A BITCH!
SPLOOSH
THIS SPOT TAKEN?
ACTUALLY...
GOOD.
BECAUSE I HAVE SAWDUST IN MY SHOES--
CAN YOU BELIEVE THE SAWDUST IN THERE?
AND YOU AND I, WE NEED TO TALK.
WE DO?
WHO THE FUCK ARE YOU?
MY GOD-GIVEN NAME IS MOLLY.
I REPRESENT A CERTAIN PARTY.
THIS PARTY IS RATHER KEEN ON YOUR RECENT DISCOVERY.
REALLY?
MOLLY, HUH?
DAILY EXPRESS
ELVIS IS DEAD

THE *NAME*, DON'T WORRY ABOUT *IT*.

I WEAR IT WITH *PRIDE*. USED TO HATE IT--DIDN'T DO ANY *GOOD*.

YEAH?

WELL, I'M ABOUT *DONE* HERE.

WE *KNOW* ABOUT YOU, *MR. BRUCE*.

HOW DO YOU KNOW MY *NAME?*

BECAUSE OF *WHAT* YOU'RE *AFTER*.

I KNEW A MAN *ONCE*, NOT UNLIKE *YOURSELF*.

THE *ONLY* THING KEEPING HIM *ALIVE* WAS HIS *THIRST* FOR REVENGE.

IT KEPT HIS HEART *BEATING*, HIS LEGS *MOVING*.

I CAN'T SAY I *CARE* FOR THIS *MUCH*...

I'M *MIDSTREAM* HERE, MAN.

BUT WHEN HE DISCOVERED HOW UNSATISFYING HIS *VENGEANCE* WOULD BE...

THE *WILL* LEFT HIM, AND HE *DIED*.

ALONE.

WITH A *GLASSY* LOOK IN HIS *EMPTY* EYE.

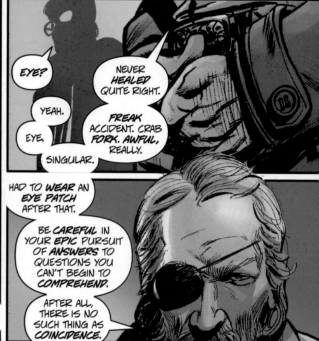

EYE?

YEAH. EYE.

SINGULAR.

NEVER *HEALED* QUITE RIGHT.

FREAK ACCIDENT. CRAB *FORK*. AWFUL, REALLY.

HAD TO *WEAR* AN *EYE PATCH* AFTER THAT.

BE *CAREFUL* IN YOUR *EPIC* PURSUIT OF *ANSWERS* TO QUESTIONS YOU CAN'T BEGIN TO *COMPREHEND*.

AFTER ALL, THERE IS NO SUCH THING AS *COINCIDENCE*.

WHAT ARE YOU *STARING* AT?

OH, HER.

DON'T *BRING* HER *DOWN* WITH YOU, *BRUCE*.

SHE HAS ENOUGH *PROBLEMS* OF HER OWN.

SHE'S A *GOOD* GIRL, THOUGH. ORIGINALLY FROM *TEXAS*.

SO SHE SAYS, BUT SOME OF US KNOW DIFFERENT.

I KNOW *NORMA JEAN* PRETTY DAMNED WELL, *STRANGER*--

MOLLY.

MOLLY, RIGHT?

SO WHATRE YA HERE TO *TELL* ME, *MOLLY?*

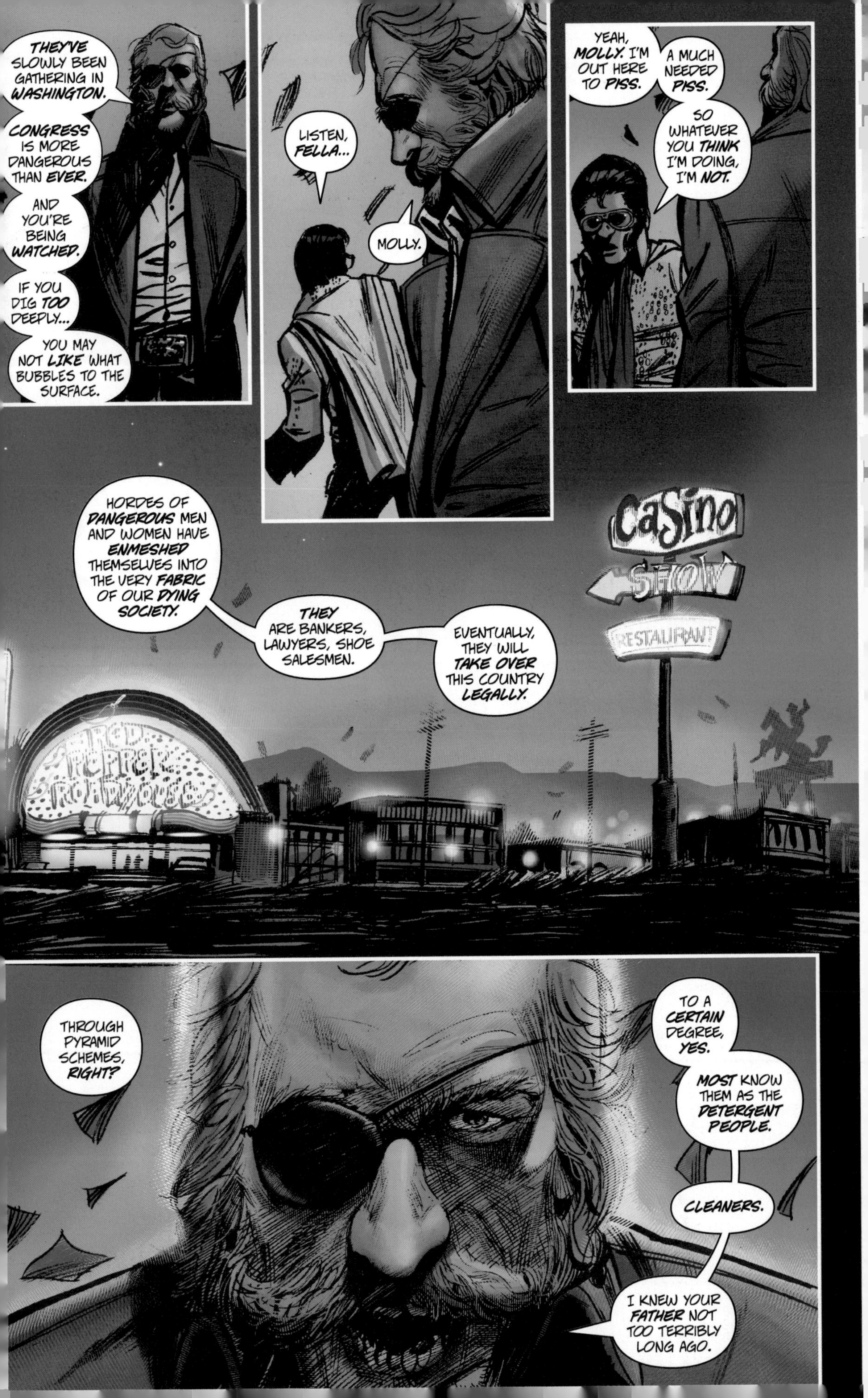

THEY'VE SLOWLY BEEN GATHERING IN WASHINGTON.
CONGRESS IS MORE DANGEROUS THAN EVER.
AND YOU'RE BEING WATCHED.
IF YOU DIG TOO DEEPLY...
YOU MAY NOT LIKE WHAT BUBBLES TO THE SURFACE.
LISTEN, FELLA...
MOLLY.
YEAH, MOLLY. I'M OUT HERE TO PISS.
A MUCH NEEDED PISS.
SO WHATEVER YOU THINK I'M DOING, I'M NOT.
CASINO
SHOW
RESTAURANT
RED PEPPER ROADHOUSE
HORDES OF DANGEROUS MEN AND WOMEN HAVE ENMESHED THEMSELVES INTO THE VERY FABRIC OF OUR DYING SOCIETY.
THEY ARE BANKERS, LAWYERS, SHOE SALESMEN.
EVENTUALLY, THEY WILL TAKE OVER THIS COUNTRY LEGALLY.
THROUGH PYRAMID SCHEMES, RIGHT?
TO A CERTAIN DEGREE, YES.
MOST KNOW THEM AS THE DETERGENT PEOPLE.
CLEANERS.
I KNEW YOUR FATHER NOT TOO TERRIBLY LONG AGO.

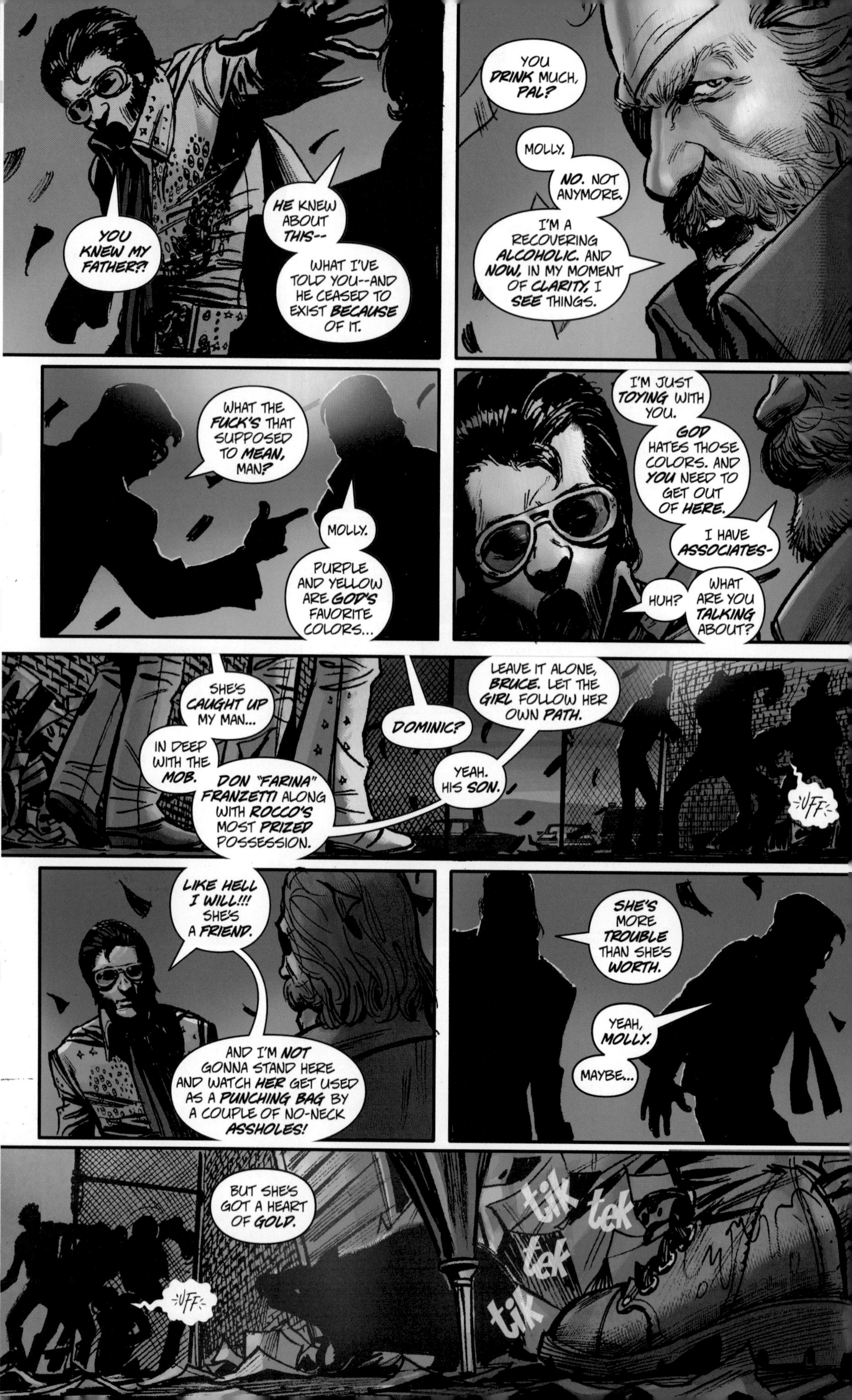
YOU KNEW MY FATHER?!
HE KNEW ABOUT THIS--
WHAT I'VE TOLD YOU--AND HE CEASED TO EXIST BECAUSE OF IT.
YOU DRINK MUCH, PAL?
MOLLY.
NO. NOT ANYMORE.
I'M A RECOVERING ALCOHOLIC. AND NOW, IN MY MOMENT OF CLARITY, I SEE THINGS.
WHAT THE FUCK'S THAT SUPPOSED TO MEAN, MAN?
MOLLY.
PURPLE AND YELLOW ARE GOD'S FAVORITE COLORS...
I'M JUST TOYING WITH YOU.
GOD HATES THOSE COLORS. AND YOU NEED TO GET OUT OF HERE.
I HAVE ASSOCIATES-
HUH?
WHAT ARE YOU TALKING ABOUT?
SHE'S CAUGHT UP MY MAN...
IN DEEP WITH THE MOB.
DON "FARINA" FRANZETTI ALONG WITH ROCCO'S MOST PRIZED POSSESSION.
DOMINIC?
YEAH. HIS SON.
LEAVE IT ALONE, BRUCE. LET THE GIRL FOLLOW HER OWN PATH.
UFF
LIKE HELL I WILL!!! SHE'S A FRIEND.
AND I'M NOT GONNA STAND HERE AND WATCH HER GET USED AS A PUNCHING BAG BY A COUPLE OF NO-NECK ASSHOLES!
SHE'S MORE TROUBLE THAN SHE'S WORTH.
YEAH, MOLLY.
MAYBE...
BUT SHE'S GOT A HEART OF GOLD.
UFF
tik tek tek tik

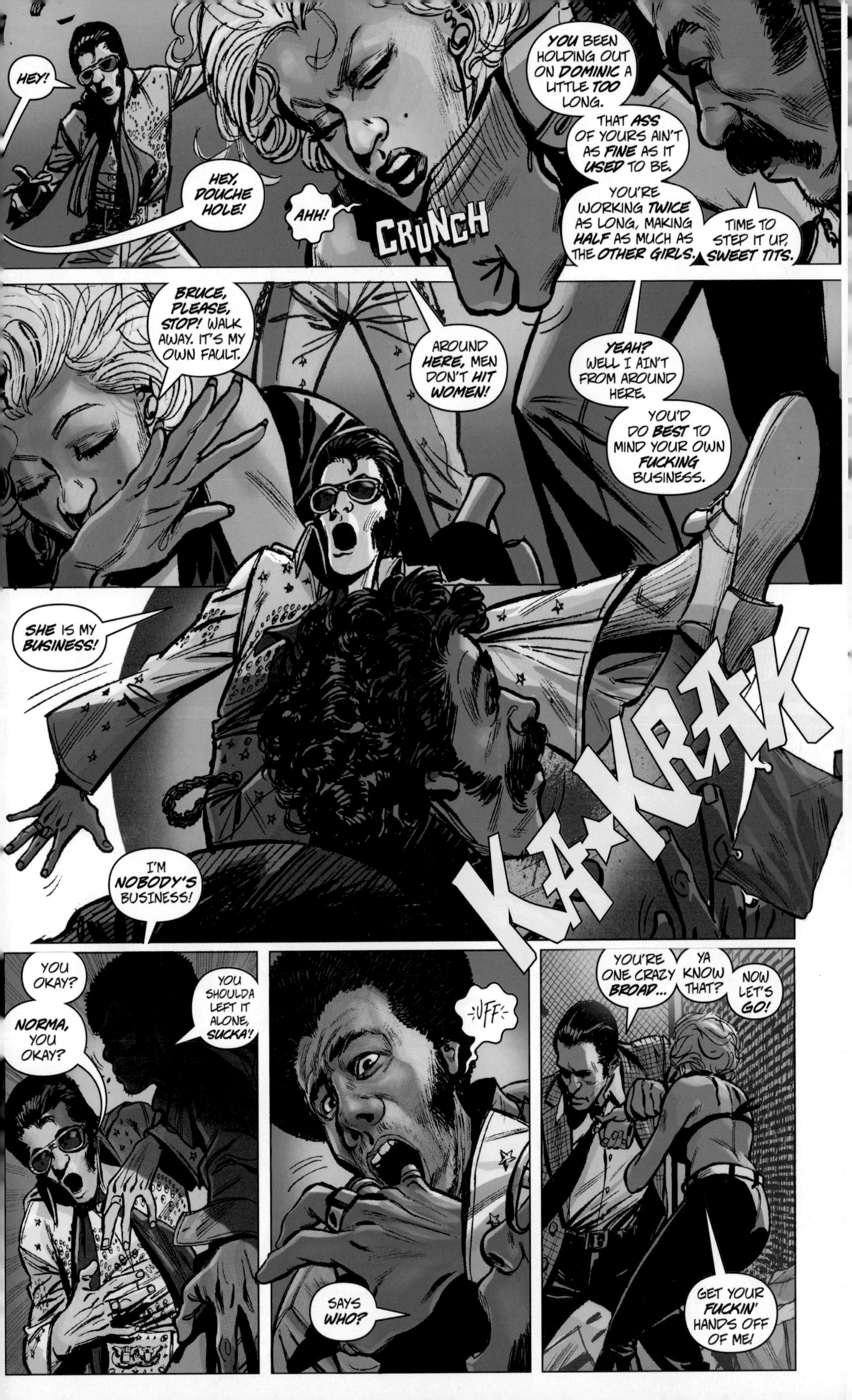
HEY!
HEY, DOUCHE HOLE!
AHH!
CRUNCH
YOU BEEN HOLDING OUT ON DOMINIC A LITTLE TOO LONG.
THAT ASS OF YOURS AIN'T AS FINE AS IT USED TO BE.
YOU'RE WORKING TWICE AS LONG, MAKING HALF AS MUCH AS THE OTHER GIRLS.
TIME TO STEP IT UP, SWEET TITS.
BRUCE, PLEASE, STOP! WALK AWAY. IT'S MY OWN FAULT.
AROUND HERE, MEN DON'T HIT WOMEN!
YEAH? WELL I AIN'T FROM AROUND HERE.
YOU'D DO BEST TO MIND YOUR OWN FUCKING BUSINESS.
SHE IS MY BUSINESS!
KA-KRAK
I'M NOBODY'S BUSINESS!
YOU OKAY?
NORMA, YOU OKAY?
YOU SHOULDA LEFT IT ALONE, SUCKA'!
UFF
SAYS WHO?
YOU'RE ONE CRAZY BROAD...
YA KNOW THAT?
NOW LET'S GO!
GET YOUR FUCKIN' HANDS OFF OF ME!

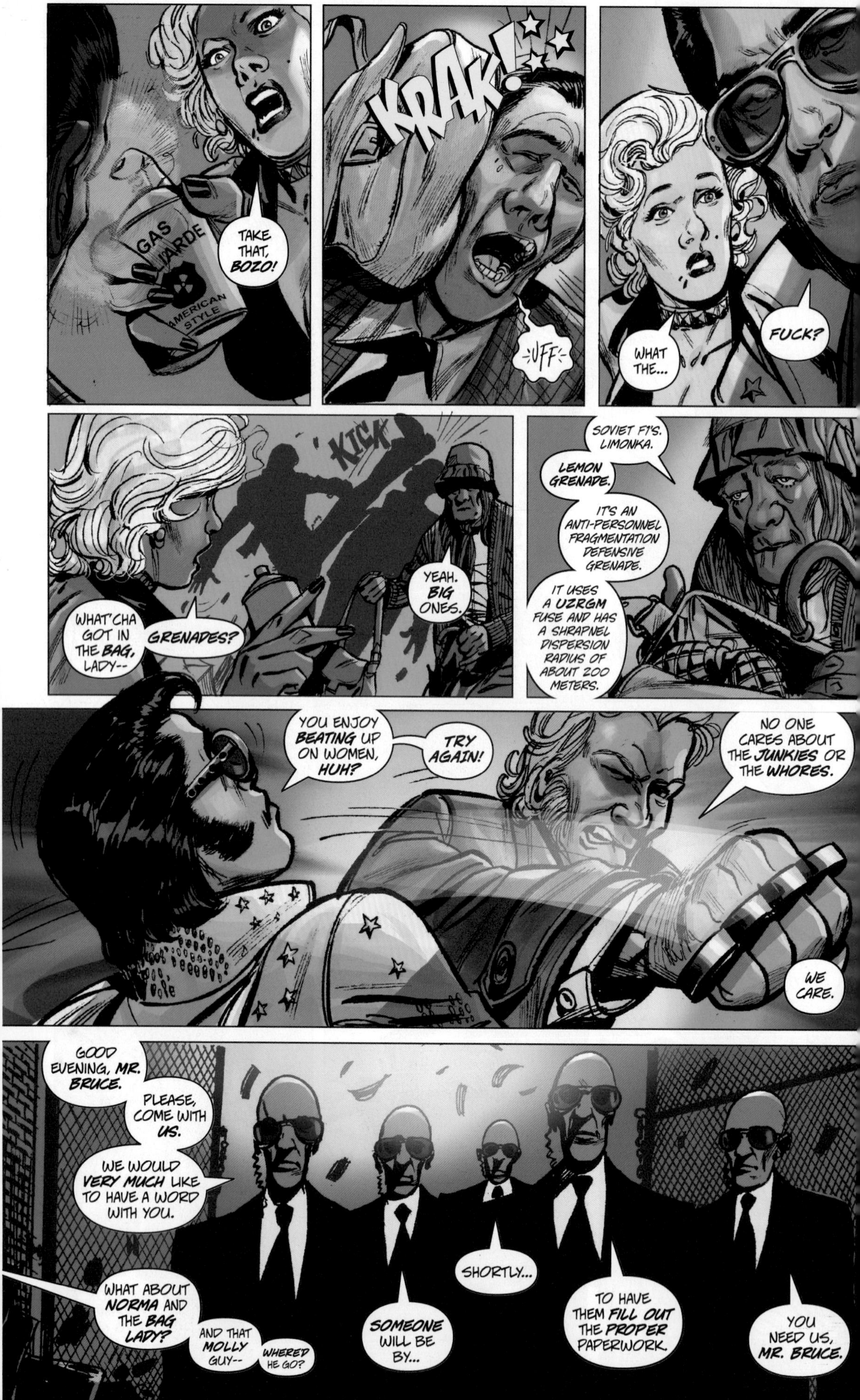
GAS LARDE
AMERICAN STYLE
TAKE THAT, BOZO!
KRAK!
UFF
WHAT THE...
FUCK?
KICK
WHAT'CHA GOT IN THE BAG, LADY--
GRENADES?
YEAH. BIG ONES.
SOVIET F1'S. LIMONKA.
LEMON GRENADE.
IT'S AN ANTI-PERSONNEL FRAGMENTATION DEFENSIVE GRENADE.
IT USES A UZRGM FUSE AND HAS A SHRAPNEL DISPERSION RADIUS OF ABOUT 200 METERS.
YOU ENJOY BEATING UP ON WOMEN, HUH?
TRY AGAIN!
NO ONE CARES ABOUT THE JUNKIES OR THE WHORES.
WE CARE.
GOOD EVENING, MR. BRUCE.
PLEASE, COME WITH US.
WE WOULD VERY MUCH LIKE TO HAVE A WORD WITH YOU.
WHAT ABOUT NORMA AND THE BAG LADY?
AND THAT MOLLY GUY--
WHERE'D HE GO?
SOMEONE WILL BE BY...
SHORTLY...
TO HAVE THEM FILL OUT THE PROPER PAPERWORK.
YOU NEED US, MR. BRUCE.

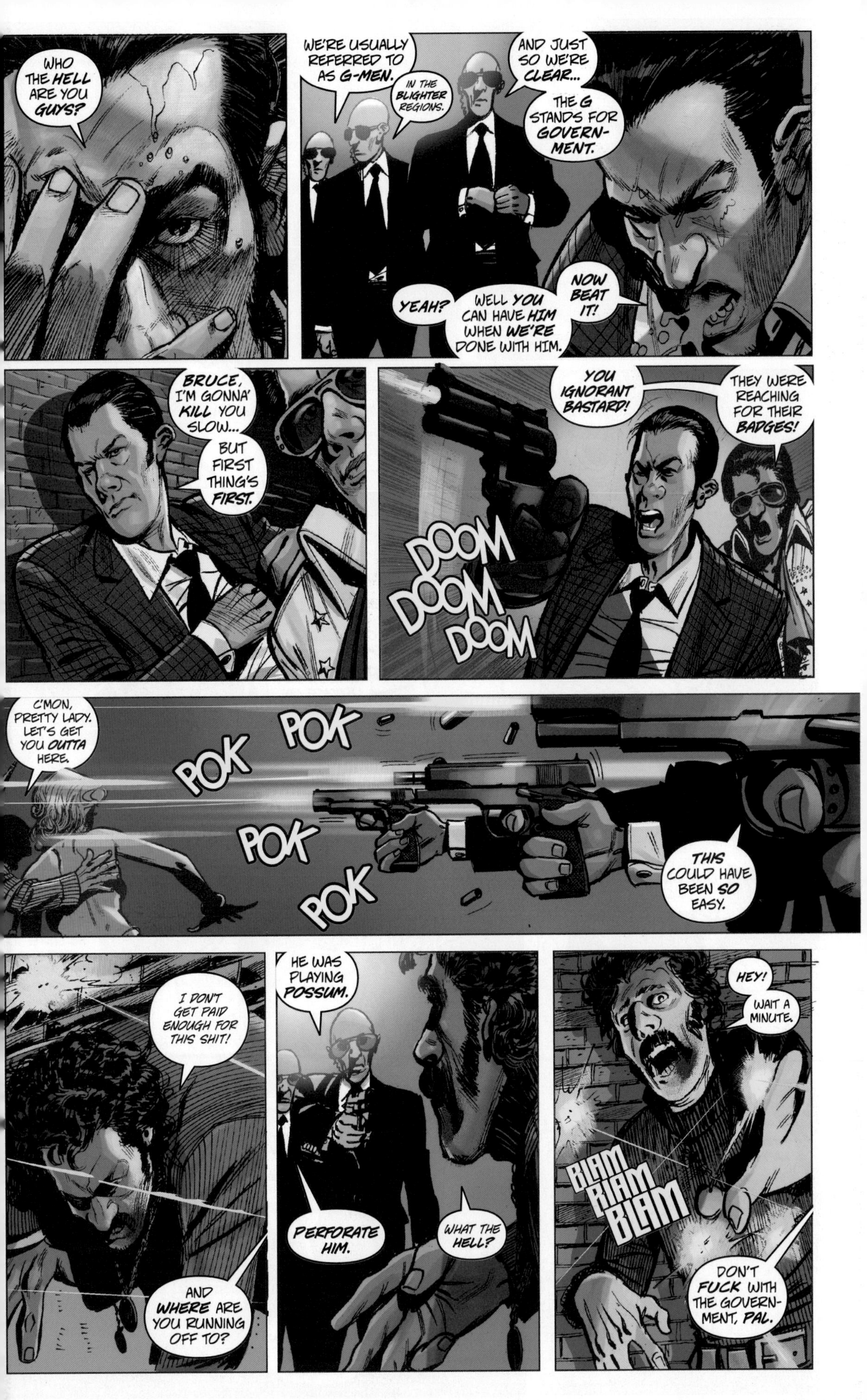

WHO THE HELL ARE YOU GUYS?
WE'RE USUALLY REFERRED TO AS G-MEN.
IN THE BLIGHTER REGIONS.
AND JUST SO WE'RE CLEAR...
THE G STANDS FOR GOVERN-MENT.
YEAH?
WELL YOU CAN HAVE HIM WHEN WE'RE DONE WITH HIM.
NOW BEAT IT!
BRUCE, I'M GONNA' KILL YOU SLOW...
BUT FIRST THING'S FIRST.
YOU IGNORANT BASTARD!
THEY WERE REACHING FOR THEIR BADGES!
DOOM DOOM DOOM
C'MON, PRETTY LADY. LET'S GET YOU OUTTA HERE.
POK POK
POK
POK
THIS COULD HAVE BEEN SO EASY.
I DON'T GET PAID ENOUGH FOR THIS SHIT!
AND WHERE ARE YOU RUNNING OFF TO?
HE WAS PLAYING POSSUM.
PERFORATE HIM.
WHAT THE HELL?
HEY!
WAIT A MINUTE.
BLAM BLAM BLAM
DON'T FUCK WITH THE GOVERN-MENT, PAL.

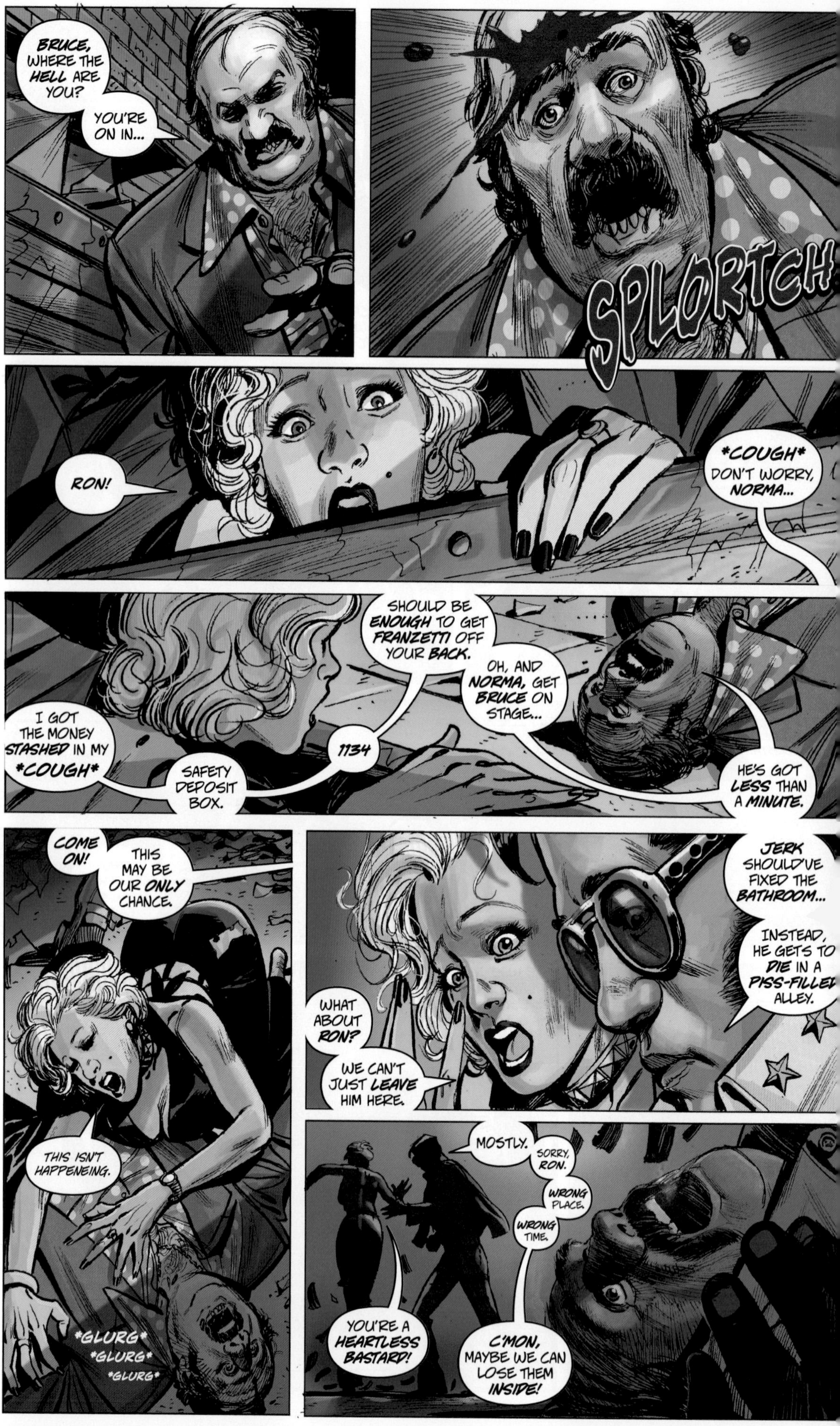
BRUCE, WHERE THE HELL ARE YOU?
YOU'RE ON IN...
SPLORTCH
RON!
COUGH DON'T WORRY, NORMA...
I GOT THE MONEY STASHED IN MY *COUGH*
SAFETY DEPOSIT BOX.
1134
SHOULD BE ENOUGH TO GET FRANZETTI OFF YOUR BACK.
OH, AND NORMA, GET BRUCE ON STAGE...
HE'S GOT LESS THAN A MINUTE.
COME ON!
THIS MAY BE OUR ONLY CHANCE.
THIS ISN'T HAPPENEING.
GLURG
GLURG
GLURG
JERK SHOULD'VE FIXED THE BATHROOM...
INSTEAD, HE GETS TO DIE IN A PISS-FILLED ALLEY.
WHAT ABOUT RON?
WE CAN'T JUST LEAVE HIM HERE.
YOU'RE A HEARTLESS BASTARD!
MOSTLY.
SORRY, RON.
WRONG PLACE.
WRONG TIME.
C'MON, MAYBE WE CAN LOSE THEM INSIDE!

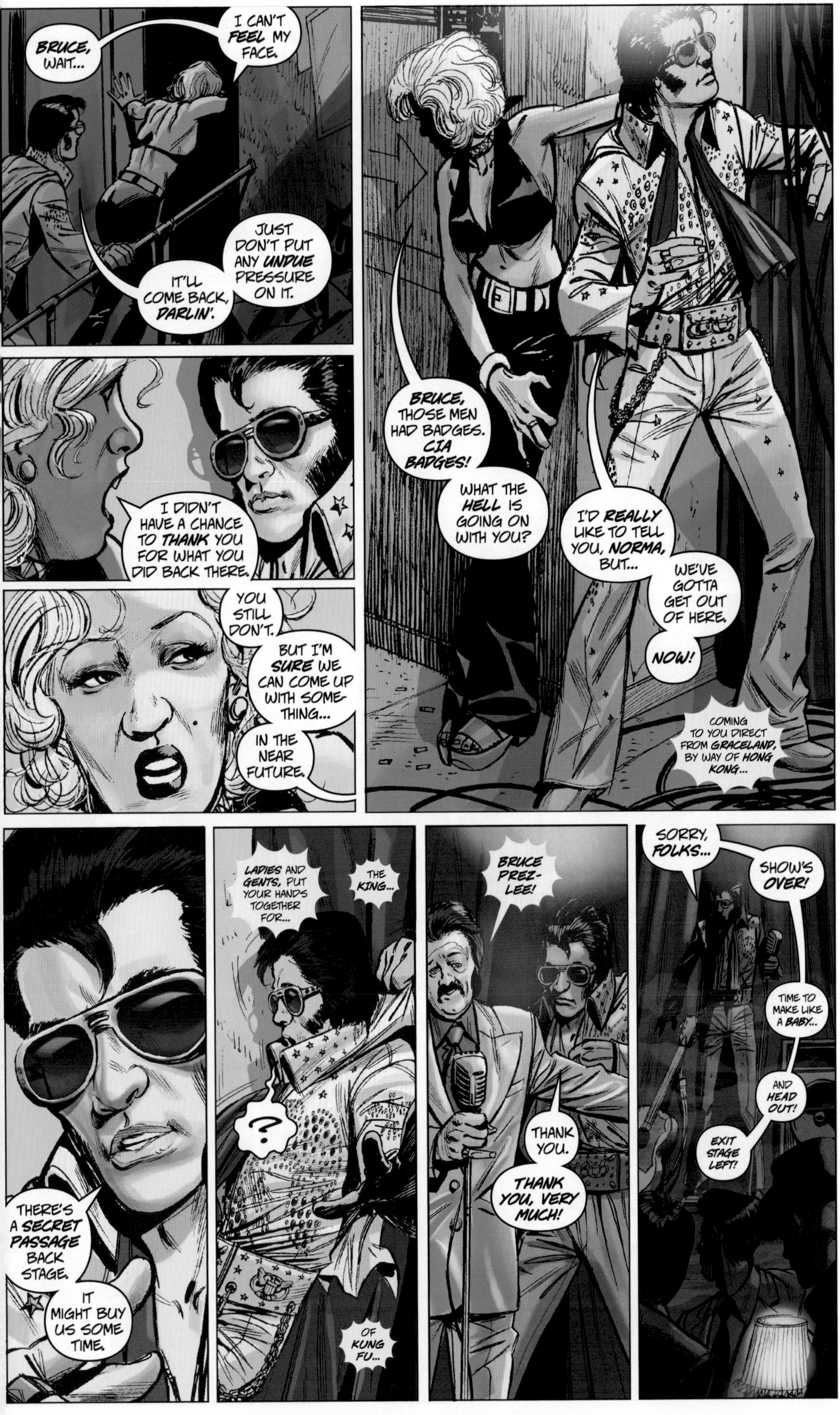
BRUCE, WAIT...
I CAN'T FEEL MY FACE.
IT'LL COME BACK, DARLIN'.
JUST DON'T PUT ANY UNDUE PRESSURE ON IT.
I DIDN'T HAVE A CHANCE TO THANK YOU FOR WHAT YOU DID BACK THERE.
YOU STILL DON'T.
BUT I'M SURE WE CAN COME UP WITH SOME-THING...
IN THE NEAR FUTURE.
BRUCE, THOSE MEN HAD BADGES. CIA BADGES!
WHAT THE HELL IS GOING ON WITH YOU?
I'D REALLY LIKE TO TELL YOU, NORMA, BUT...
WE'VE GOTTA GET OUT OF HERE.
NOW!
COMING TO YOU DIRECT FROM GRACELAND, BY WAY OF HONG KONG...
THERE'S A SECRET PASSAGE BACK STAGE.
IT MIGHT BUY US SOME TIME.
LADIES AND GENTS, PUT YOUR HANDS TOGETHER FOR...
THE KING...
?
OF KUNG FU...
BRUCE PREZ-LEE!
THANK YOU.
THANK YOU, VERY MUCH!
SORRY, FOLKS...
SHOW'S OVER!
TIME TO MAKE LIKE A BABY...
AND HEAD OUT!
EXIT STAGE LEFT!

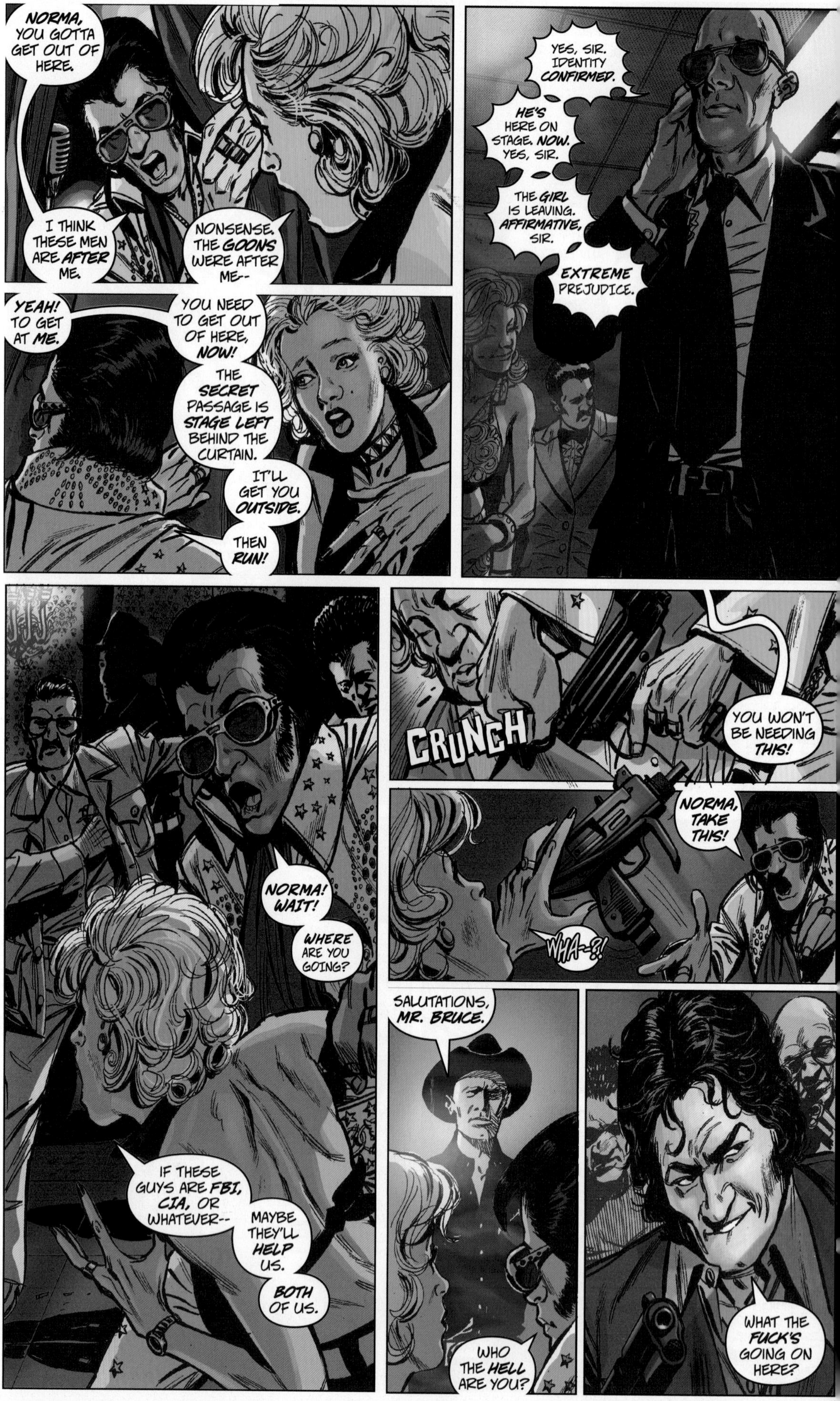
NORMA, YOU GOTTA GET OUT OF HERE.
I THINK THESE MEN ARE AFTER ME.
NONSENSE. THE GOONS WERE AFTER ME--
YES, SIR. IDENTITY CONFIRMED.
HE'S HERE ON STAGE. NOW. YES, SIR.
THE GIRL IS LEAVING. AFFIRMATIVE, SIR.
EXTREME PREJUDICE.
YEAH! TO GET AT ME.
YOU NEED TO GET OUT OF HERE, NOW!
THE SECRET PASSAGE IS STAGE LEFT BEHIND THE CURTAIN.
IT'LL GET YOU OUTSIDE.
THEN RUN!
NORMA! WAIT!
WHERE ARE YOU GOING?
IF THESE GUYS ARE FBI, CIA, OR WHATEVER--
MAYBE THEY'LL HELP US.
BOTH OF US.
CRUNCH
YOU WON'T BE NEEDING THIS!
NORMA, TAKE THIS!
WHA--?!
SALUTATIONS, MR. BRUCE.
WHO THE HELL ARE YOU?
WHAT THE FUCK'S GOING ON HERE?

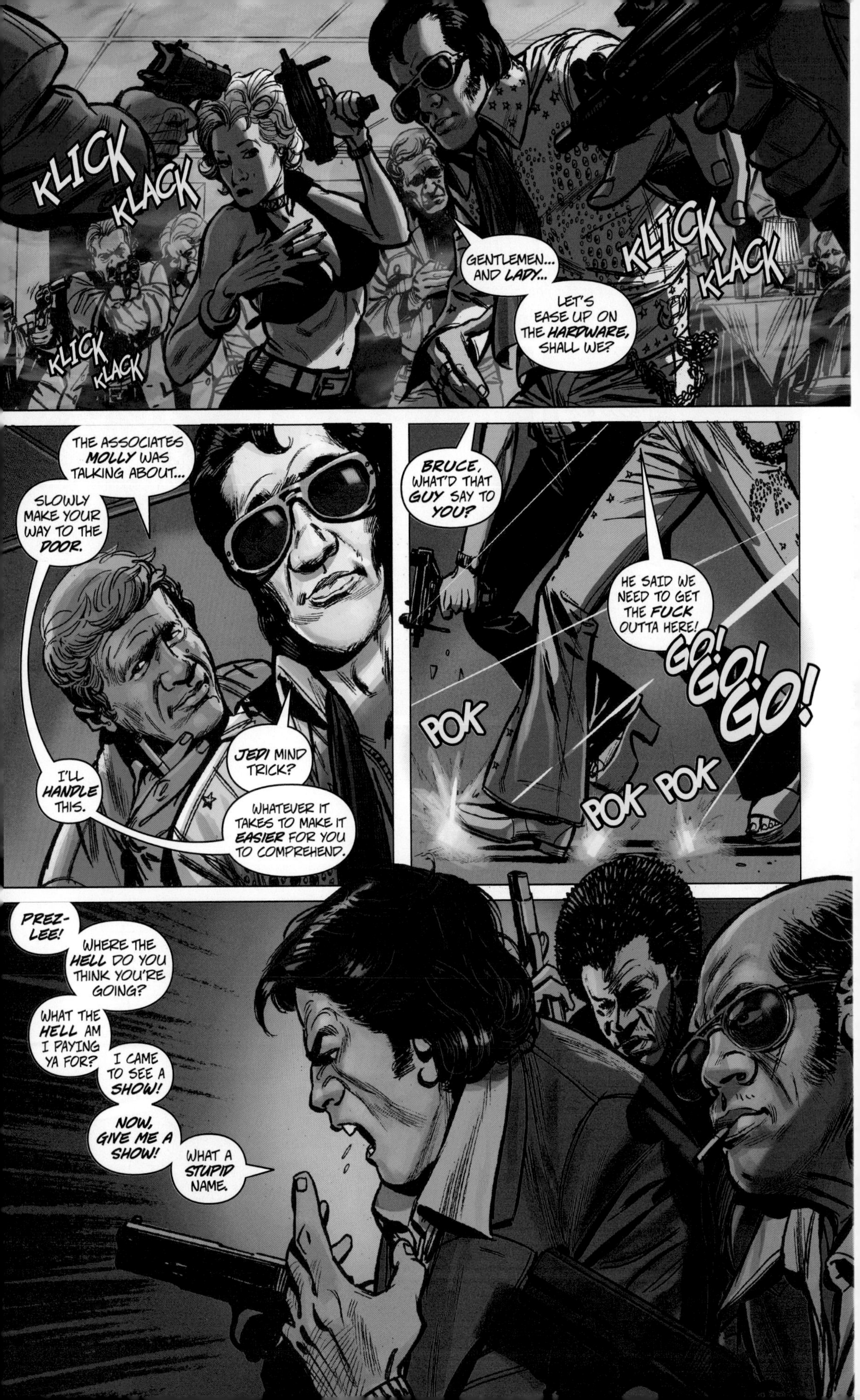
KLICK KLACK
KLICK KLACK
KLICK KLACK
GENTLEMEN... AND LADY...
LET'S EASE UP ON THE HARDWARE, SHALL WE?
THE ASSOCIATES MOLLY WAS TALKING ABOUT...
SLOWLY MAKE YOUR WAY TO THE DOOR.
I'LL HANDLE THIS.
JEDI MIND TRICK?
WHATEVER IT TAKES TO MAKE IT EASIER FOR YOU TO COMPREHEND.
BRUCE, WHAT'D THAT GUY SAY TO YOU?
HE SAID WE NEED TO GET THE FUCK OUTTA HERE!
GO! GO! GO!
POK
POK POK
PREZ-LEE!
WHERE THE HELL DO YOU THINK YOU'RE GOING?
WHAT THE HELL AM I PAYING YA FOR?
I CAME TO SEE A SHOW!
NOW, GIVE ME A SHOW!
WHAT A STUPID NAME.

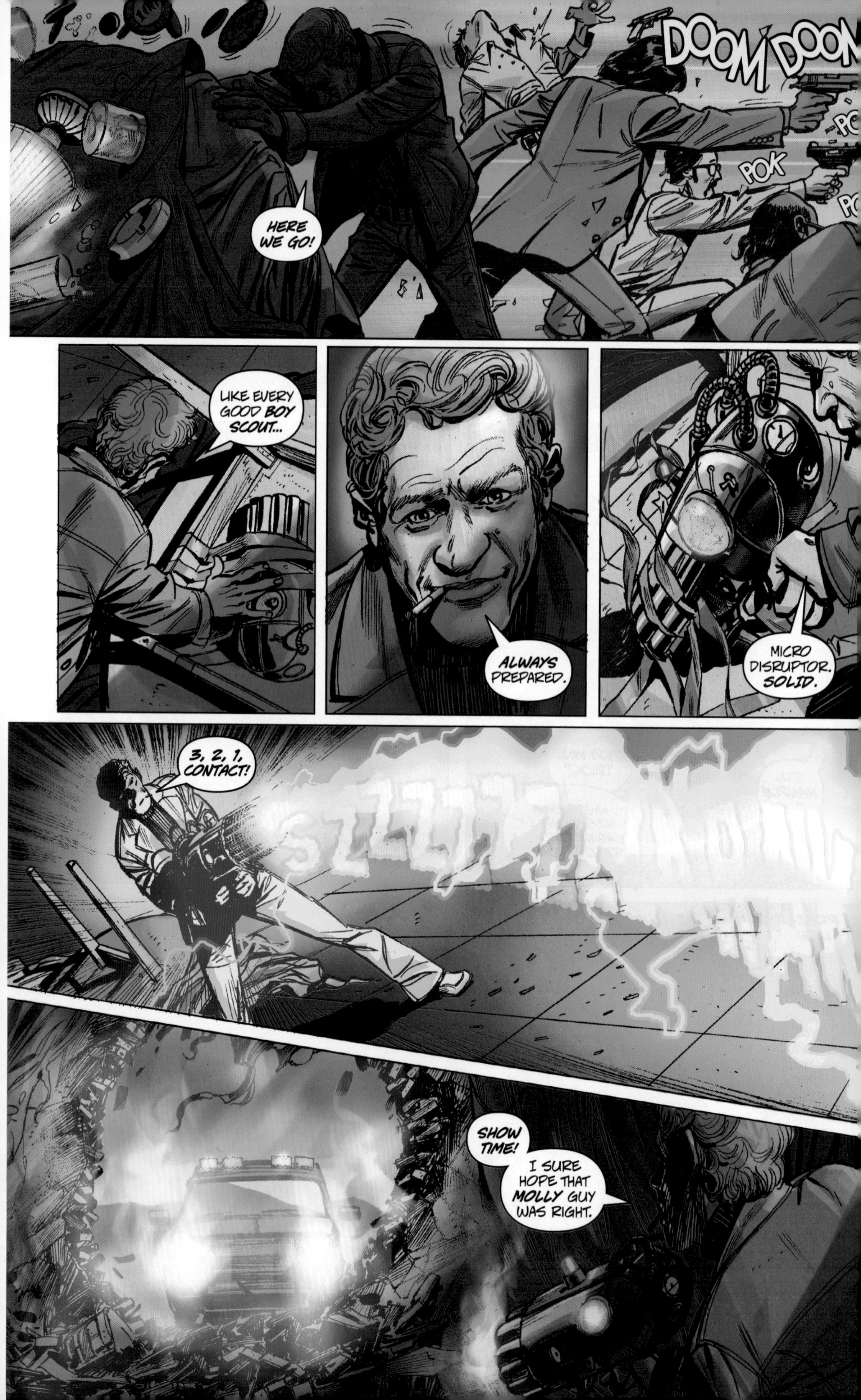
DOOM DOOM
POK
HERE WE GO!
LIKE EVERY GOOD BOY SCOUT...
ALWAYS PREPARED.
MICRO DISRUPTOR. SOLID.
3, 2, 1, CONTACT!
SHOW TIME!
I SURE HOPE THAT MOLLY GUY WAS RIGHT.

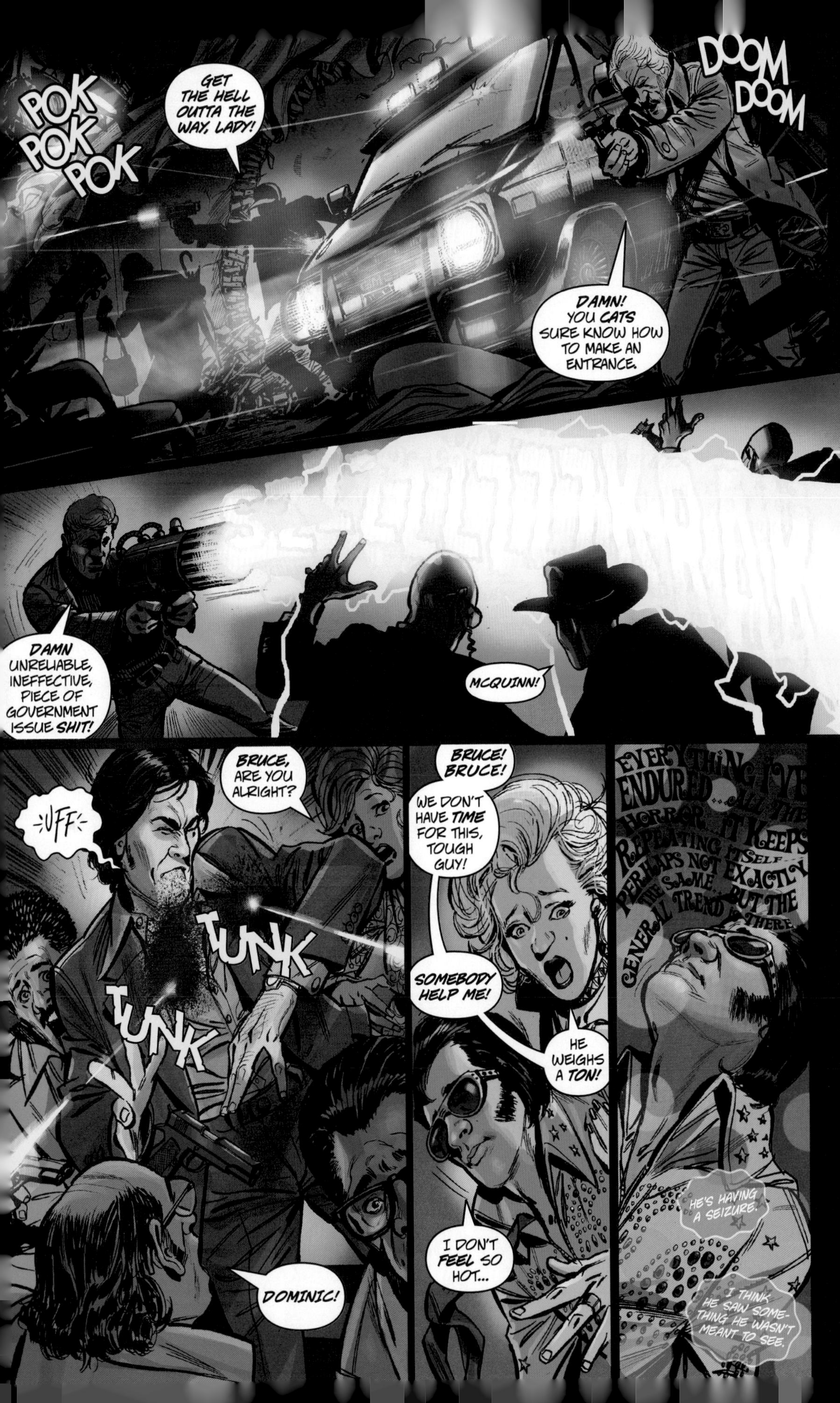
POK POK POK
GET THE HELL OUTTA THE WAY, LADY!
DOOM DOOM
DAMN! YOU CATS SURE KNOW HOW TO MAKE AN ENTRANCE.
DAMN UNRELIABLE, INEFFECTIVE, PIECE OF GOVERNMENT ISSUE SHIT!
MCQUINN!
UFF
BRUCE, ARE YOU ALRIGHT?
TUNK
TUNK
DOMINIC!
BRUCE! BRUCE!
WE DON'T HAVE TIME FOR THIS, TOUGH GUY!
SOMEBODY HELP ME!
HE WEIGHS A TON!
I DON'T FEEL SO HOT...
EVERYTHING I'VE ENDURED... ALL THE HORROR... IT KEEPS REPEATING ITSELF— PERHAPS NOT EXACTLY THE SAME... BUT THE GENERAL TREND IS THERE.
HE'S HAVING A SEIZURE.
I THINK HE SAW SOMETHING HE WASN'T MEANT TO SEE.

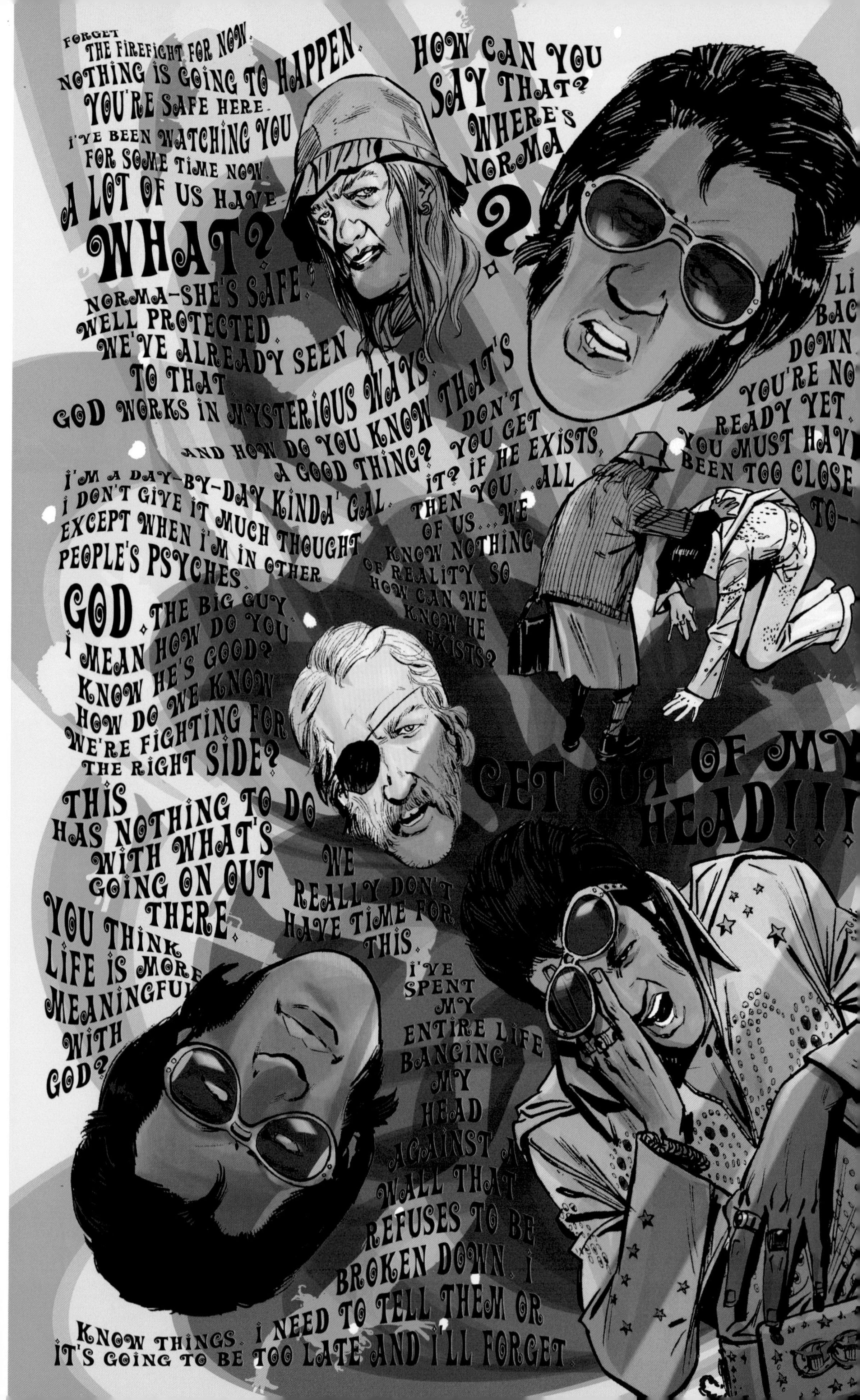
FORGET THE FIREFIGHT FOR NOW. NOTHING IS GOING TO HAPPEN. YOU'RE SAFE HERE. I'VE BEEN WATCHING YOU FOR SOME TIME NOW. A LOT OF US HAVE.
HOW CAN YOU SAY THAT? WHERE'S NORMA?
WHAT?
NORMA—SHE'S SAFE. WELL PROTECTED. WE'VE ALREADY SEEN TO THAT.
GOD WORKS IN MYSTERIOUS WAYS.
AND HOW DO YOU KNOW THAT'S A GOOD THING?
DON'T YOU GET IT? IF HE EXISTS, THEN YOU... ALL OF US... WE KNOW NOTHING OF REALITY. SO HOW CAN WE KNOW HE EXISTS?
I'M A DAY-BY-DAY KINDA' GAL. I DON'T GIVE IT MUCH THOUGHT EXCEPT WHEN I'M IN OTHER PEOPLE'S PSYCHES.
GOD. THE BIG GUY. I MEAN HOW DO YOU KNOW HE'S GOOD? HOW DO WE KNOW WE'RE FIGHTING FOR THE RIGHT SIDE?
LI BAC DOWN YOU'RE NO READY YET. YOU MUST HAV BEEN TOO CLOSE TO--
GET OUT OF MY HEAD!!!
THIS HAS NOTHING TO DO WITH WHAT'S GOING ON OUT THERE.
WE REALLY DON'T HAVE TIME FOR THIS.
YOU THINK LIFE IS MORE MEANINGFU WITH GOD?
I'VE SPENT MY ENTIRE LIFE BANGING MY HEAD AGAINST A WALL THAT REFUSES TO BE BROKEN DOWN. I KNOW THINGS. I NEED TO TELL THEM OR IT'S GOING TO BE TOO LATE AND I'LL FORGET.

FROM THIS DAY FORWARD, THE PAST IS NO LONGER TRUE.

THERE IS NO NATURAL ORDER OF THINGS.

NOT ANYMORE.

POK

WE FINISHED HERE.

YOU'LL SEE.

I DID WHAT THE WORK ORDER TOLD ME TO DO.

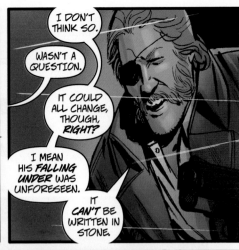

I DON'T THINK SO.

WASN'T A QUESTION.

IT COULD ALL CHANGE, THOUGH, RIGHT?

I MEAN HIS FALLING UNDER WAS UNFORESEEN.

IT CAN'T BE WRITTEN IN STONE.

BEST NOT TO SPECULATE AT THIS JUNCTURE, REALLY.

YOU'RE DEAD WRONG. WITH GOD, YOU'RE A MEANINGLESS TOY HE PLAYS WITH AND THROWS AWAY. TO THE INFINITE, THE FINITE IS INFINITELY MINISCULE

BUT DEFINITIVES ARE NO LONGER.

BRUCE SAW TO THAT.

ACCIDENTALLY.

THAT DOESN'T COUNT REALLY.

WHAT DID I SEE?

POK

YOU REALLY MUST ADMIT TO THIS BEING AN EXCITING TIME...

POK POK

WHAT THE HELL DID I SEE?

FOR ALL OF US.

NO...

NOT REALLY.

DOESN'T SURPRISE ME YOU THINK IT IS THOUGH.

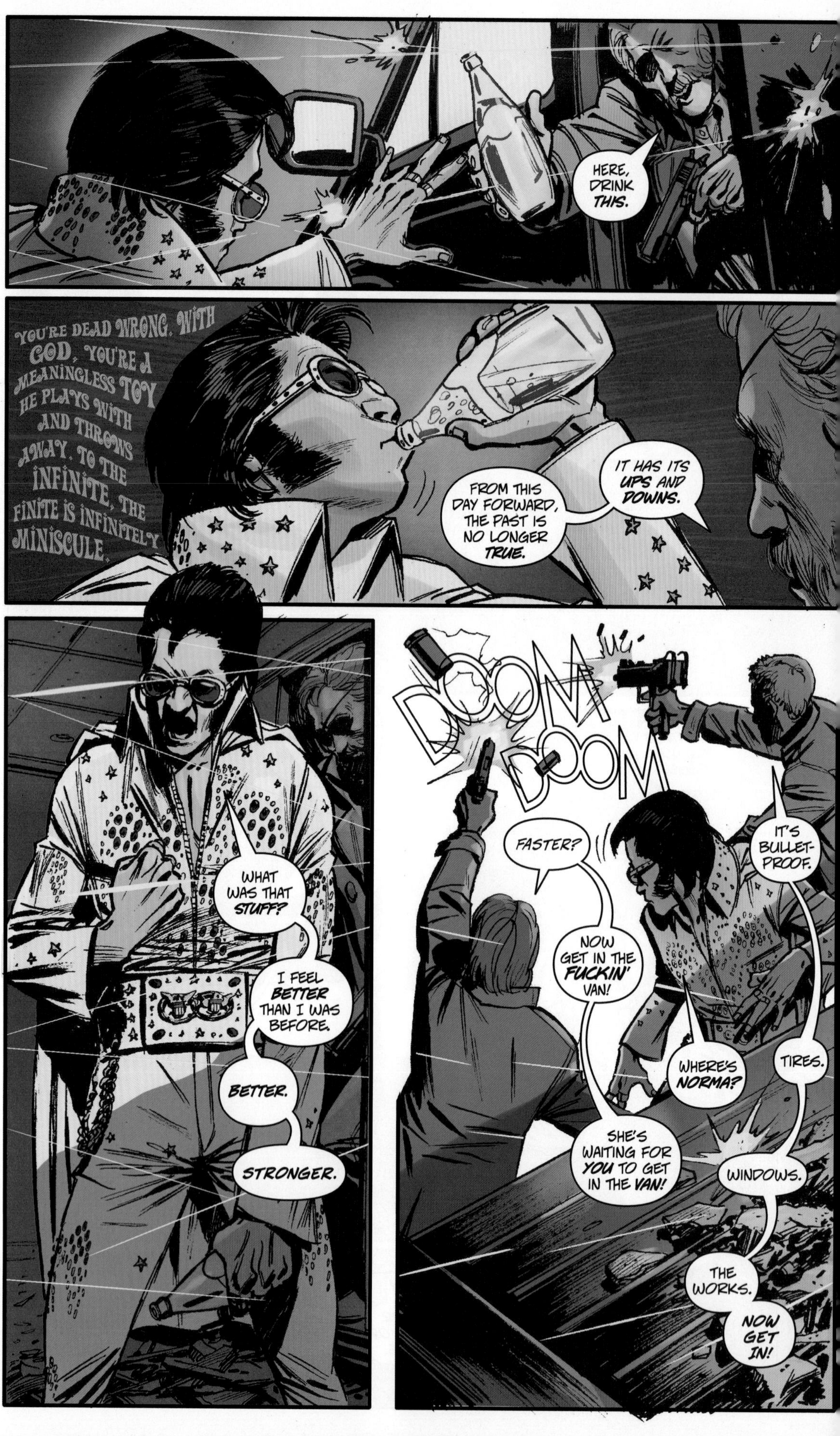
HERE, DRINK THIS.
YOU'RE DEAD WRONG. WITH GOD, YOU'RE A MEANINGLESS TOY HE PLAYS WITH AND THROWS AWAY. TO THE INFINITE, THE FINITE IS INFINITELY MINISCULE.
FROM THIS DAY FORWARD, THE PAST IS NO LONGER TRUE.
IT HAS ITS UPS AND DOWNS.
WHAT WAS THAT STUFF?
I FEEL BETTER THAN I WAS BEFORE.
BETTER.
STRONGER.
DOOM DOOM
FASTER?
NOW GET IN THE FUCKIN' VAN!
IT'S BULLET-PROOF.
WHERE'S NORMA?
TIRES.
SHE'S WAITING FOR YOU TO GET IN THE VAN!
WINDOWS.
THE WORKS.
NOW GET IN!

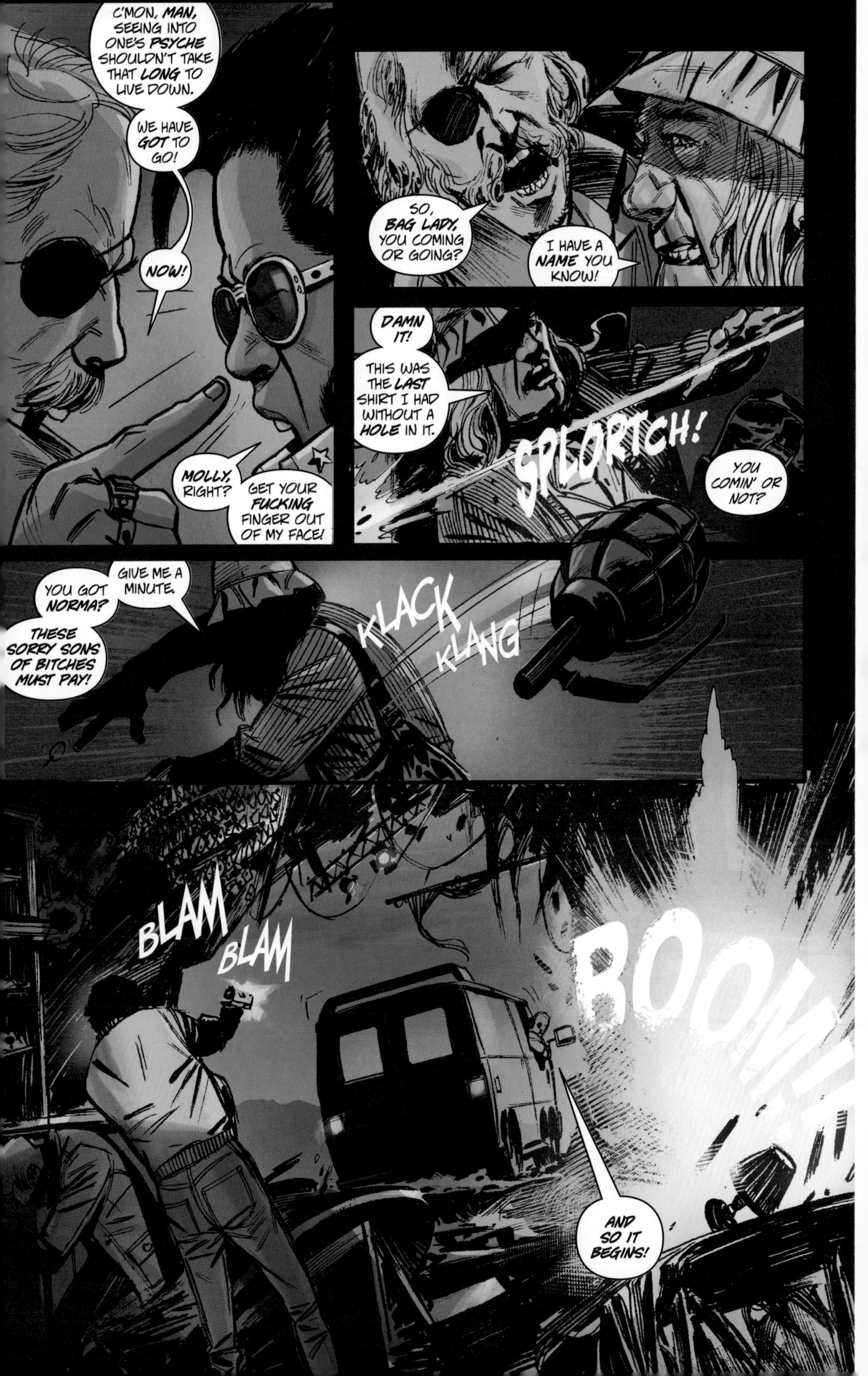
C'MON, MAN, SEEING INTO ONE'S PSYCHE SHOULDN'T TAKE THAT LONG TO LIVE DOWN.
WE HAVE GOT TO GO!
NOW!
MOLLY, RIGHT?
GET YOUR FUCKING FINGER OUT OF MY FACE!
SO, BAG LADY, YOU COMING OR GOING?
I HAVE A NAME YOU KNOW!
DAMN IT!
THIS WAS THE LAST SHIRT I HAD WITHOUT A HOLE IN IT.
SPLORTCH!
YOU COMIN' OR NOT?
YOU GOT NORMA?
GIVE ME A MINUTE.
THESE SORRY SONS OF BITCHES MUST PAY!
KLACK
KLANG
BLAM
BLAM
BOOM!
AND SO IT BEGINS!

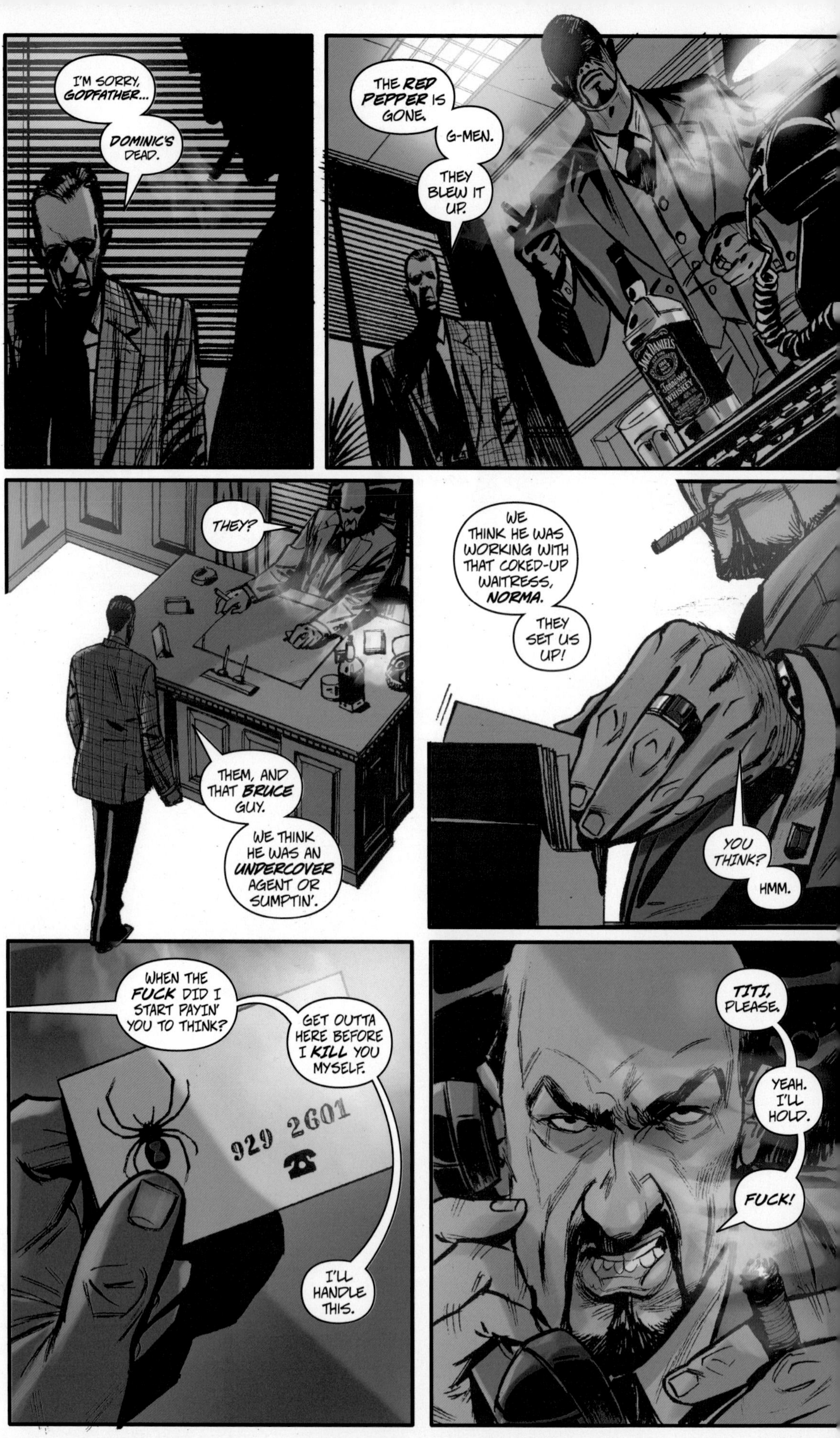
I'M SORRY, GODFATHER...
DOMINIC'S DEAD.
THE RED PEPPER IS GONE.
G-MEN.
THEY BLEW IT UP.
THEY?
WE THINK HE WAS WORKING WITH THAT COKED-UP WAITRESS, NORMA.
THEY SET US UP!
THEM, AND THAT BRUCE GUY.
WE THINK HE WAS AN UNDERCOVER AGENT OR SUMPTIN'.
YOU THINK?
HMM.
WHEN THE FUCK DID I START PAYIN' YOU TO THINK?
GET OUTTA HERE BEFORE I KILL YOU MYSELF.
I'LL HANDLE THIS.
929 2601
TITI, PLEASE.
YEAH. I'LL HOLD.
FUCK!

CHAPTER TWO

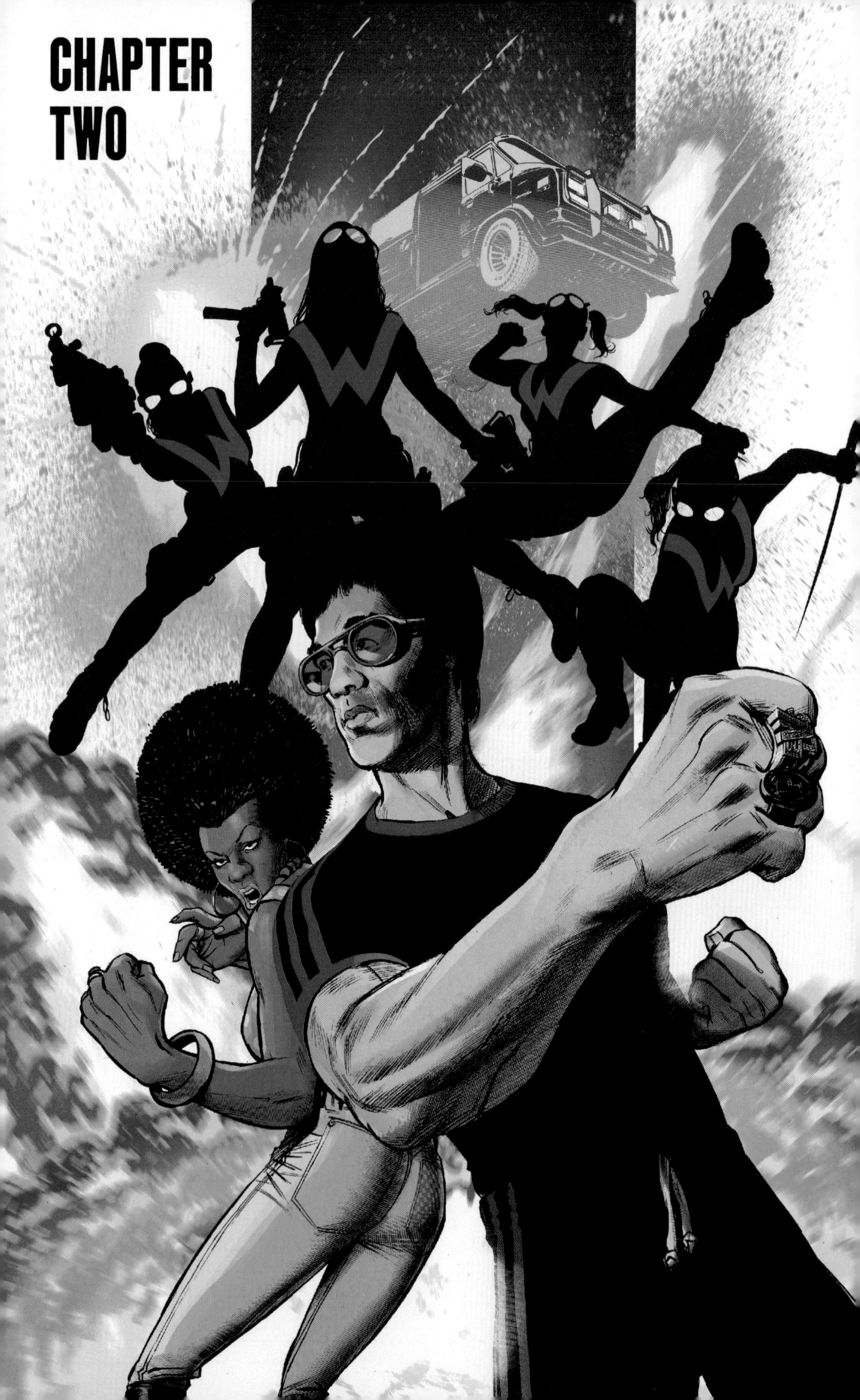

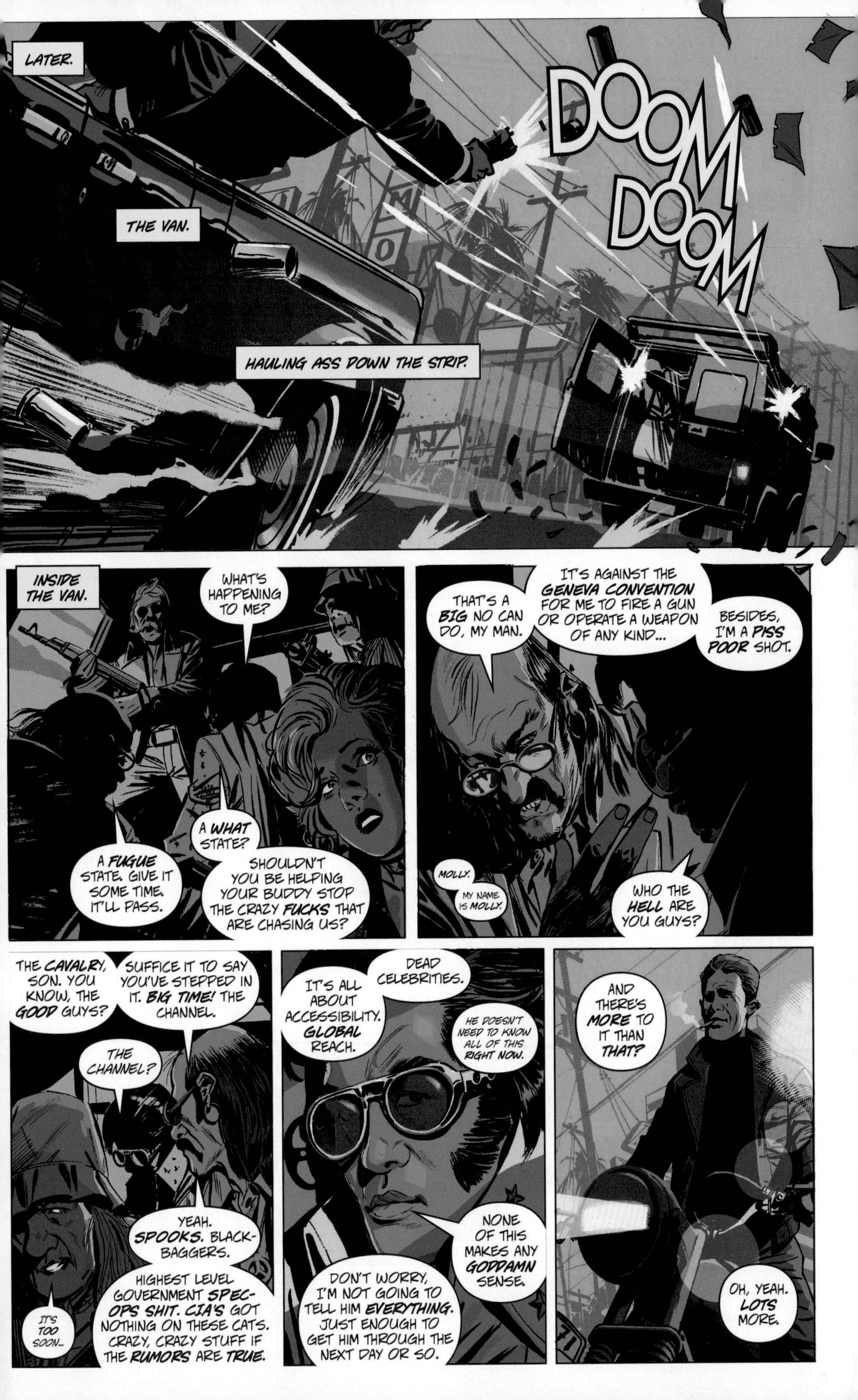
LATER.
THE VAN.
HAULING ASS DOWN THE STRIP.
DOOM DOOM DOOM
INSIDE THE VAN.
WHAT'S HAPPENING TO ME?
A FUGUE STATE. GIVE IT SOME TIME. IT'LL PASS.
A WHAT STATE?
SHOULDN'T YOU BE HELPING YOUR BUDDY STOP THE CRAZY FUCKS THAT ARE CHASING US?
THAT'S A BIG NO CAN DO, MY MAN.
IT'S AGAINST THE GENEVA CONVENTION FOR ME TO FIRE A GUN OR OPERATE A WEAPON OF ANY KIND...
BESIDES, I'M A PISS POOR SHOT.
MOLLY.
MY NAME IS MOLLY.
WHO THE HELL ARE YOU GUYS?
THE CAVALRY, SON. YOU KNOW, THE GOOD GUYS?
SUFFICE IT TO SAY YOU'VE STEPPED IN IT. BIG TIME! THE CHANNEL.
THE CHANNEL?
YEAH. SPOOKS. BLACK-BAGGERS.
HIGHEST LEVEL GOVERNMENT SPEC-OPS SHIT. CIA'S GOT NOTHING ON THESE CATS. CRAZY, CRAZY STUFF IF THE RUMORS ARE TRUE.
IT'S TOO SOON...
DEAD CELEBRITIES.
IT'S ALL ABOUT ACCESSIBILITY. GLOBAL REACH.
HE DOESN'T NEED TO KNOW ALL OF THIS RIGHT NOW.
NONE OF THIS MAKES ANY GODDAMN SENSE.
DON'T WORRY, I'M NOT GOING TO TELL HIM EVERYTHING. JUST ENOUGH TO GET HIM THROUGH THE NEXT DAY OR SO.
AND THERE'S MORE TO IT THAN THAT?
OH, YEAH. LOTS MORE.

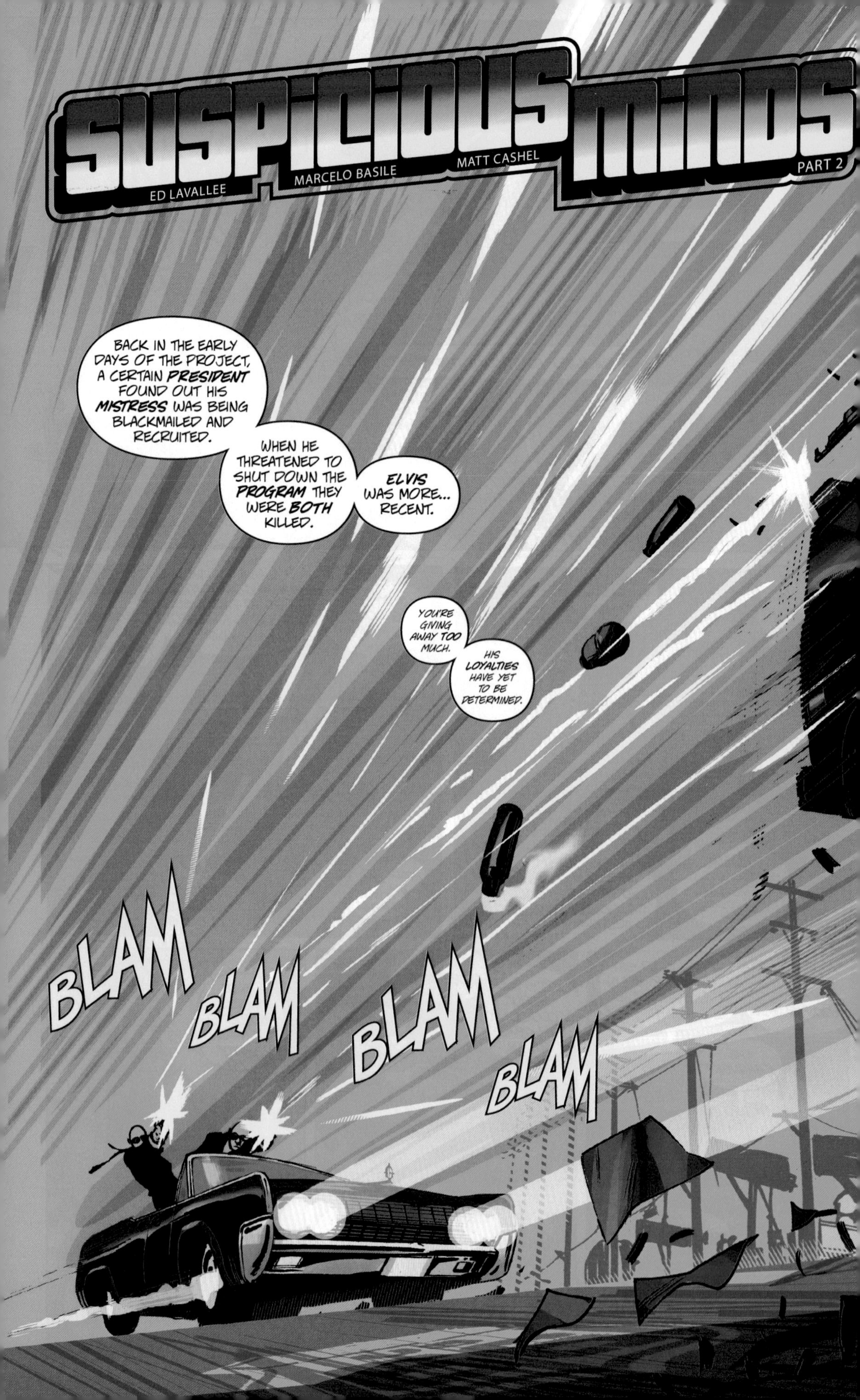
SUSPICIOUS MINDS
PART 2
ED LAVALLEE
MARCELO BASILE
MATT CASHEL
BACK IN THE EARLY DAYS OF THE PROJECT, A CERTAIN PRESIDENT FOUND OUT HIS MISTRESS WAS BEING BLACKMAILED AND RECRUITED.
WHEN HE THREATENED TO SHUT DOWN THE PROGRAM THEY WERE BOTH KILLED.
ELVIS WAS MORE... RECENT.
YOU'RE GIVING AWAY TOO MUCH.
HIS LOYALTIES HAVE YET TO BE DETERMINED.
BLAM
BLAM
BLAM
BLAM

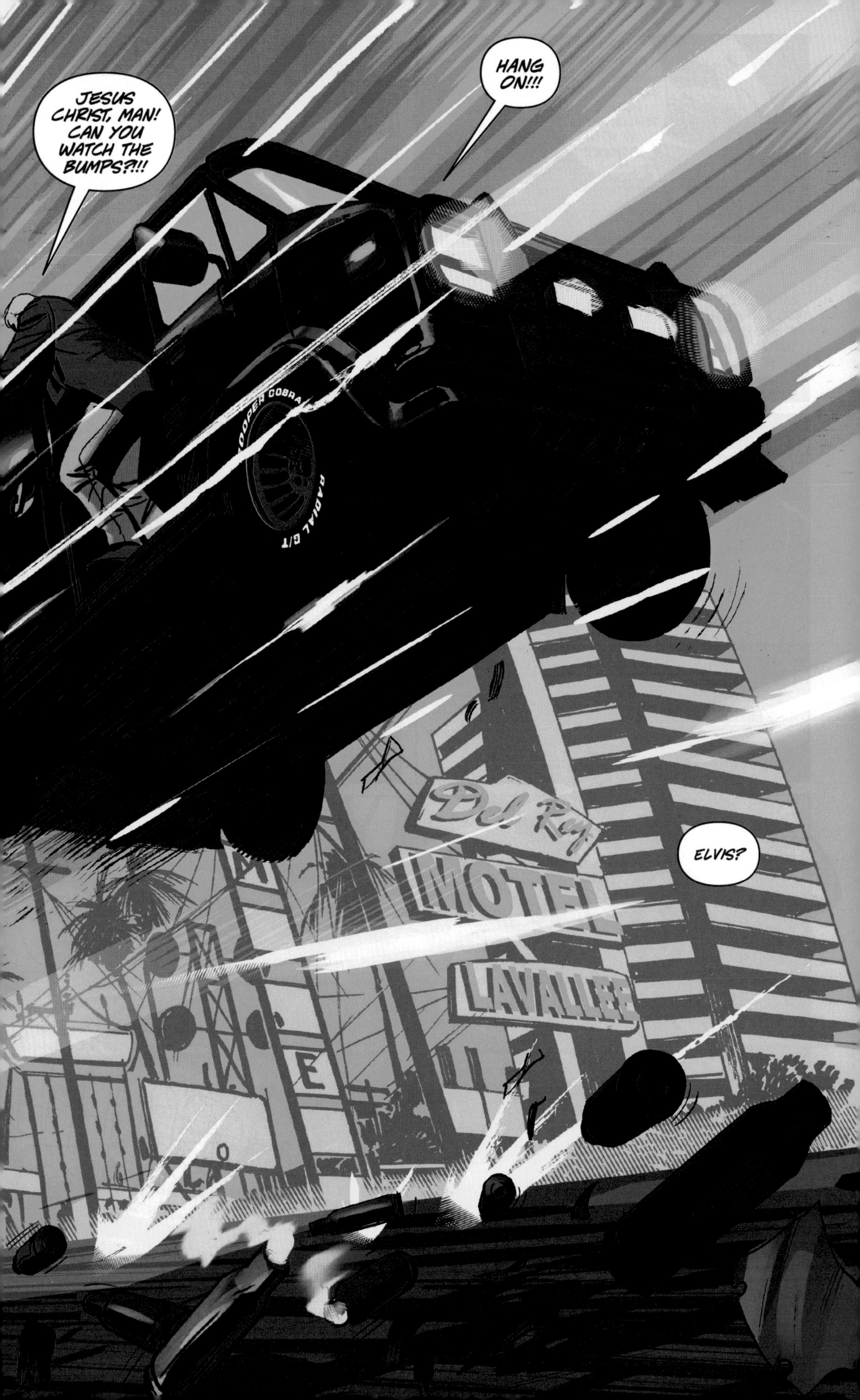
JESUS CHRIST, MAN! CAN YOU WATCH THE BUMPS?!!!
HANG ON!!!
COOPER COBRA RADIAL G/T
Del Rey
MOTEL
LAVALLEE
ELVIS?

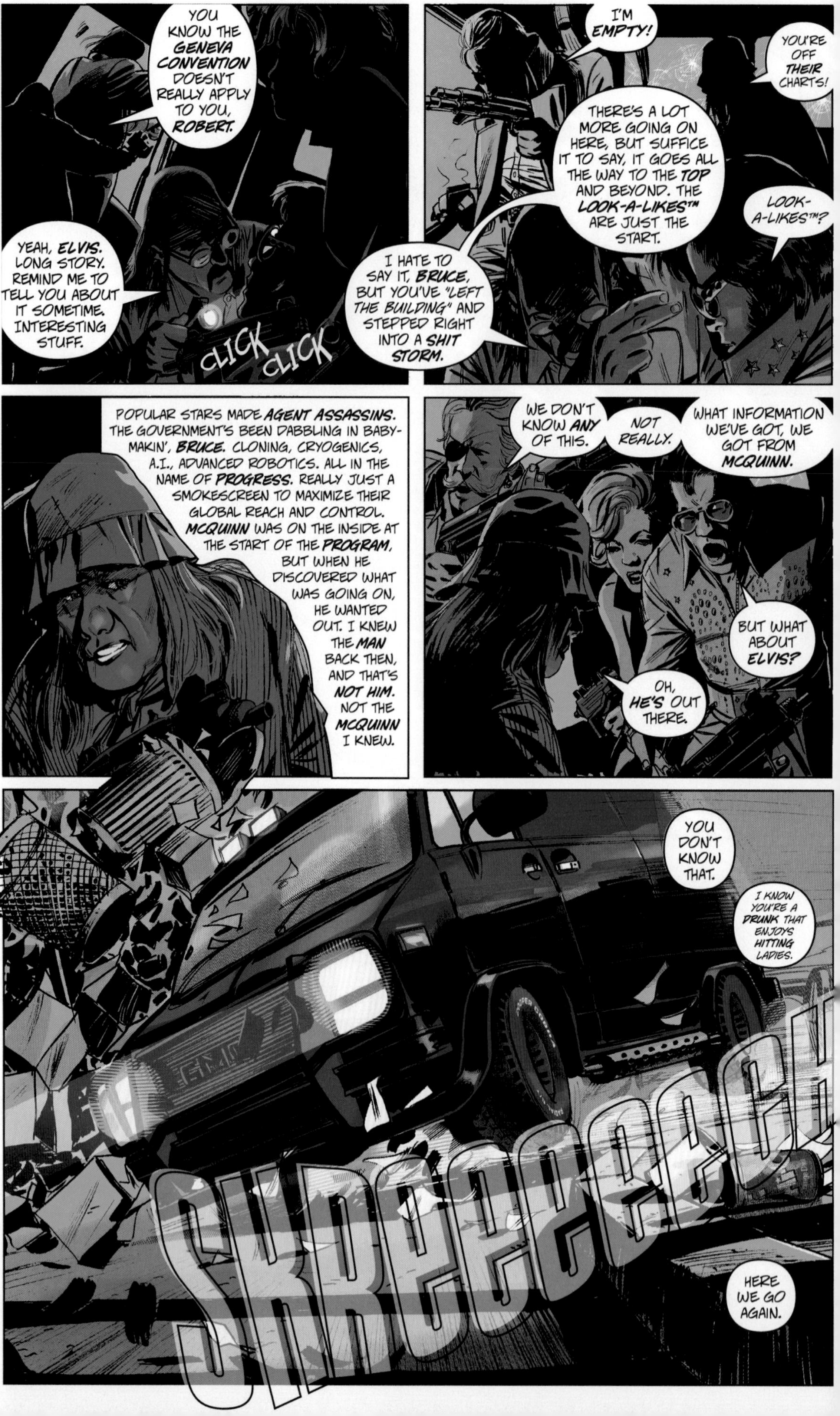

YOU KNOW THE GENEVA CONVENTION DOESN'T REALLY APPLY TO YOU, ROBERT.
YEAH, ELVIS. LONG STORY. REMIND ME TO TELL YOU ABOUT IT SOMETIME. INTERESTING STUFF.
CLICK CLICK
I'M EMPTY!
YOU'RE OFF THEIR CHARTS!
I HATE TO SAY IT, BRUCE, BUT YOU'VE "LEFT THE BUILDING" AND STEPPED RIGHT INTO A SHIT STORM.
THERE'S A LOT MORE GOING ON HERE, BUT SUFFICE IT TO SAY, IT GOES ALL THE WAY TO THE TOP AND BEYOND. THE LOOK-A-LIKES™ ARE JUST THE START.
LOOK-A-LIKES™?
POPULAR STARS MADE AGENT ASSASSINS. THE GOVERNMENT'S BEEN DABBLING IN BABY-MAKIN', BRUCE. CLONING, CRYOGENICS, A.I., ADVANCED ROBOTICS. ALL IN THE NAME OF PROGRESS. REALLY JUST A SMOKESCREEN TO MAXIMIZE THEIR GLOBAL REACH AND CONTROL. MCQUINN WAS ON THE INSIDE AT THE START OF THE PROGRAM, BUT WHEN HE DISCOVERED WHAT WAS GOING ON, HE WANTED OUT. I KNEW THE MAN BACK THEN, AND THAT'S NOT HIM. NOT THE MCQUINN I KNEW.
WE DON'T KNOW ANY OF THIS.
NOT REALLY.
WHAT INFORMATION WE'VE GOT, WE GOT FROM MCQUINN.
BUT WHAT ABOUT ELVIS?
OH, HE'S OUT THERE.
YOU DON'T KNOW THAT.
I KNOW YOU'RE A DRUNK THAT ENJOYS HITTING LADIES.
HERE WE GO AGAIN.
SHREEEEECH

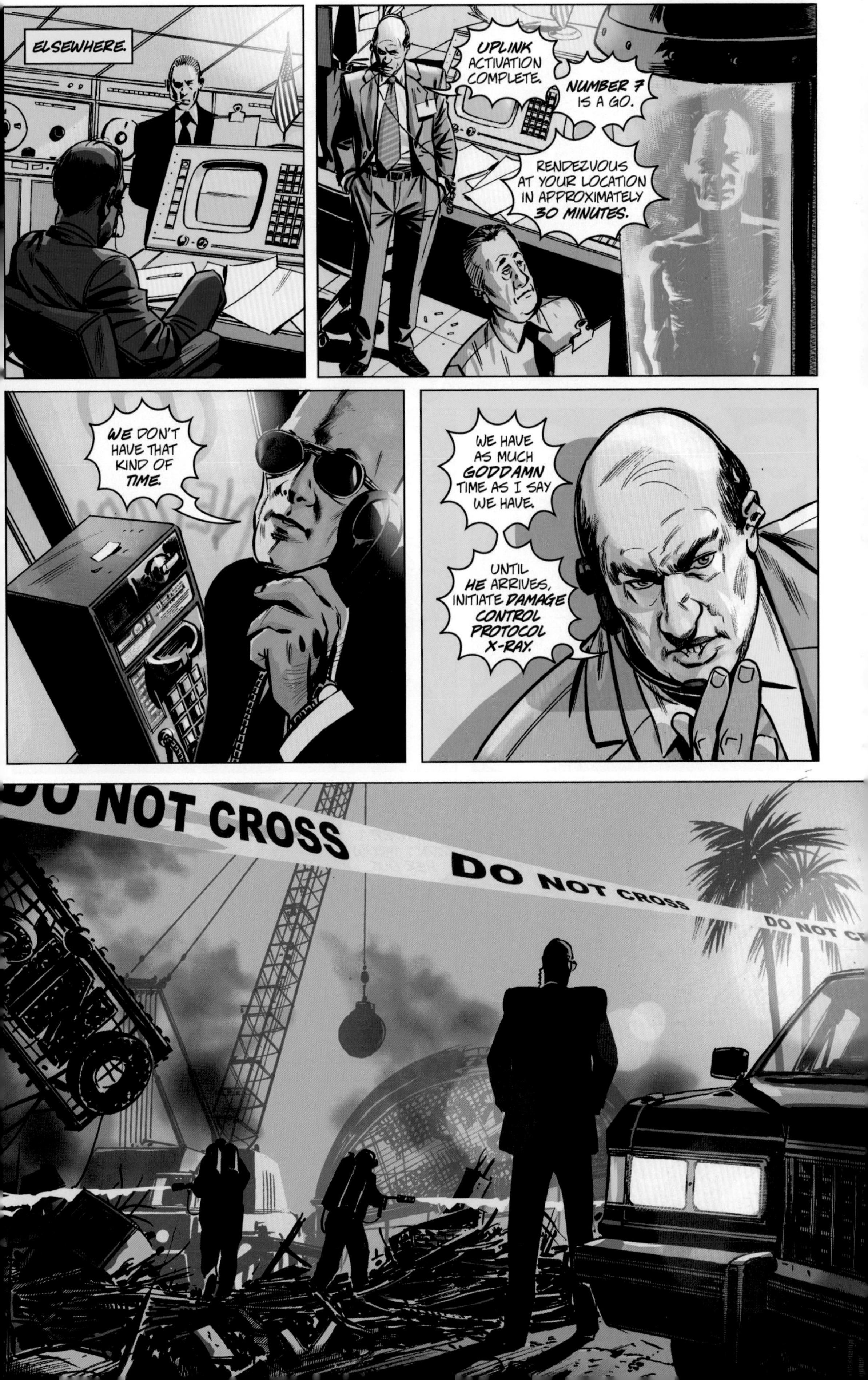
ELSEWHERE.
UPLINK ACTIVATION COMPLETE.
NUMBER 7 IS A GO.
RENDEZVOUS AT YOUR LOCATION IN APPROXIMATELY 30 MINUTES.
WE DON'T HAVE THAT KIND OF TIME.
WE HAVE AS MUCH GODDAMN TIME AS I SAY WE HAVE.
UNTIL HE ARRIVES, INITIATE DAMAGE CONTROL PROTOCOL X-RAY.
DO NOT CROSS
DO NOT CROSS

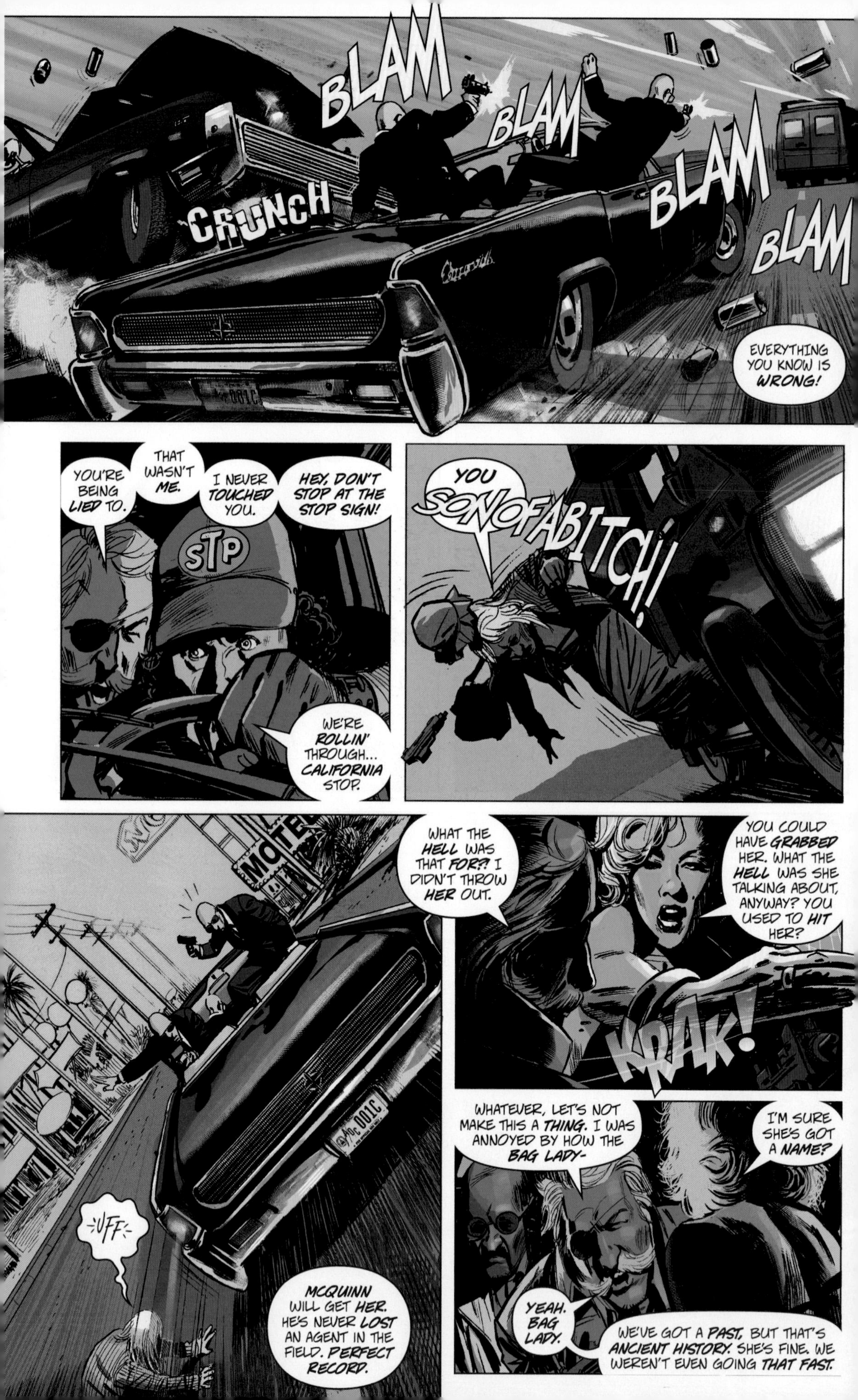
BLAM
BLAM
CRUNCH
BLAM
BLAM
EVERYTHING YOU KNOW IS WRONG!
YOU'RE BEING LIED TO.
THAT WASN'T ME.
I NEVER TOUCHED YOU.
HEY, DON'T STOP AT THE STOP SIGN!
STP
WE'RE ROLLIN' THROUGH... CALIFORNIA STOP.
YOU SONOFABITCH!
MOTEL
UFF
MCQUINN WILL GET HER. HE'S NEVER LOST AN AGENT IN THE FIELD. PERFECT RECORD.
WHAT THE HELL WAS THAT FOR?! I DIDN'T THROW HER OUT.
YOU COULD HAVE GRABBED HER. WHAT THE HELL WAS SHE TALKING ABOUT, ANYWAY? YOU USED TO HIT HER?
KRAK!
WHATEVER, LET'S NOT MAKE THIS A THING. I WAS ANNOYED BY HOW THE BAG LADY-
I'M SURE SHE'S GOT A NAME?
YEAH. BAG LADY.
WE'VE GOT A PAST, BUT THAT'S ANCIENT HISTORY. SHE'S FINE. WE WEREN'T EVEN GOING THAT FAST.

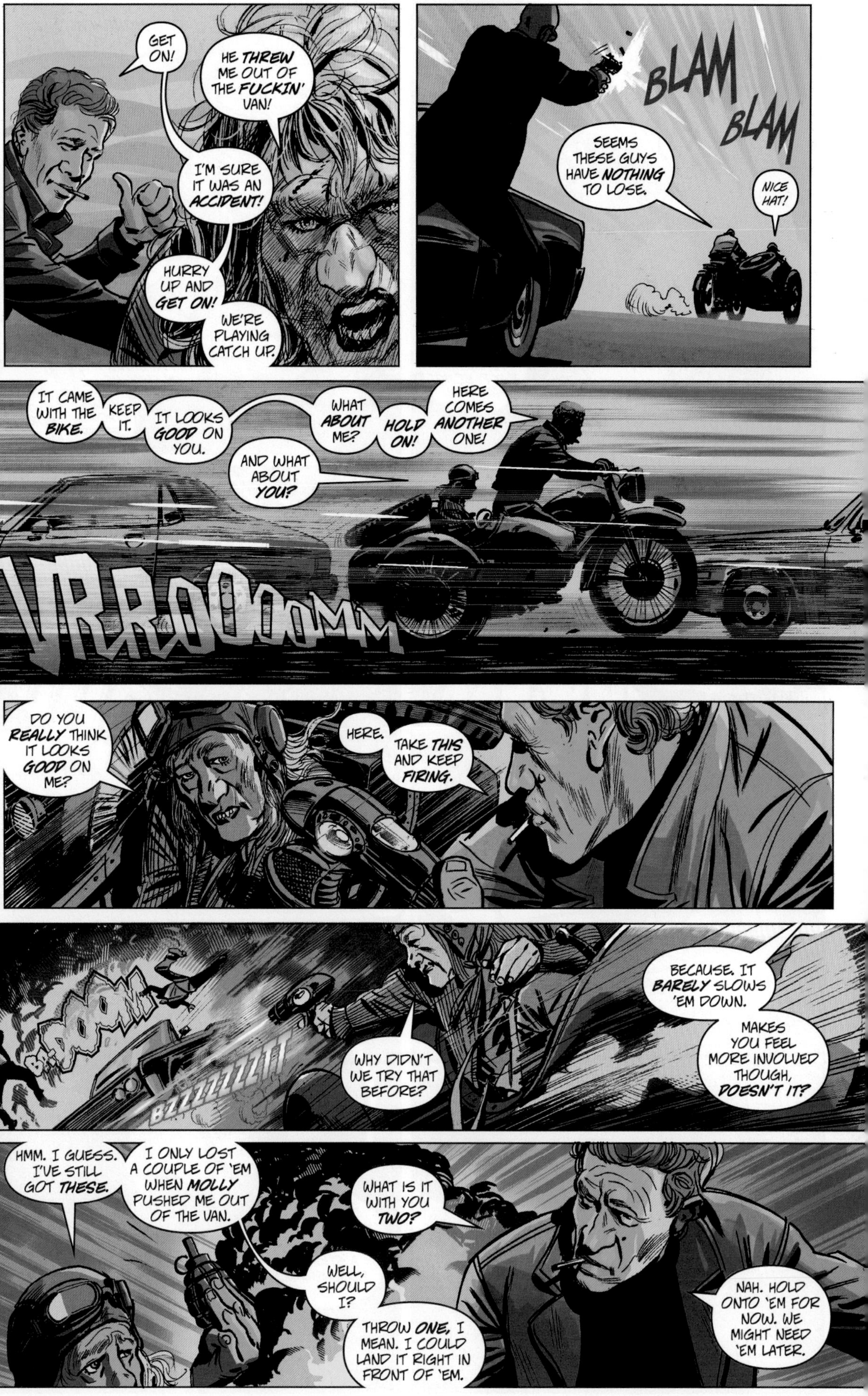
GET ON!
HE THREW ME OUT OF THE FUCKIN' VAN!
I'M SURE IT WAS AN ACCIDENT!
HURRY UP AND GET ON!
WE'RE PLAYING CATCH UP.
BLAM
BLAM
SEEMS THESE GUYS HAVE NOTHING TO LOSE.
NICE HAT!
IT CAME WITH THE BIKE.
KEEP IT.
IT LOOKS GOOD ON YOU.
WHAT ABOUT ME?
HOLD ON!
HERE COMES ANOTHER ONE!
AND WHAT ABOUT YOU?
VRROOOOMM
DO YOU REALLY THINK IT LOOKS GOOD ON ME?
HERE.
TAKE THIS AND KEEP FIRING.
B-DOOM
BZZZZZZZZTT
WHY DIDN'T WE TRY THAT BEFORE?
BECAUSE. IT BARELY SLOWS 'EM DOWN.
MAKES YOU FEEL MORE INVOLVED THOUGH, DOESN'T IT?
HMM. I GUESS. I'VE STILL GOT THESE.
I ONLY LOST A COUPLE OF 'EM WHEN MOLLY PUSHED ME OUT OF THE VAN.
WHAT IS IT WITH YOU TWO?
WELL, SHOULD I?
THROW ONE, I MEAN. I COULD LAND IT RIGHT IN FRONT OF 'EM.
NAH. HOLD ONTO 'EM FOR NOW. WE MIGHT NEED 'EM LATER.

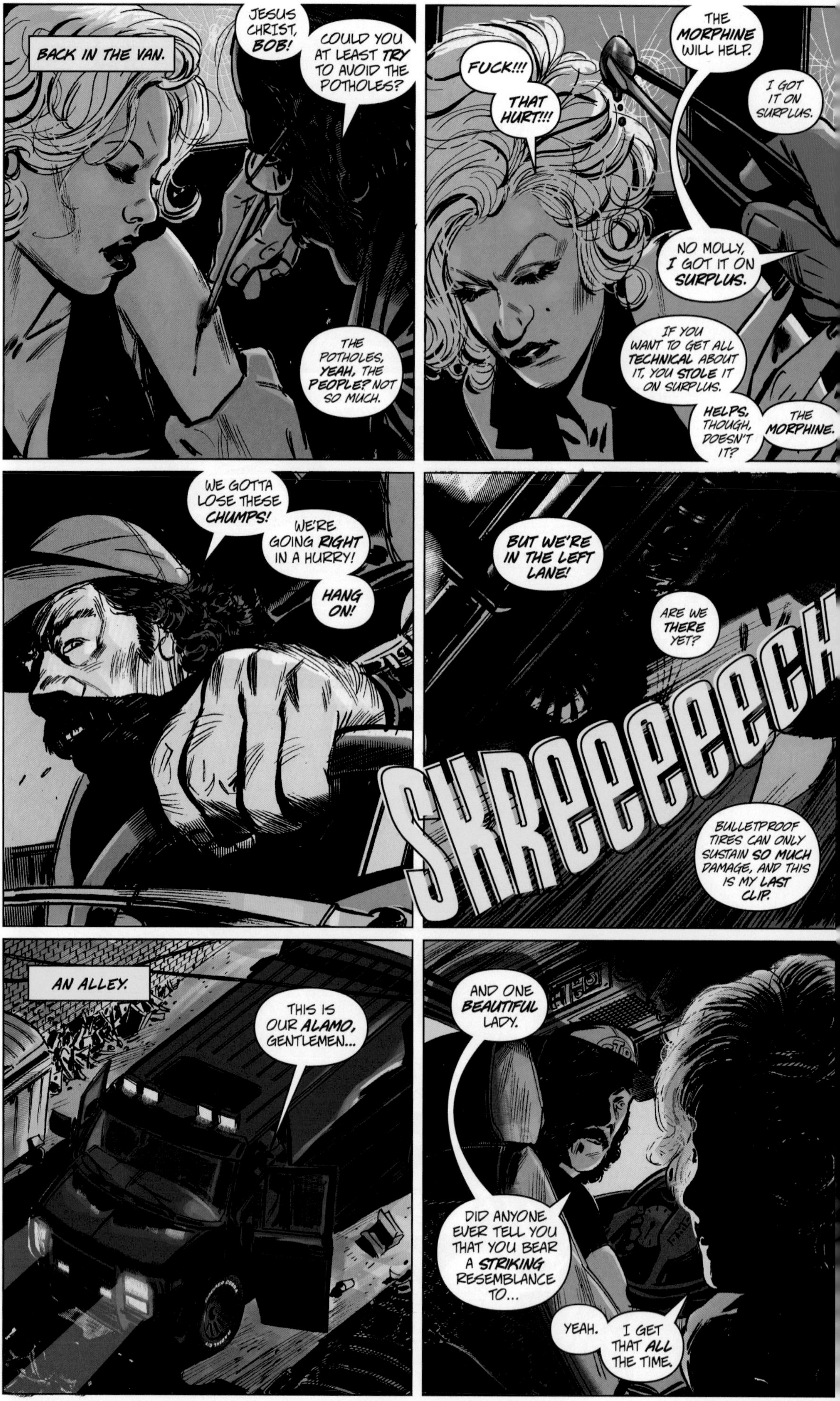
BACK IN THE VAN.
JESUS CHRIST, BOB!
COULD YOU AT LEAST TRY TO AVOID THE POTHOLES?
THE POTHOLES, YEAH. THE PEOPLE? NOT SO MUCH.
FUCK!!!
THAT HURT!!!
THE MORPHINE WILL HELP.
I GOT IT ON SURPLUS.
NO MOLLY, I GOT IT ON SURPLUS.
IF YOU WANT TO GET ALL TECHNICAL ABOUT IT, YOU STOLE IT ON SURPLUS.
HELPS, THOUGH, DOESN'T IT?
THE MORPHINE.
WE GOTTA LOSE THESE CHUMPS!
WE'RE GOING RIGHT IN A HURRY!
HANG ON!
BUT WE'RE IN THE LEFT LANE!
ARE WE THERE YET?
SKREEEEECH
BULLETPROOF TIRES CAN ONLY SUSTAIN SO MUCH DAMAGE, AND THIS IS MY LAST CLIP.
AN ALLEY.
THIS IS OUR ALAMO, GENTLEMEN...
AND ONE BEAUTIFUL LADY.
DID ANYONE EVER TELL YOU THAT YOU BEAR A STRIKING RESEMBLANCE TO...
YEAH.
I GET THAT ALL THE TIME.

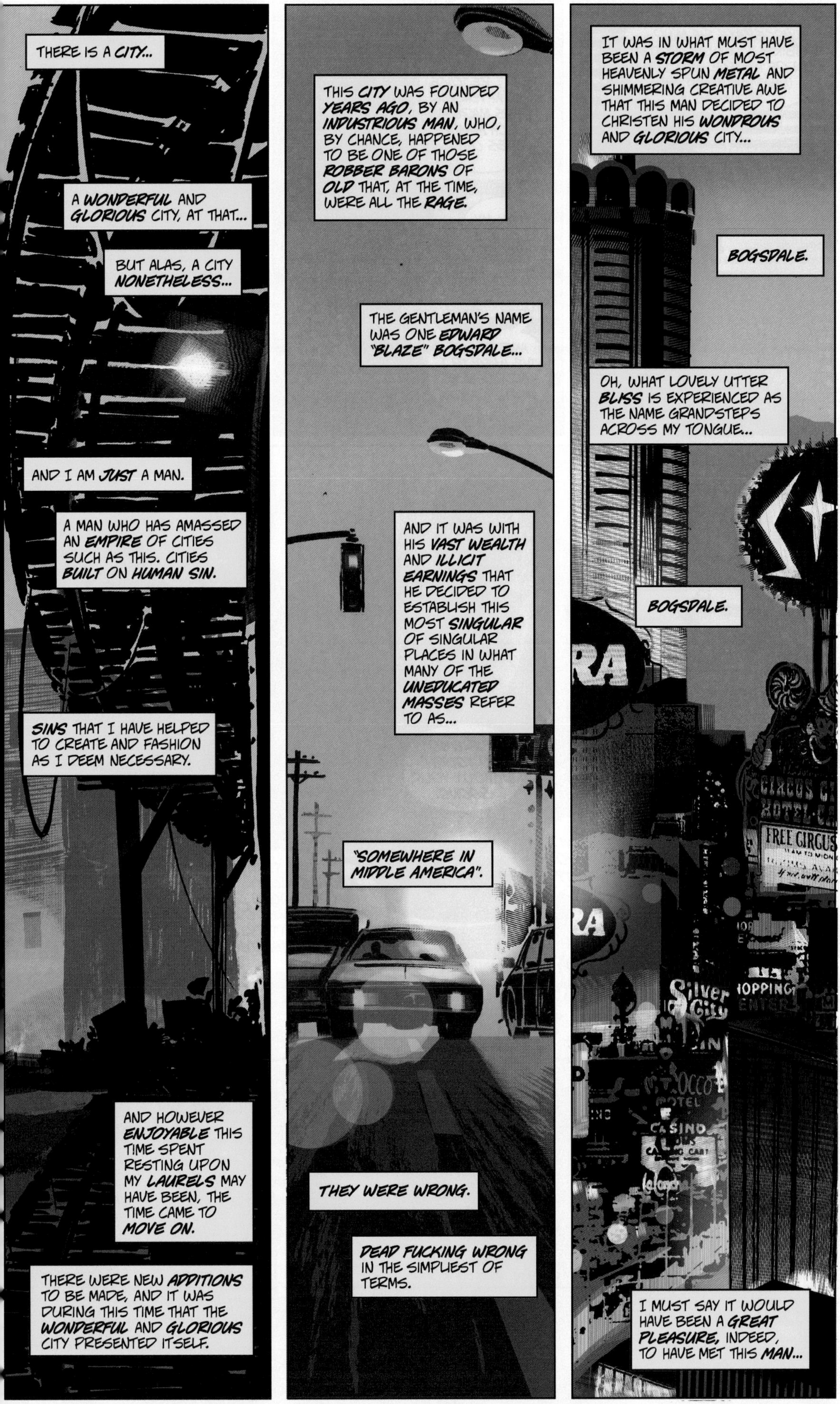
THERE IS A CITY...
A WONDERFUL AND GLORIOUS CITY, AT THAT...
BUT ALAS, A CITY NONETHELESS...
AND I AM JUST A MAN.
A MAN WHO HAS AMASSED AN EMPIRE OF CITIES SUCH AS THIS. CITIES BUILT ON HUMAN SIN.
SINS THAT I HAVE HELPED TO CREATE AND FASHION AS I DEEM NECESSARY.
AND HOWEVER ENJOYABLE THIS TIME SPENT RESTING UPON MY LAURELS MAY HAVE BEEN, THE TIME CAME TO MOVE ON.
THERE WERE NEW ADDITIONS TO BE MADE, AND IT WAS DURING THIS TIME THAT THE WONDERFUL AND GLORIOUS CITY PRESENTED ITSELF.
THIS CITY WAS FOUNDED YEARS AGO, BY AN INDUSTRIOUS MAN, WHO, BY CHANCE, HAPPENED TO BE ONE OF THOSE ROBBER BARONS OF OLD THAT, AT THE TIME, WERE ALL THE RAGE.
THE GENTLEMAN'S NAME WAS ONE EDWARD "BLAZE" BOGSDALE...
AND IT WAS WITH HIS VAST WEALTH AND ILLICIT EARNINGS THAT HE DECIDED TO ESTABLISH THIS MOST SINGULAR OF SINGULAR PLACES IN WHAT MANY OF THE UNEDUCATED MASSES REFER TO AS...
"SOMEWHERE IN MIDDLE AMERICA".
THEY WERE WRONG.
DEAD FUCKING WRONG IN THE SIMPLIEST OF TERMS.
IT WAS IN WHAT MUST HAVE BEEN A STORM OF MOST HEAVENLY SPUN METAL AND SHIMMERING CREATIVE AWE THAT THIS MAN DECIDED TO CHRISTEN HIS WONDROUS AND GLORIOUS CITY...
BOGSDALE.
OH, WHAT LOVELY UTTER BLISS IS EXPERIENCED AS THE NAME GRANDSTEPS ACROSS MY TONGUE...
BOGSDALE.
FREE CIRCUS
Silver City
CASINO
I MUST SAY IT WOULD HAVE BEEN A GREAT PLEASURE, INDEED, TO HAVE MET THIS MAN...

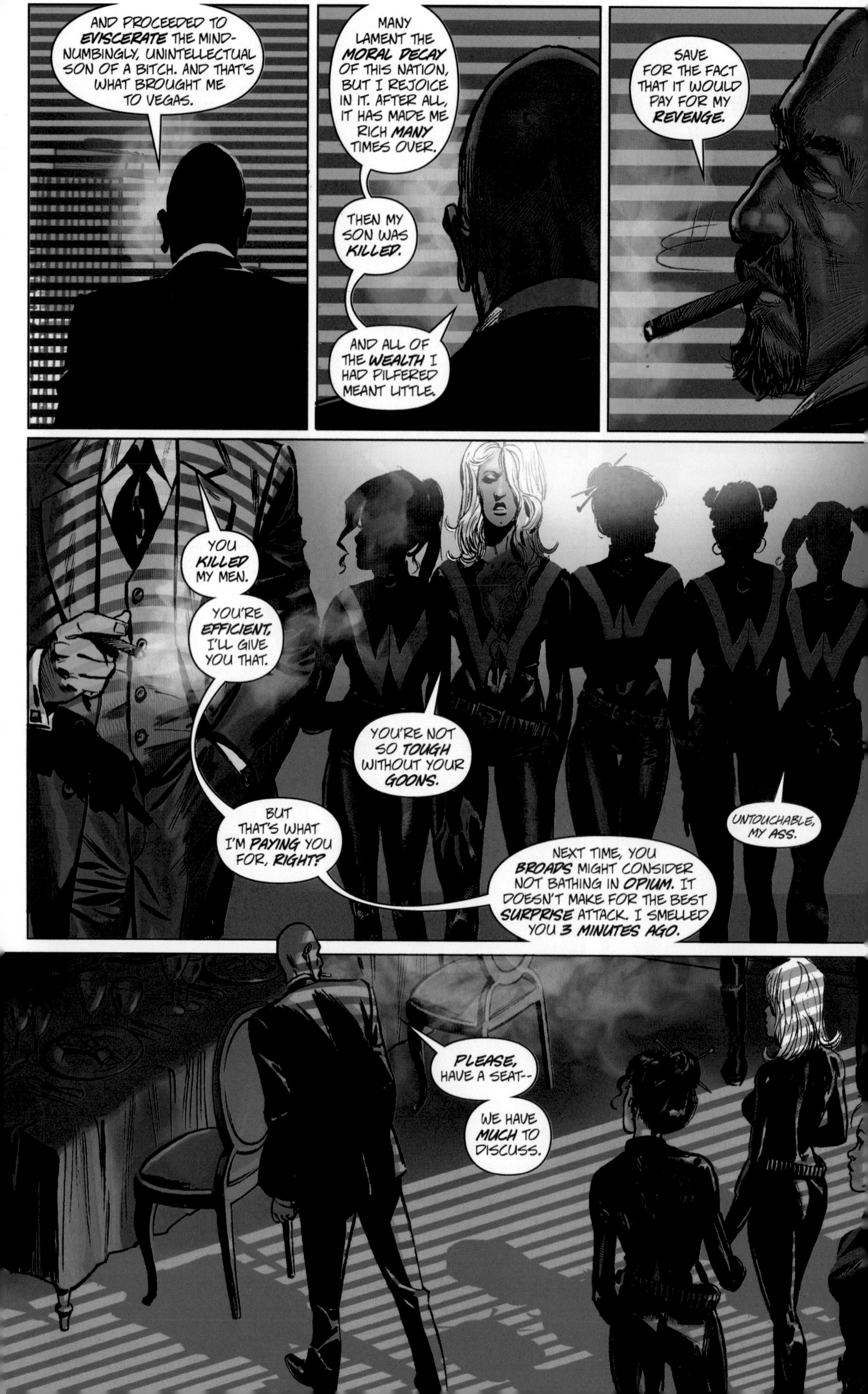
AND PROCEEDED TO EVISCERATE THE MIND-NUMBINGLY, UNINTELLECTUAL SON OF A BITCH. AND THAT'S WHAT BROUGHT ME TO VEGAS.
MANY LAMENT THE MORAL DECAY OF THIS NATION, BUT I REJOICE IN IT. AFTER ALL, IT HAS MADE ME RICH MANY TIMES OVER.
THEN MY SON WAS KILLED.
AND ALL OF THE WEALTH I HAD PILFERED MEANT LITTLE.
SAVE FOR THE FACT THAT IT WOULD PAY FOR MY REVENGE.
YOU KILLED MY MEN.
YOU'RE EFFICIENT, I'LL GIVE YOU THAT.
BUT THAT'S WHAT I'M PAYING YOU FOR, RIGHT?
YOU'RE NOT SO TOUGH WITHOUT YOUR GOONS.
UNTOUCHABLE, MY ASS.
NEXT TIME, YOU BROADS MIGHT CONSIDER NOT BATHING IN OPIUM. IT DOESN'T MAKE FOR THE BEST SURPRISE ATTACK. I SMELLED YOU 3 MINUTES AGO.
PLEASE, HAVE A SEAT--
WE HAVE MUCH TO DISCUSS.

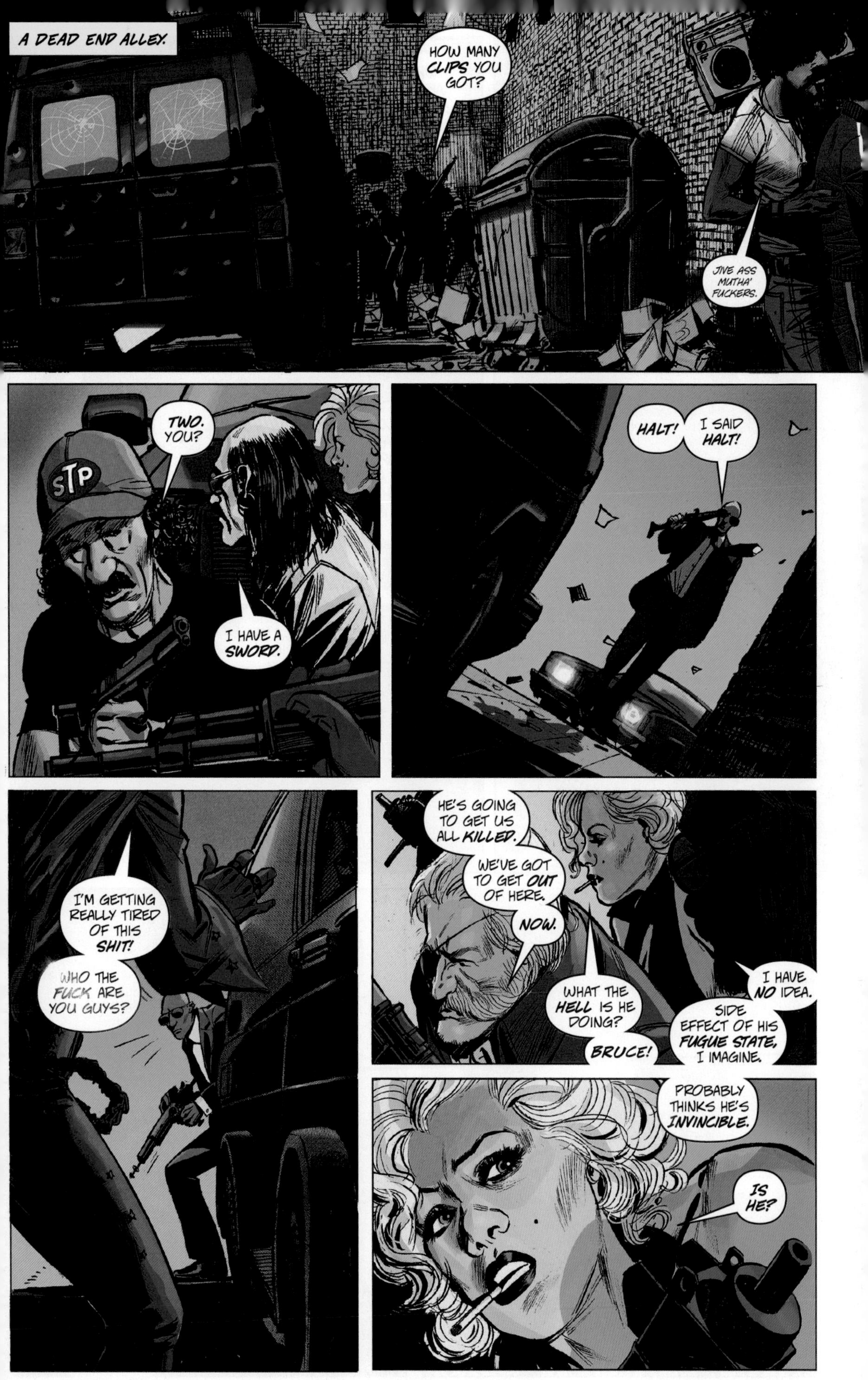
A DEAD END ALLEY.
HOW MANY CLIPS YOU GOT?
JIVE ASS MUTHA' FUCKERS.
TWO. YOU?
I HAVE A SWORD.
HALT!
I SAID HALT!
I'M GETTING REALLY TIRED OF THIS SHIT!
WHO THE FUCK ARE YOU GUYS?
HE'S GOING TO GET US ALL KILLED.
WE'VE GOT TO GET OUT OF HERE.
NOW.
WHAT THE HELL IS HE DOING?
BRUCE!
I HAVE NO IDEA.
SIDE EFFECT OF HIS FUGUE STATE, I IMAGINE.
PROBABLY THINKS HE'S INVINCIBLE.
IS HE?

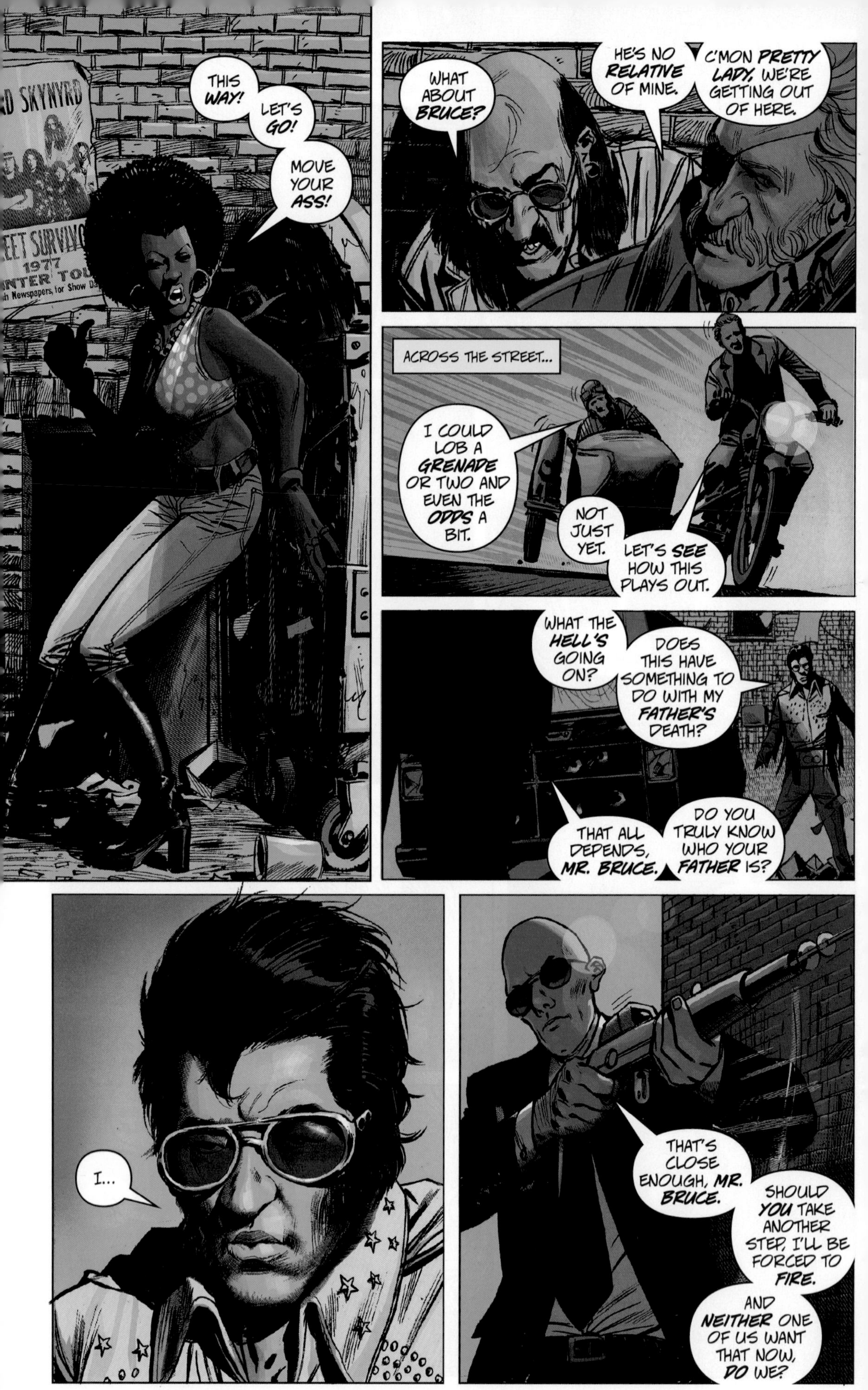

RD SKYNYRD
EET SURVIVO
1977
NTER TOU
h Newspapers for Show Da
THIS WAY!
LET'S GO!
MOVE YOUR ASS!
WHAT ABOUT BRUCE?
HE'S NO RELATIVE OF MINE.
C'MON PRETTY LADY, WE'RE GETTING OUT OF HERE.
ACROSS THE STREET...
I COULD LOB A GRENADE OR TWO AND EVEN THE ODDS A BIT.
NOT JUST YET.
LET'S SEE HOW THIS PLAYS OUT.
WHAT THE HELL'S GOING ON?
DOES THIS HAVE SOMETHING TO DO WITH MY FATHER'S DEATH?
THAT ALL DEPENDS, MR. BRUCE.
DO YOU TRULY KNOW WHO YOUR FATHER IS?
I...
THAT'S CLOSE ENOUGH, MR. BRUCE.
SHOULD YOU TAKE ANOTHER STEP, I'LL BE FORCED TO FIRE.
AND NEITHER ONE OF US WANT THAT NOW, DO WE?

HOW MANY MORE OF *THESE* DO YOU HAVE?

NONE.

AND YOURS IS LOSING *ITS* CHARGE.

YOU WANT *CRAZY*? I'LL SHOW YOU *CRAZY*!

C'MON!

BZZZZTZZZ!

BZZZZZZZZZT!

BRUCE, IS IT? WHY DIDN'T YOU FOLLOW MISS BROWN?

WHO'S *MISS BROWN*?

I DIDN'T *SEE* ANYONE.

CAN SHE BE *TRUSTED*?

SUDDENLY, THERE WAS THE SMELL OF *OZONE* AND *BURNING RUBBER* AS THE LONE AGENT FELL TO THE GROUND AT *BRUCE'S* FEET. THIS WAS GOOD FOR BRUCE.

THIS WAS GOOD FOR *EVERYONE*.

YOU'RE ON FIRE.

SAME CIRCLES, *HER* AND I.

SIMILAR *AGENDAS*, BUT DIFFERENT.

I'M *MISS BROWN*!

BARELY.

SHE *SAVED* YOUR FRIENDS. YOU CAN *TRUST* HER.

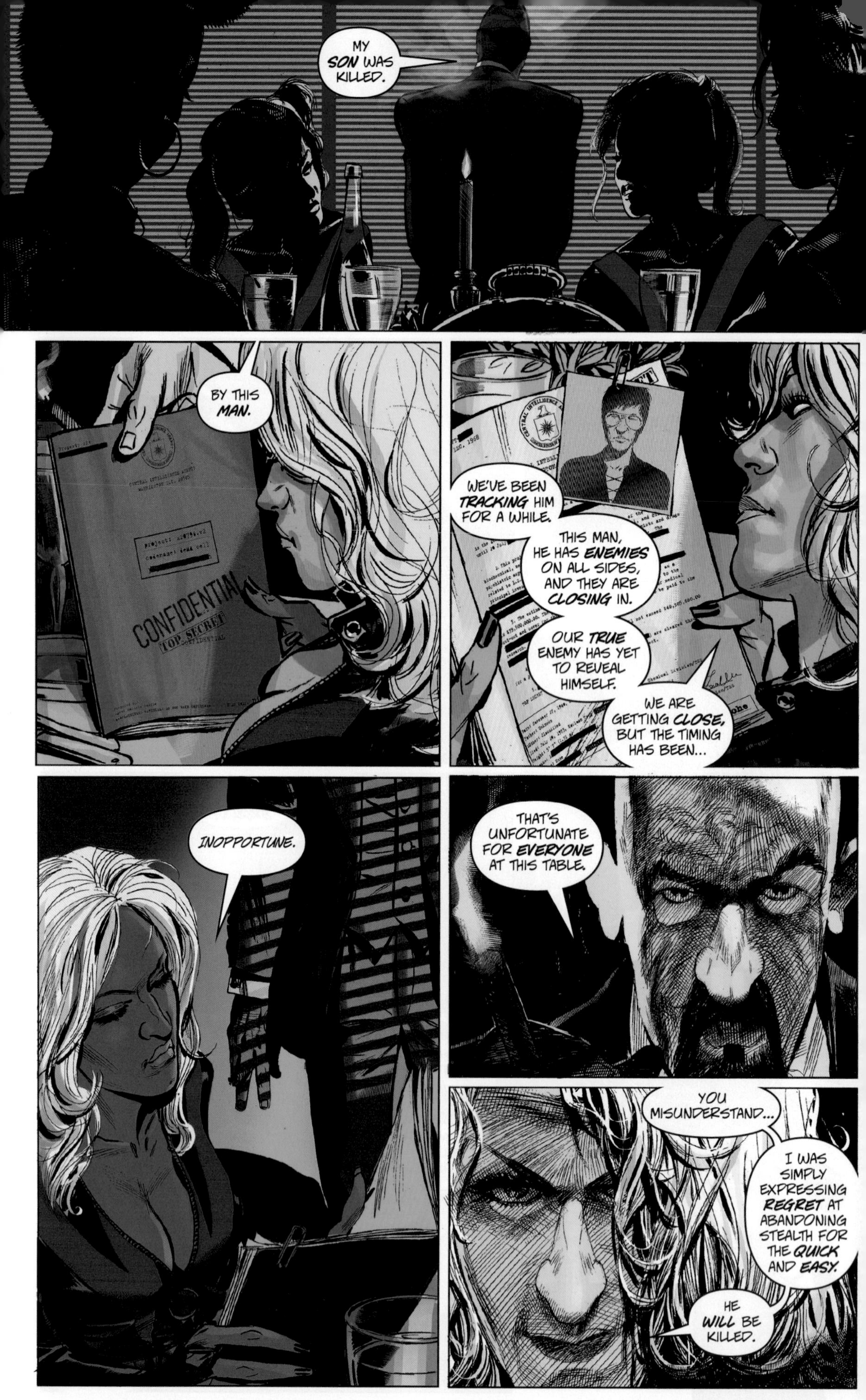
MY SON WAS KILLED.
BY THIS MAN.
CONFIDENTIAL
TOP SECRET
WE'VE BEEN TRACKING HIM FOR A WHILE.
THIS MAN, HE HAS ENEMIES ON ALL SIDES, AND THEY ARE CLOSING IN.
OUR TRUE ENEMY HAS YET TO REVEAL HIMSELF.
WE ARE GETTING CLOSE, BUT THE TIMING HAS BEEN...
INOPPORTUNE.
THAT'S UNFORTUNATE FOR EVERYONE AT THIS TABLE.
YOU MISUNDERSTAND...
I WAS SIMPLY EXPRESSING REGRET AT ABANDONING STEALTH FOR THE QUICK AND EASY.
HE WILL BE KILLED.

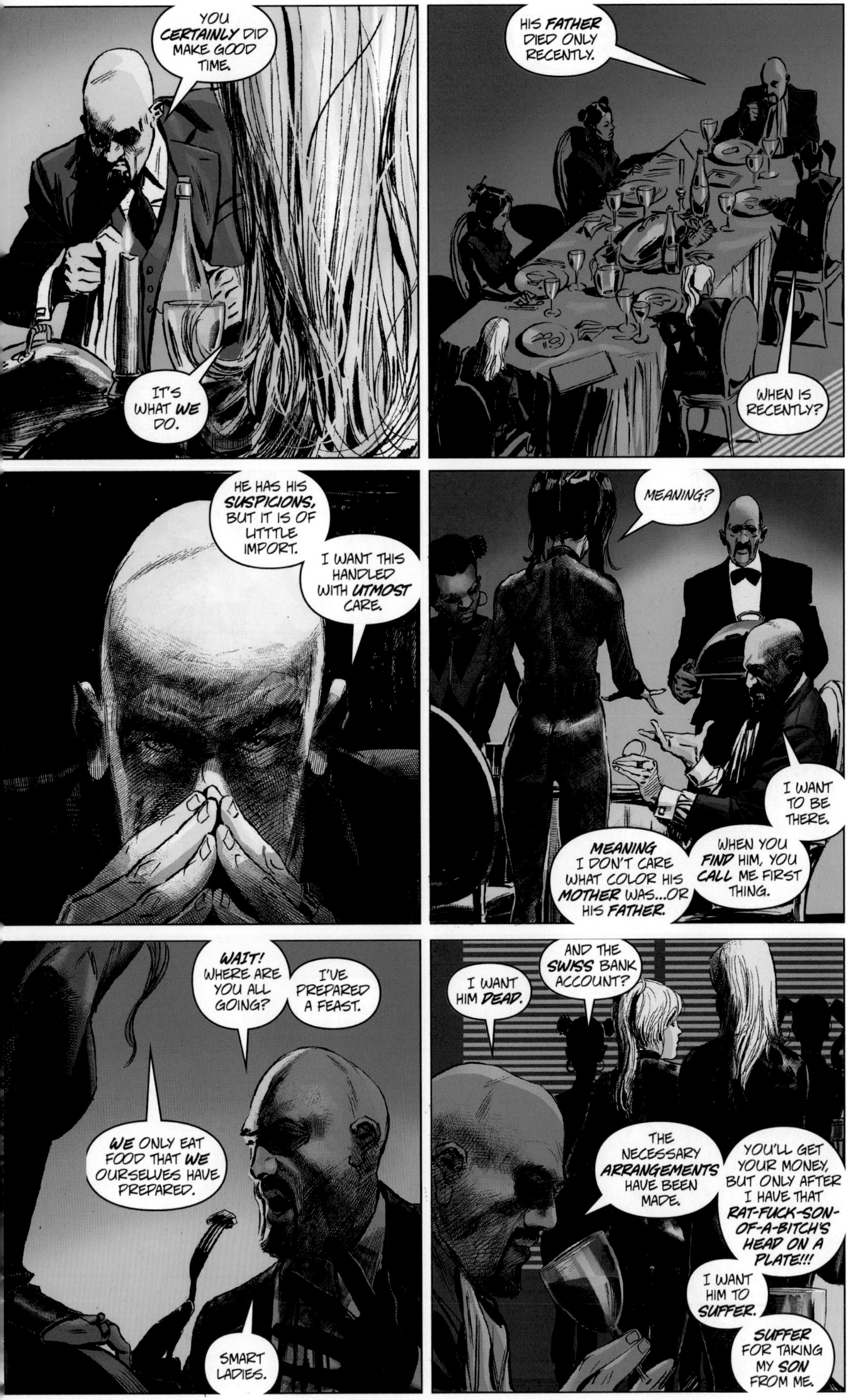

YOU CERTAINLY DID MAKE GOOD TIME.
IT'S WHAT WE DO.
HIS FATHER DIED ONLY RECENTLY.
WHEN IS RECENTLY?
HE HAS HIS SUSPICIONS, BUT IT IS OF LITTLE IMPORT.
I WANT THIS HANDLED WITH UTMOST CARE.
MEANING?
I WANT TO BE THERE.
WHEN YOU FIND HIM, YOU CALL ME FIRST THING.
MEANING I DON'T CARE WHAT COLOR HIS MOTHER WAS...OR HIS FATHER.
WAIT! WHERE ARE YOU ALL GOING?
I'VE PREPARED A FEAST.
WE ONLY EAT FOOD THAT WE OURSELVES HAVE PREPARED.
SMART LADIES.
AND THE SWISS BANK ACCOUNT?
I WANT HIM DEAD.
THE NECESSARY ARRANGEMENTS HAVE BEEN MADE.
YOU'LL GET YOUR MONEY, BUT ONLY AFTER I HAVE THAT RAT-FUCK-SON-OF-A-BITCH'S HEAD ON A PLATE!!!
I WANT HIM TO SUFFER.
SUFFER FOR TAKING MY SON FROM ME.

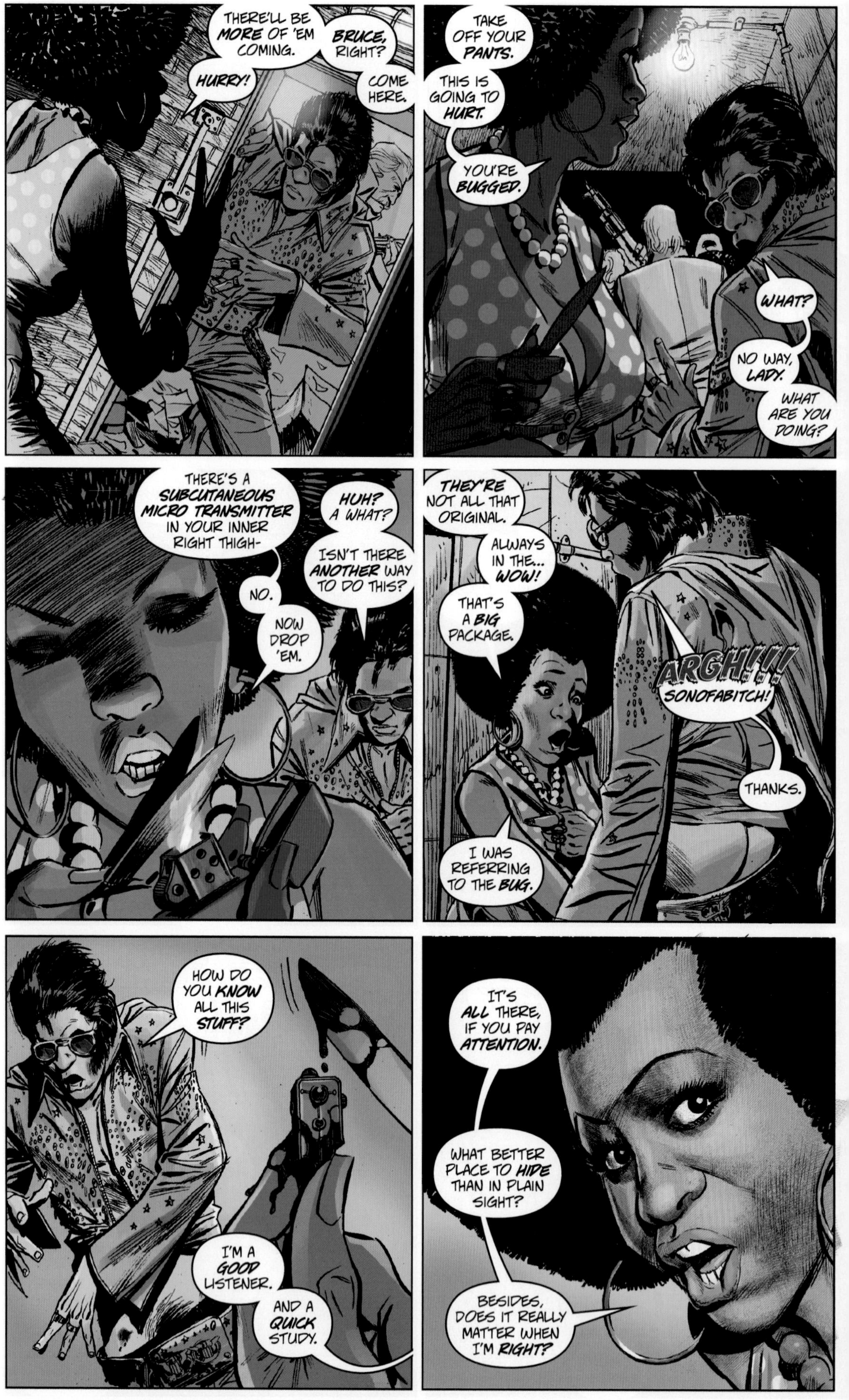
THERE'LL BE MORE OF 'EM COMING.
HURRY!
BRUCE, RIGHT?
COME HERE.
TAKE OFF YOUR PANTS.
THIS IS GOING TO HURT.
YOU'RE BUGGED.
WHAT?
NO WAY, LADY.
WHAT ARE YOU DOING?
THERE'S A SUBCUTANEOUS MICRO TRANSMITTER IN YOUR INNER RIGHT THIGH-
HUH? A WHAT?
ISN'T THERE ANOTHER WAY TO DO THIS?
NO.
NOW DROP 'EM.
THEY'RE NOT ALL THAT ORIGINAL.
ALWAYS IN THE... WOW!
THAT'S A BIG PACKAGE.
ARGH!!!
SONOFABITCH!
THANKS.
I WAS REFERRING TO THE BUG.
HOW DO YOU KNOW ALL THIS STUFF?
I'M A GOOD LISTENER.
AND A QUICK STUDY.
IT'S ALL THERE, IF YOU PAY ATTENTION.
WHAT BETTER PLACE TO HIDE THAN IN PLAIN SIGHT?
BESIDES, DOES IT REALLY MATTER WHEN I'M RIGHT?

NOW, I'M GOING TO HAVE TO ASK YOU *ALL* TO HIDE.

HIDE?

WHERE?

OLD *BOOTLEGGER* STORAGE UNDER THE FLOOR.

THEY'RE EQUIPPED FOR ALL KINDS OF *SHIT*.

AND ILLEGAL *ALIENS?*

WHY ARE YOU HELPING US?

WHAT'S *YOUR* STORY?

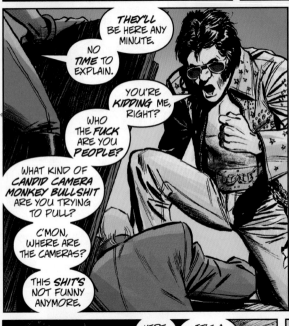

THEY'LL BE HERE ANY MINUTE.

NO *TIME* TO EXPLAIN.

YOU'RE *KIDDING* ME, RIGHT?

WHO THE *FUCK* ARE YOU *PEOPLE?*

WHAT KIND OF *CANDID CAMERA MONKEY BULLSHIT* ARE YOU TRYING TO PULL?

C'MON, WHERE ARE THE CAMERAS?

THIS *SHIT'S* NOT FUNNY ANYMORE.

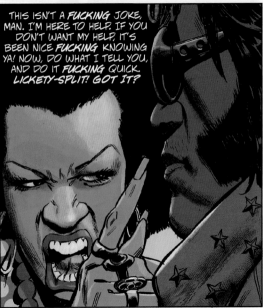

THIS ISN'T A *FUCKING* JOKE, MAN. I'M HERE TO HELP. IF YOU DON'T WANT MY HELP, IT'S BEEN NICE *FUCKING* KNOWING YA! NOW, DO WHAT I TELL YOU, AND DO IT *FUCKING* QUICK. LICKETY-SPLIT! GOT IT?

HERE, TAKE THIS.

IT'S A CHANGE OF CLOTHES. I CAN'T IMAGINE THAT GETUP IS COMFORTABLE OR PRACTICAL GIVEN OUR CURRENT SITUATION.

FUCK!

I'M STILL IN *COSTUME!*

SURPRISED THE *WIG* STAYED ON THIS LONG!

YO, *ROBERT!* YOU GONNA HELP OUT HERE?

YOU FIGURE THERE'RE *SPIDERS* IN HERE?

WHAT'S *THAT* LOOK FOR?

COSTUME CHANGE?

IN THE MIDDLE OF ALL OF *THIS?*

YOU'VE GOT TO BE *FUCKING* KIDDING ME!

WHAT?

DOES IT LOOK *BAD?*

BEATS THE HELL OUT OF *POLYESTER!*

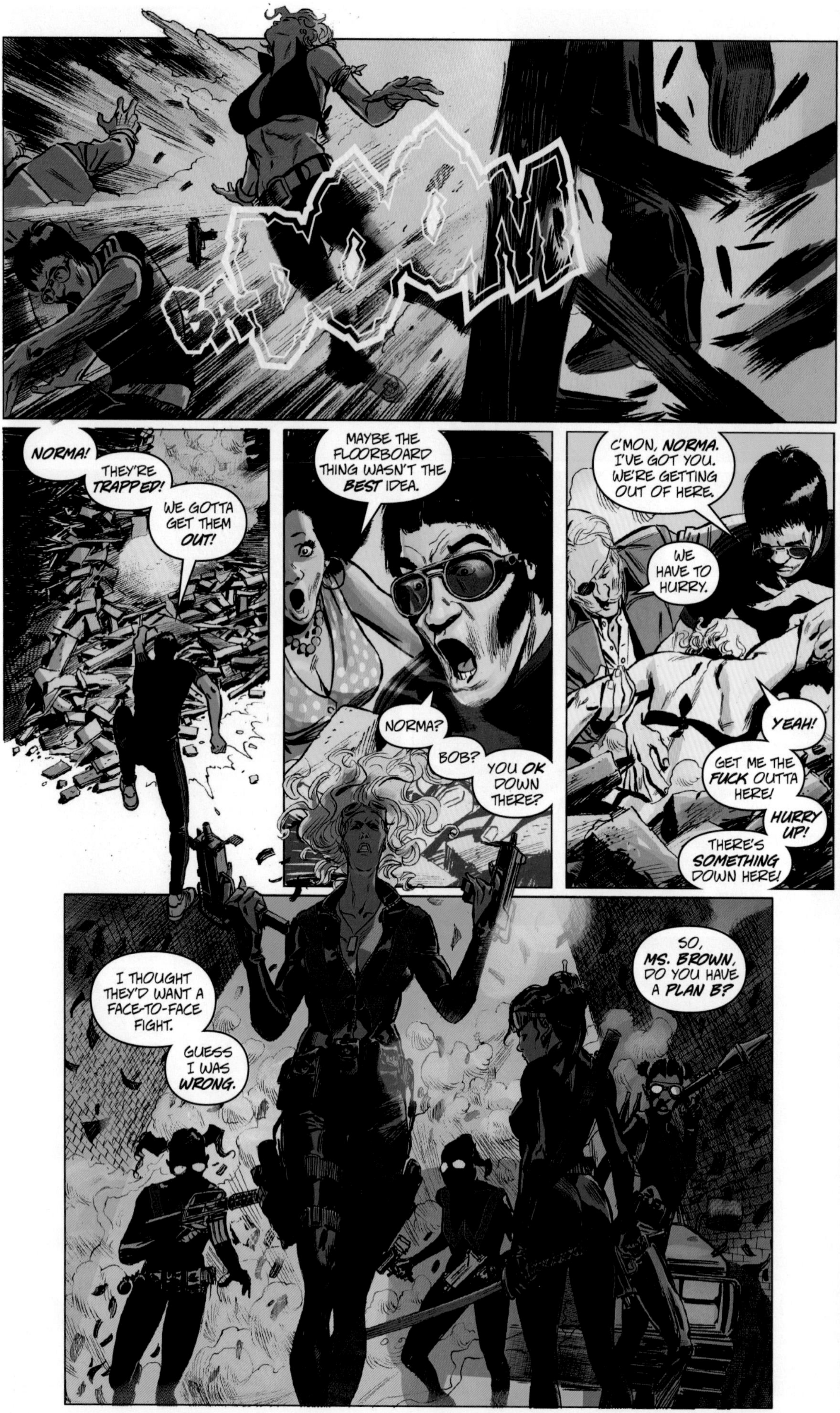
NORMA!
THEY'RE TRAPPED!
WE GOTTA GET THEM OUT!
MAYBE THE FLOORBOARD THING WASN'T THE BEST IDEA.
NORMA?
BOB?
YOU OK DOWN THERE?
C'MON, NORMA. I'VE GOT YOU. WE'RE GETTING OUT OF HERE.
WE HAVE TO HURRY.
YEAH!
GET ME THE FUCK OUTTA HERE!
HURRY UP!
THERE'S SOMETHING DOWN HERE!
I THOUGHT THEY'D WANT A FACE-TO-FACE FIGHT.
GUESS I WAS WRONG.
SO, MS. BROWN, DO YOU HAVE A PLAN B?

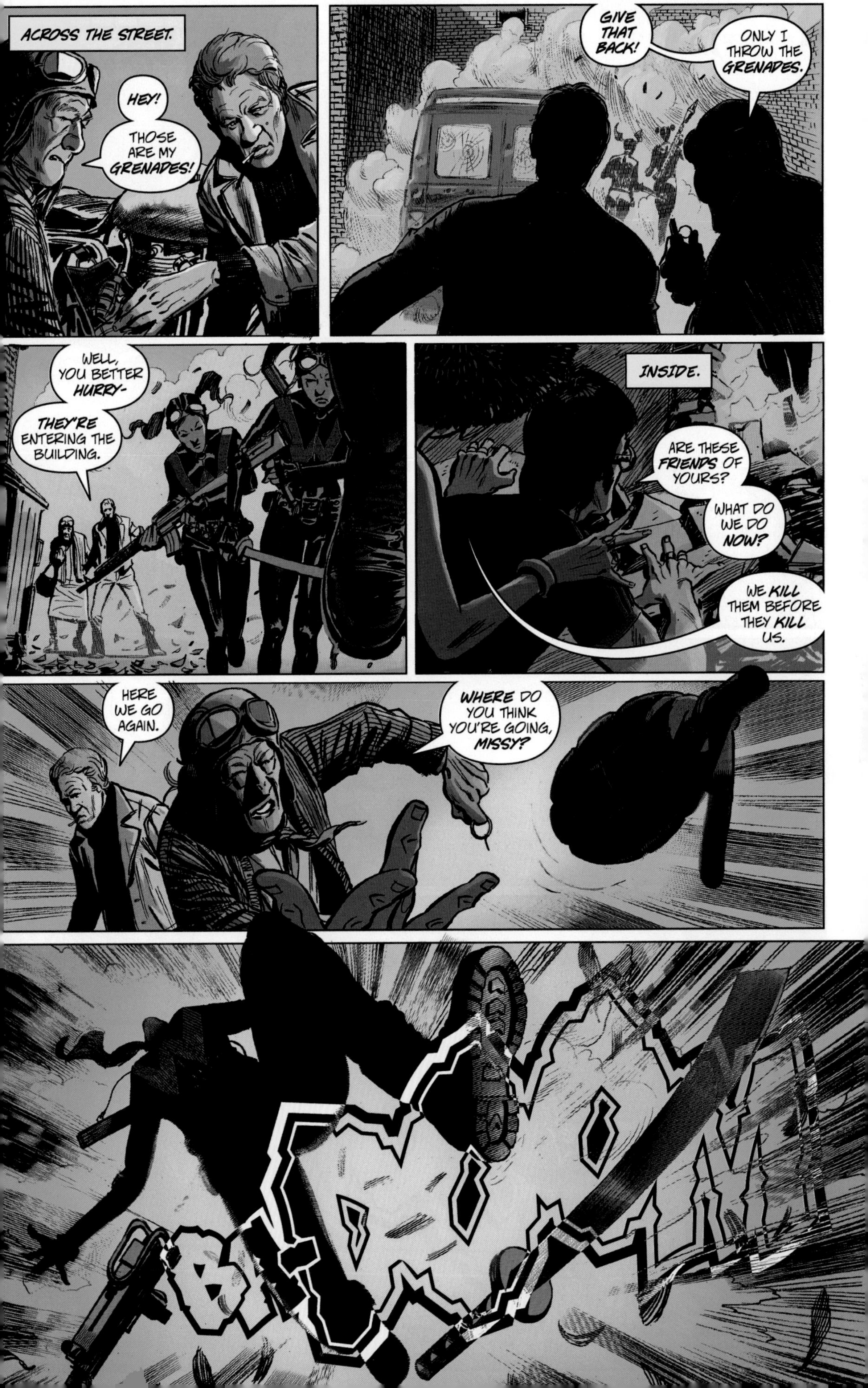

ACROSS THE STREET.
HEY!
THOSE ARE MY GRENADES!
GIVE THAT BACK!
ONLY I THROW THE GRENADES.
WELL, YOU BETTER HURRY-
THEY'RE ENTERING THE BUILDING.
INSIDE.
ARE THESE FRIENDS OF YOURS?
WHAT DO WE DO NOW?
WE KILL THEM BEFORE THEY KILL US.
HERE WE GO AGAIN.
WHERE DO YOU THINK YOU'RE GOING, MISSY?
BOOM!

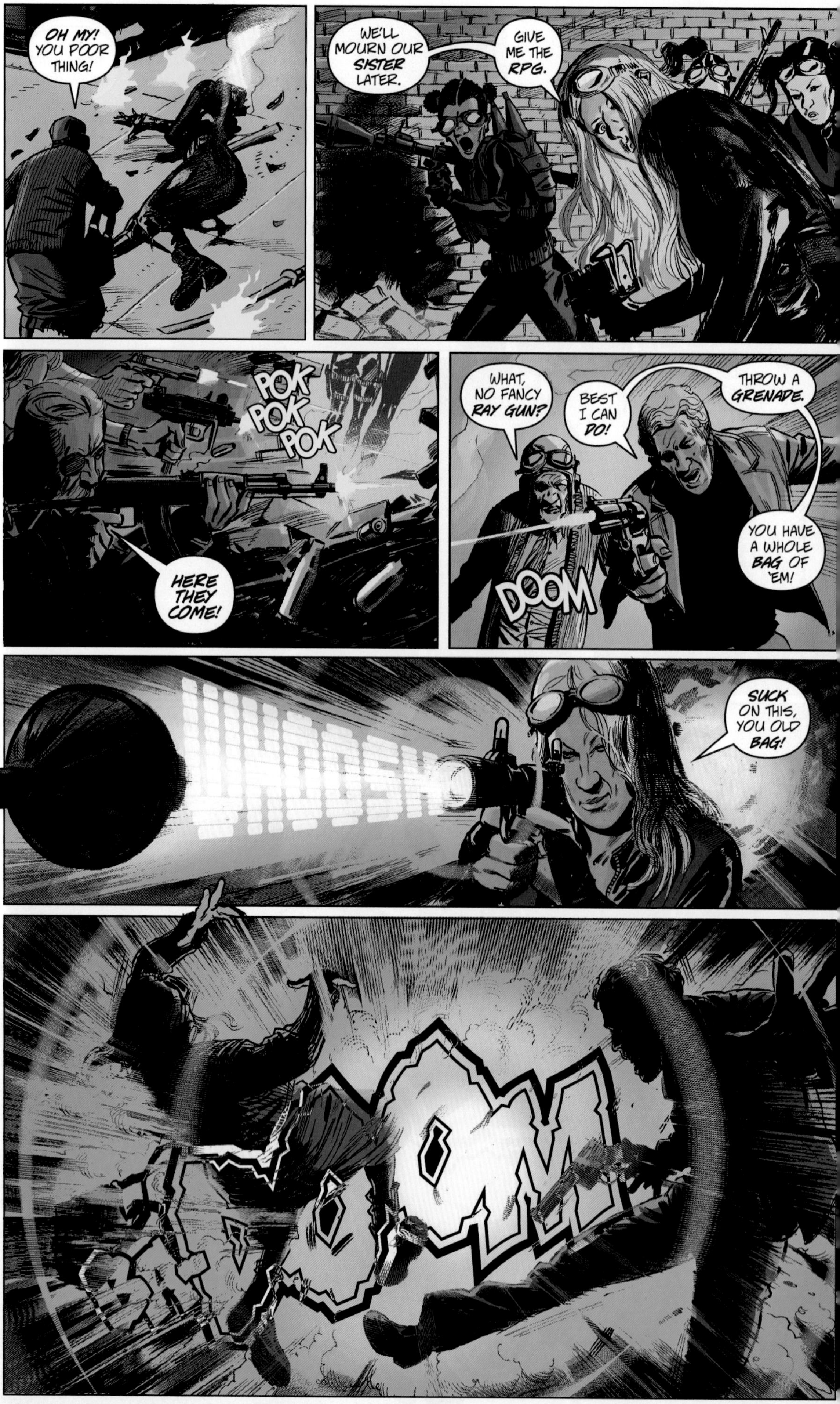
OH MY! YOU POOR THING!
WE'LL MOURN OUR SISTER LATER.
GIVE ME THE RPG.
POK POK POK
HERE THEY COME!
WHAT, NO FANCY RAY GUN?
BEST I CAN DO!
THROW A GRENADE.
DOOM
YOU HAVE A WHOLE BAG OF 'EM!
SUCK ON THIS, YOU OLD BAG!

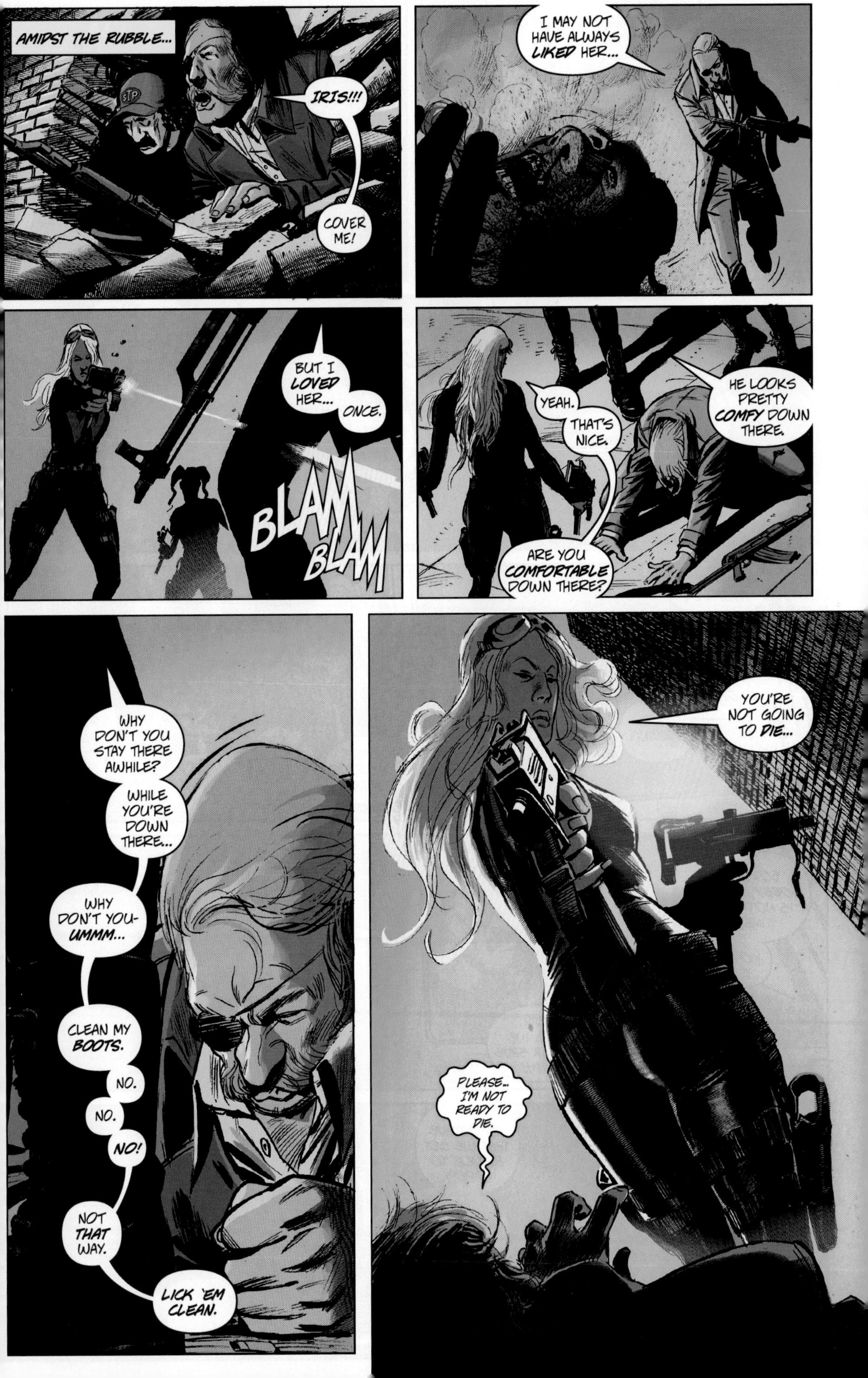
AMIDST THE RUBBLE...
IRIS!!!
COVER ME!
I MAY NOT HAVE ALWAYS LIKED HER...
BUT I LOVED HER...
ONCE.
BLAM
BLAM
YEAH.
THAT'S NICE.
HE LOOKS PRETTY COMFY DOWN THERE.
ARE YOU COMFORTABLE DOWN THERE?
WHY DON'T YOU STAY THERE AWHILE?
WHILE YOU'RE DOWN THERE...
WHY DON'T YOU- UMMM...
CLEAN MY BOOTS.
NO.
NO.
NO!
NOT THAT WAY.
LICK 'EM CLEAN.
YOU'RE NOT GOING TO DIE...
PLEASE... I'M NOT READY TO DIE.

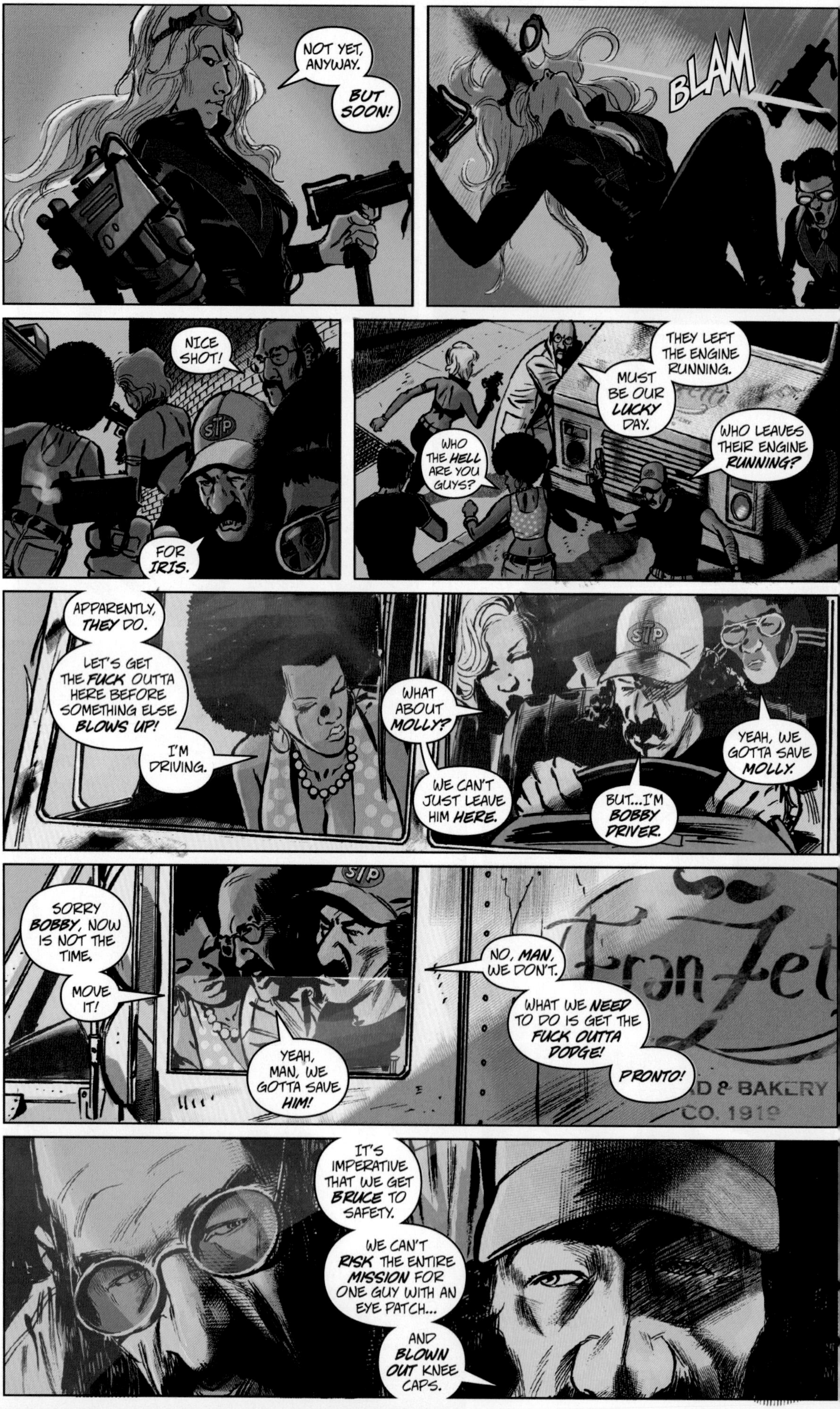

NOT YET, ANYWAY.
BUT SOON!
BLAM
NICE SHOT!
FOR IRIS.
THEY LEFT THE ENGINE RUNNING.
MUST BE OUR LUCKY DAY.
WHO THE HELL ARE YOU GUYS?
WHO LEAVES THEIR ENGINE RUNNING?
APPARENTLY, THEY DO.
LET'S GET THE FUCK OUTTA HERE BEFORE SOMETHING ELSE BLOWS UP!
I'M DRIVING.
WHAT ABOUT MOLLY?
WE CAN'T JUST LEAVE HIM HERE.
BUT...I'M BOBBY DRIVER.
YEAH, WE GOTTA SAVE MOLLY.
SORRY BOBBY, NOW IS NOT THE TIME.
MOVE IT!
YEAH, MAN, WE GOTTA SAVE HIM!
NO, MAN, WE DON'T.
WHAT WE NEED TO DO IS GET THE FUCK OUTTA DODGE!
PRONTO!
AD & BAKERY
CO. 1919
IT'S IMPERATIVE THAT WE GET BRUCE TO SAFETY.
WE CAN'T RISK THE ENTIRE MISSION FOR ONE GUY WITH AN EYE PATCH...
AND BLOWN OUT KNEE CAPS.

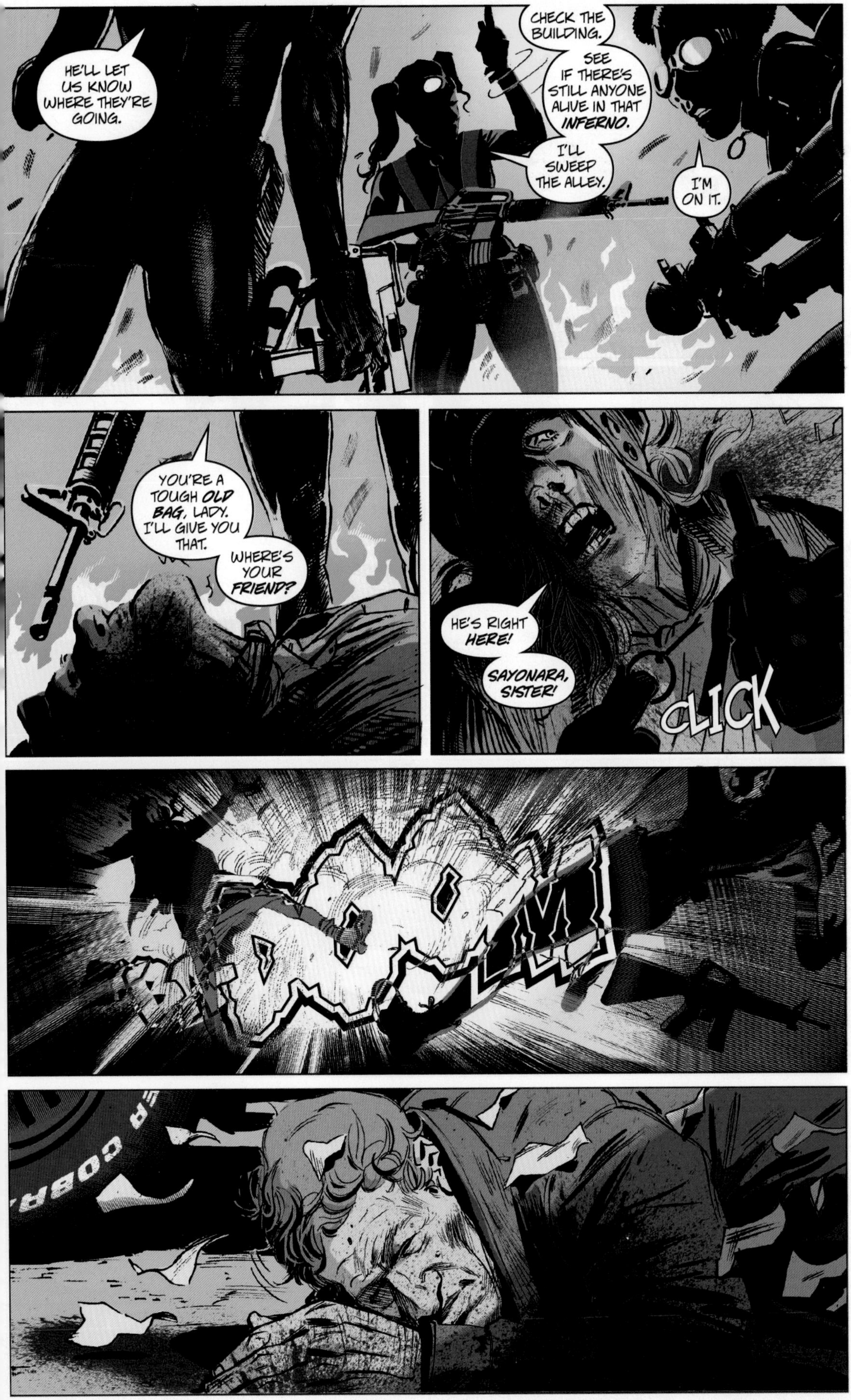
HE'LL LET US KNOW WHERE THEY'RE GOING.
CHECK THE BUILDING.
SEE IF THERE'S STILL ANYONE ALIVE IN THAT *INFERNO*.
I'LL SWEEP THE ALLEY.
I'M ON IT.
YOU'RE A TOUGH *OLD BAG*, LADY. I'LL GIVE YOU THAT.
WHERE'S YOUR *FRIEND?*
HE'S RIGHT *HERE!*
SAYONARA, SISTER!
CLICK

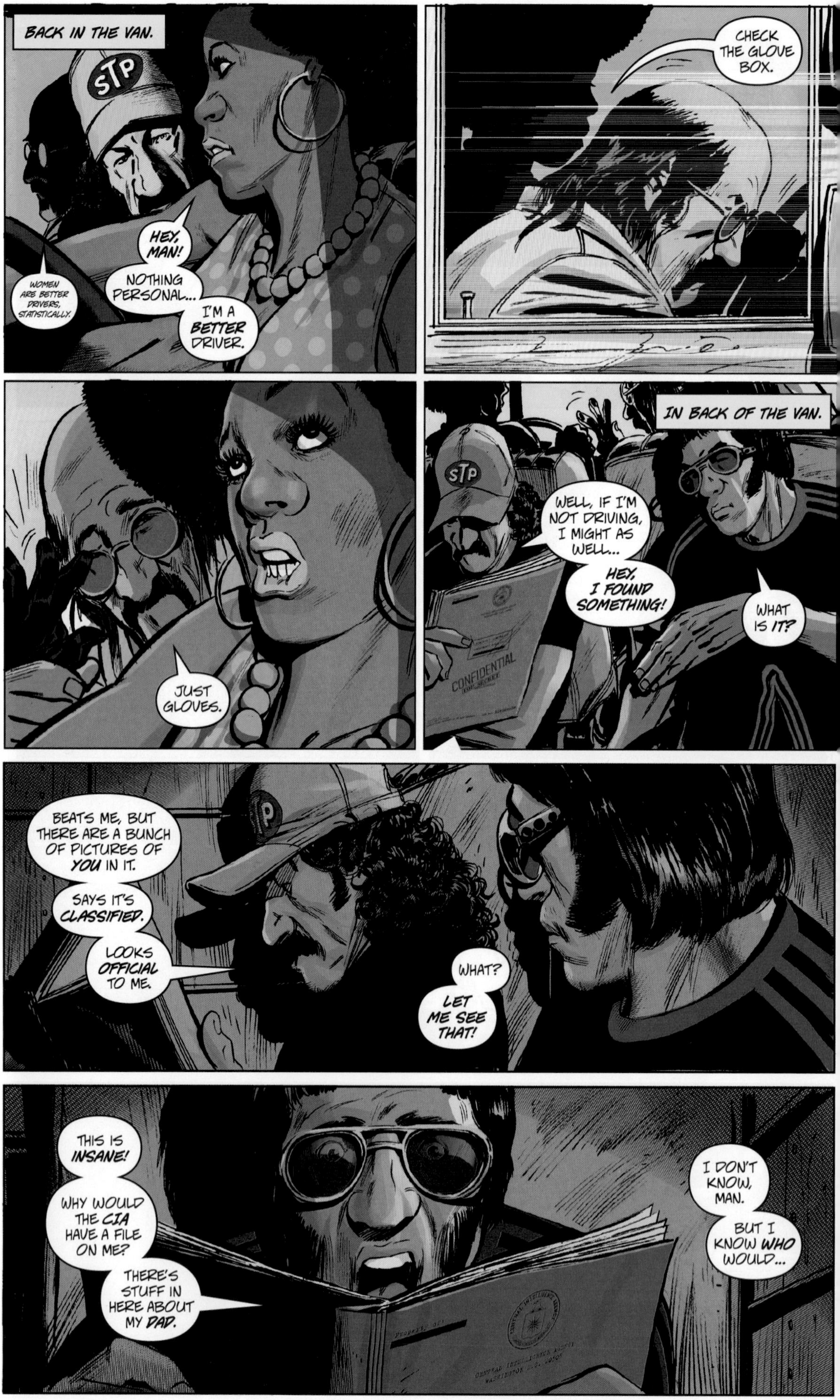
BACK IN THE VAN.
HEY, MAN!
NOTHING PERSONAL...
I'M A BETTER DRIVER.
WOMEN ARE BETTER DRIVERS, STATISTICALLY.
CHECK THE GLOVE BOX.
JUST GLOVES.
IN BACK OF THE VAN.
WELL, IF I'M NOT DRIVING, I MIGHT AS WELL...
HEY, I FOUND SOMETHING!
WHAT IS IT?
CONFIDENTIAL
BEATS ME, BUT THERE ARE A BUNCH OF PICTURES OF YOU IN IT.
SAYS IT'S CLASSIFIED.
LOOKS OFFICIAL TO ME.
WHAT?
LET ME SEE THAT!
THIS IS INSANE!
WHY WOULD THE CIA HAVE A FILE ON ME?
THERE'S STUFF IN HERE ABOUT MY DAD.
I DON'T KNOW, MAN.
BUT I KNOW WHO WOULD...

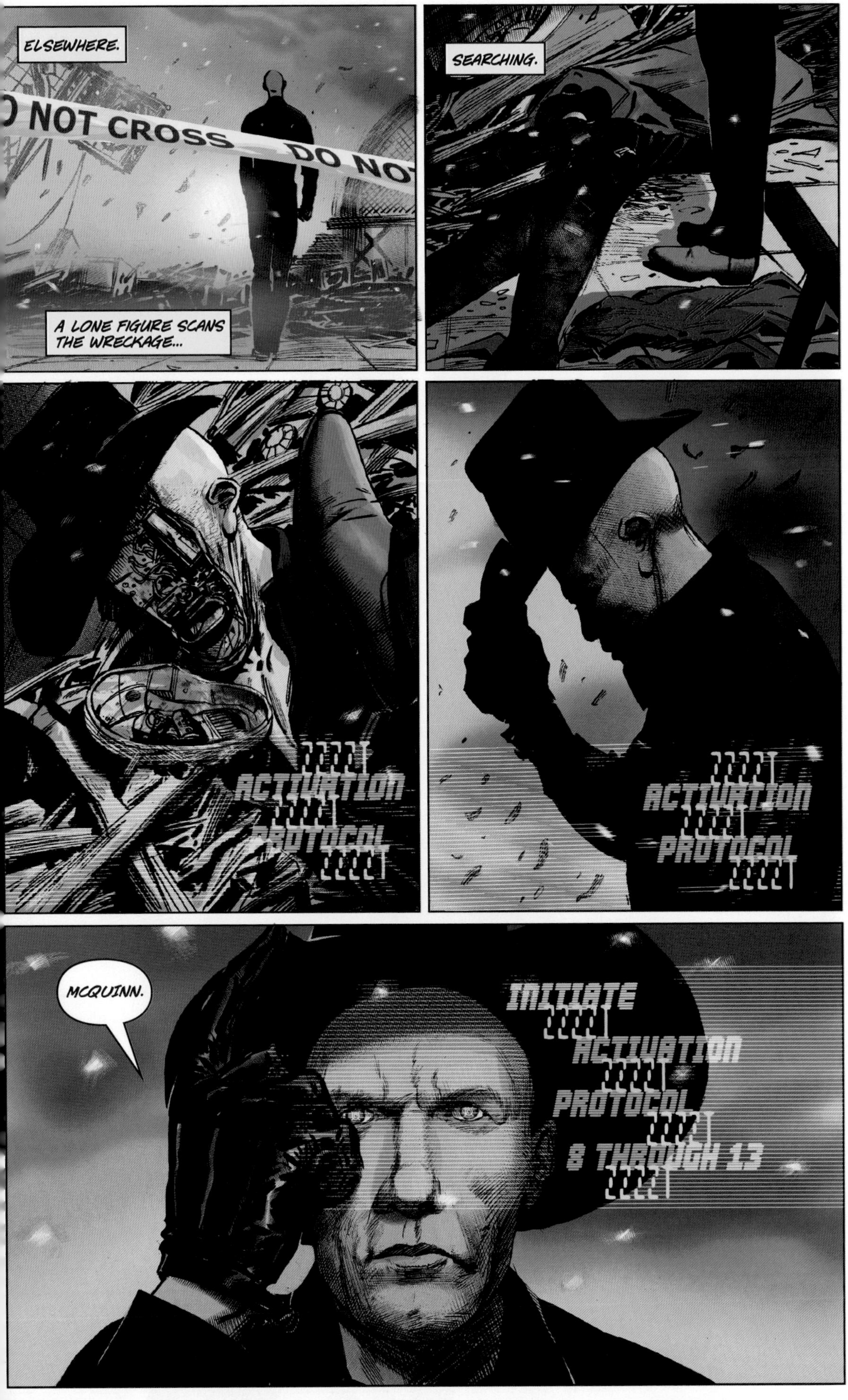
ELSEWHERE.
NOT CROSS
DO NO
A LONE FIGURE SCANS THE WRECKAGE...
SEARCHING.
ACTIVATION
PROTOCOL
ACTIVATION
PROTOCOL
MCQUINN.
INITIATE
ACTIVATION
PROTOCOL
8 THROUGH 13

CHAPTER THREE

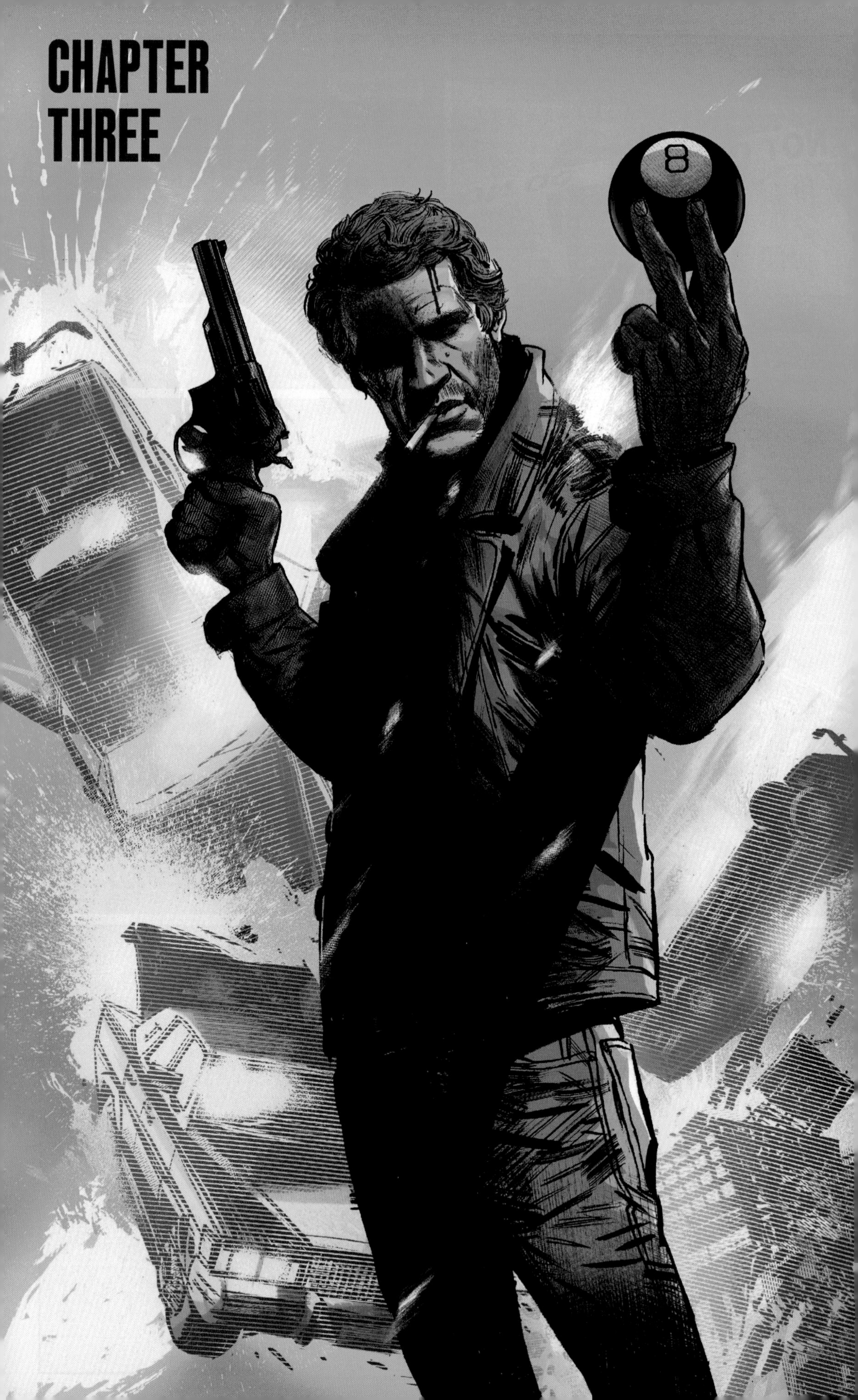
8

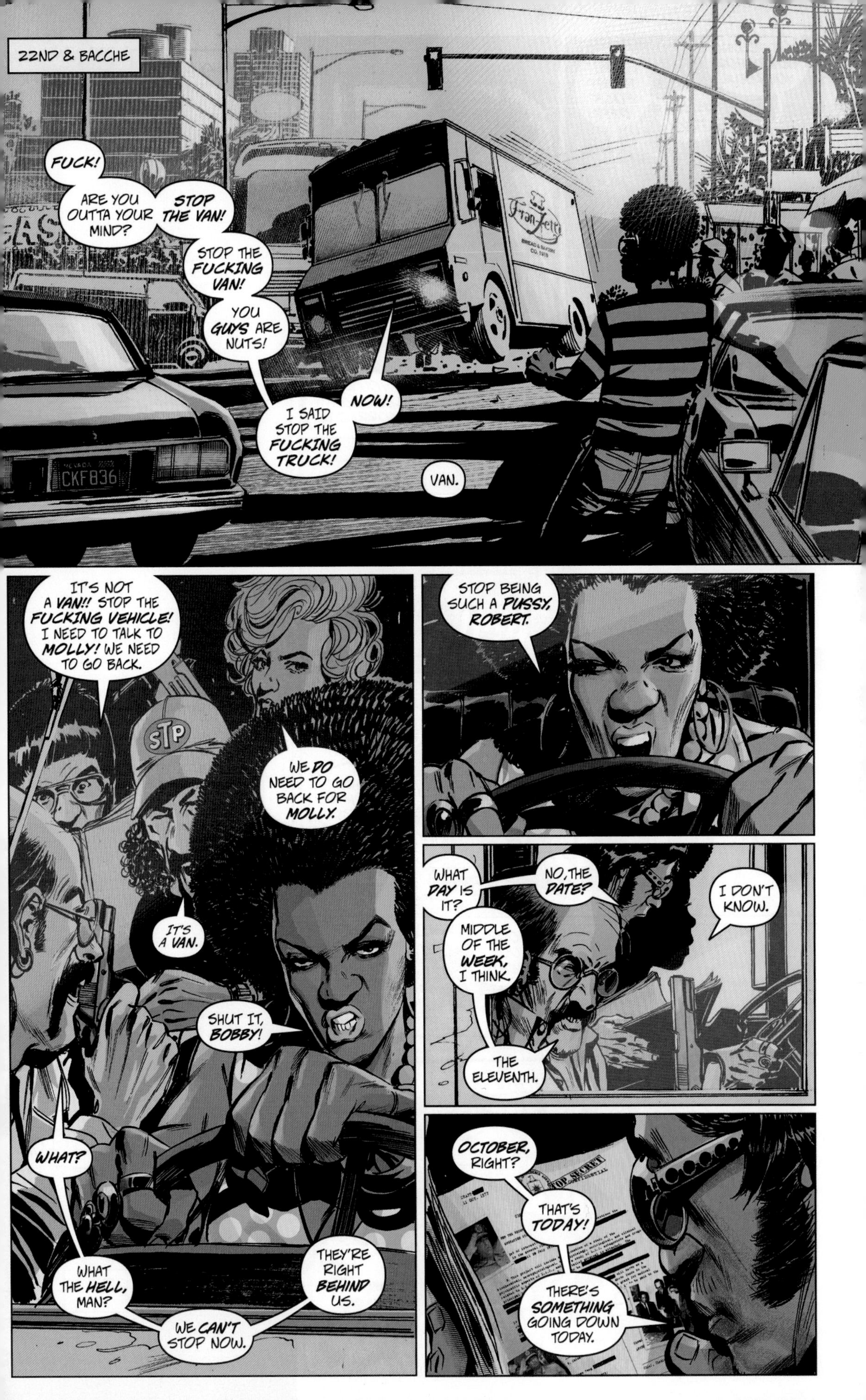
22ND & BACCHE
FUCK!
ARE YOU OUTTA YOUR MIND?
STOP THE VAN!
STOP THE FUCKING VAN!
YOU GUYS ARE NUTS!
NOW!
I SAID STOP THE FUCKING TRUCK!
VAN.
CKF 836
IT'S NOT A VAN!! STOP THE FUCKING VEHICLE! I NEED TO TALK TO MOLLY! WE NEED TO GO BACK.
WE DO NEED TO GO BACK FOR MOLLY.
IT'S A VAN.
SHUT IT, BOBBY!
WHAT?
WHAT THE HELL, MAN?
THEY'RE RIGHT BEHIND US.
WE CAN'T STOP NOW.
STOP BEING SUCH A PUSSY, ROBERT.
WHAT DAY IS IT?
NO, THE DATE?
I DON'T KNOW.
MIDDLE OF THE WEEK, I THINK.
THE ELEVENTH.
OCTOBER, RIGHT?
TOP SECRET
THAT'S TODAY!
THERE'S SOMETHING GOING DOWN TODAY.

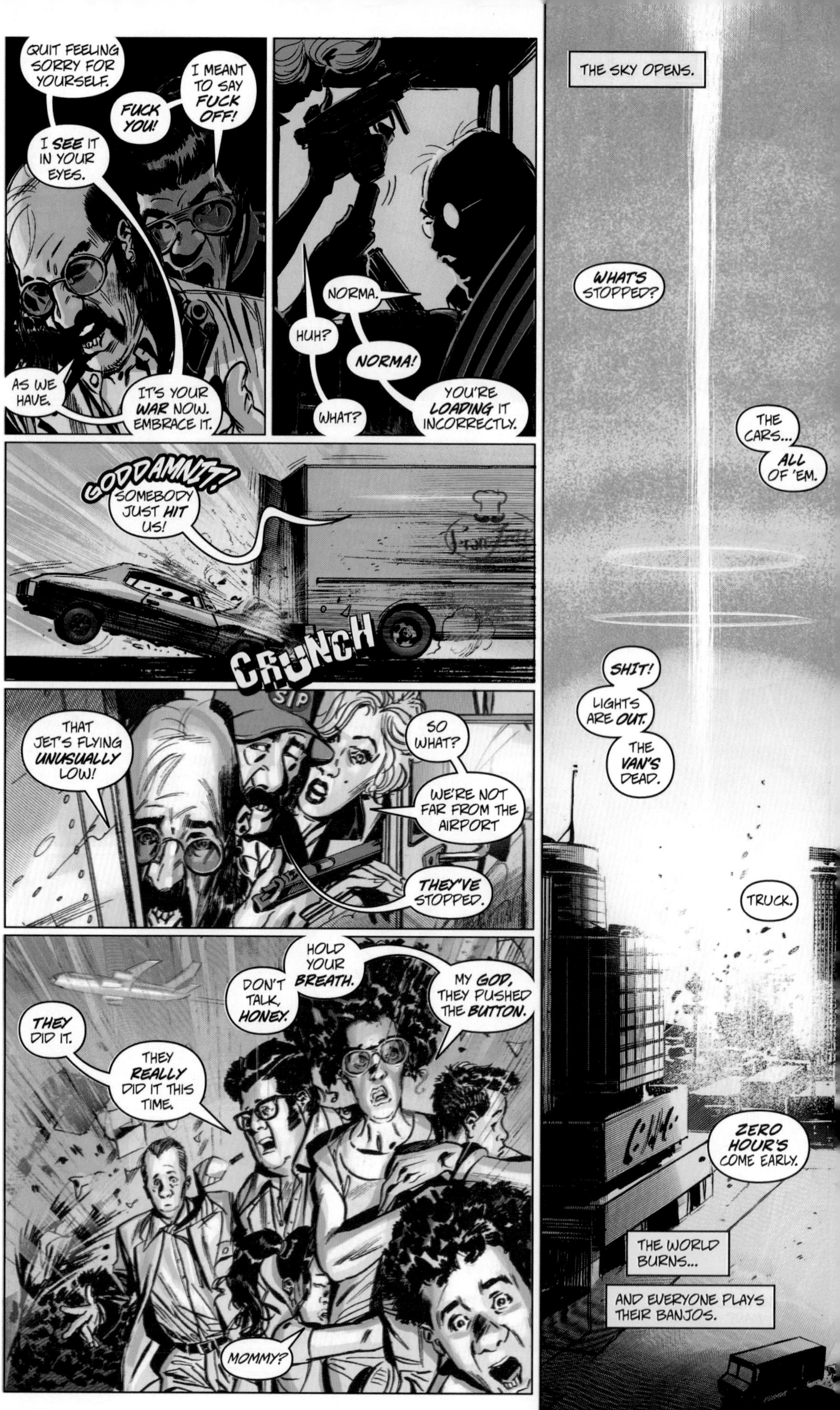
QUIT FEELING SORRY FOR YOURSELF.
I SEE IT IN YOUR EYES.
FUCK YOU!
I MEANT TO SAY FUCK OFF!
AS WE HAVE.
IT'S YOUR WAR NOW. EMBRACE IT.
NORMA.
HUH?
NORMA!
WHAT?
YOU'RE LOADING IT INCORRECTLY.
GODDAMNIT! SOMEBODY JUST HIT US!
CRUNCH
THAT JET'S FLYING UNUSUALLY LOW!
SO WHAT?
WE'RE NOT FAR FROM THE AIRPORT
THEY'VE STOPPED.
THEY DID IT.
THEY REALLY DID IT THIS TIME.
DON'T TALK, HONEY.
HOLD YOUR BREATH.
MY GOD, THEY PUSHED THE BUTTON.
MOMMY?
THE SKY OPENS.
WHAT'S STOPPED?
THE CARS... ALL OF 'EM.
SHIT!
LIGHTS ARE OUT.
THE VAN'S DEAD.
TRUCK.
ZERO HOUR'S COME EARLY.
THE WORLD BURNS...
AND EVERYONE PLAYS THEIR BANJOS.

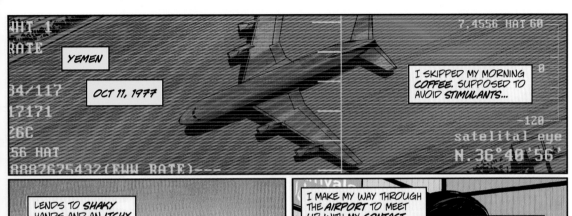

YEMEN

OCT 11, 1977

7.4556 HAT 60

I SKIPPED MY MORNING COFFEE. SUPPOSED TO AVOID STIMULANTS...

satelital eye
N. 36°40'56'

LENDS TO SHAKY HANDS AND AN ITCHY TRIGGER FINGER.

THE MARK IS ONE LIEUTENANT-COLONEL IBRAHAM AL-HAMDI.

I DON'T KNOW ANY OF THE DETAILS BEYOND THAT.

I MAKE MY WAY THROUGH THE AIRPORT TO MEET UP WITH MY CONTACT.

THE LOCALS ARE IN A FRENZY.

AFTER ALL, I'M SUPPOSED TO BE DEAD...

AM I?

I CAN'T BE CERTAIN.

//8887DDODODDPS
RDSPDPDP:GGA NSA
YEMEN- 12-10-1977

EVERYONE IS STARING IN AWE, WIDE-EYED IN AMAZEMENT.

AFTER ALL, ELVIS IS "OFFICIALLY" DEAD.

I SIGN AUTOGRAPHS.

I'M ON AUTO PILOT NOW.

IT'S ALL CLINICAL.

ELVIS OP - RATE 303#35 vie

SIR?

YEAH. LET'S GO.

SAMSONITE.

DURABLE.

GORILLA PROOF.

I SIGN MORE **AUTOGRAPHS** AS THE **OPERATION** IS EXPLAINED TO ME IN MINUTE DETAIL.

HERE'S THE **PLAN** AS IT STANDS.

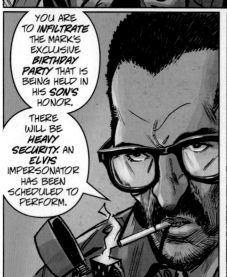

YOU ARE TO **INFILTRATE** THE MARK'S EXCLUSIVE **BIRTHDAY PARTY** THAT IS BEING HELD IN HIS **SON'S** HONOR.

THERE WILL BE **HEAVY SECURITY.** AN **ELVIS IMPERSONATOR** HAS BEEN SCHEDULED TO PERFORM.

THE SAFEHOUSE

TYPICAL **SHIT** HOLE.

AT LEAST THEY GOT THE **POSTERS** RIGHT.

MY **HEAD** HURTS.

I'M NOT SURE IF THE **PAIN** IS **REAL** OR **IMAGINARY**.

SOMETHING I'VE **CONJURED** UP FOR THE MISSION.

I TRY TO **CONVINCE** MYSELF THIS IS A **BAD MAN**.

THE PRIVATE MADE **PUBLIC**.

HOUSES...HOMES...TORN OR BLOWN IN HALF.

THE INSIDES **VISIBLE,** AND IT'S **ALL** THIS MAN'S FAULT.

BUT I **KNOW** BETTER.

THERE WILL BE CONSEQUENCES.

FAR-REACHING **CONSEQUENCES** THAT WILL COME BACK AND **BITE** US ALL ON OUR COLLECTIVE ASSES.

IT ALL STARTS IN **YEMEN**...

NOT EVEN A **BLIP** ON THE RADAR.

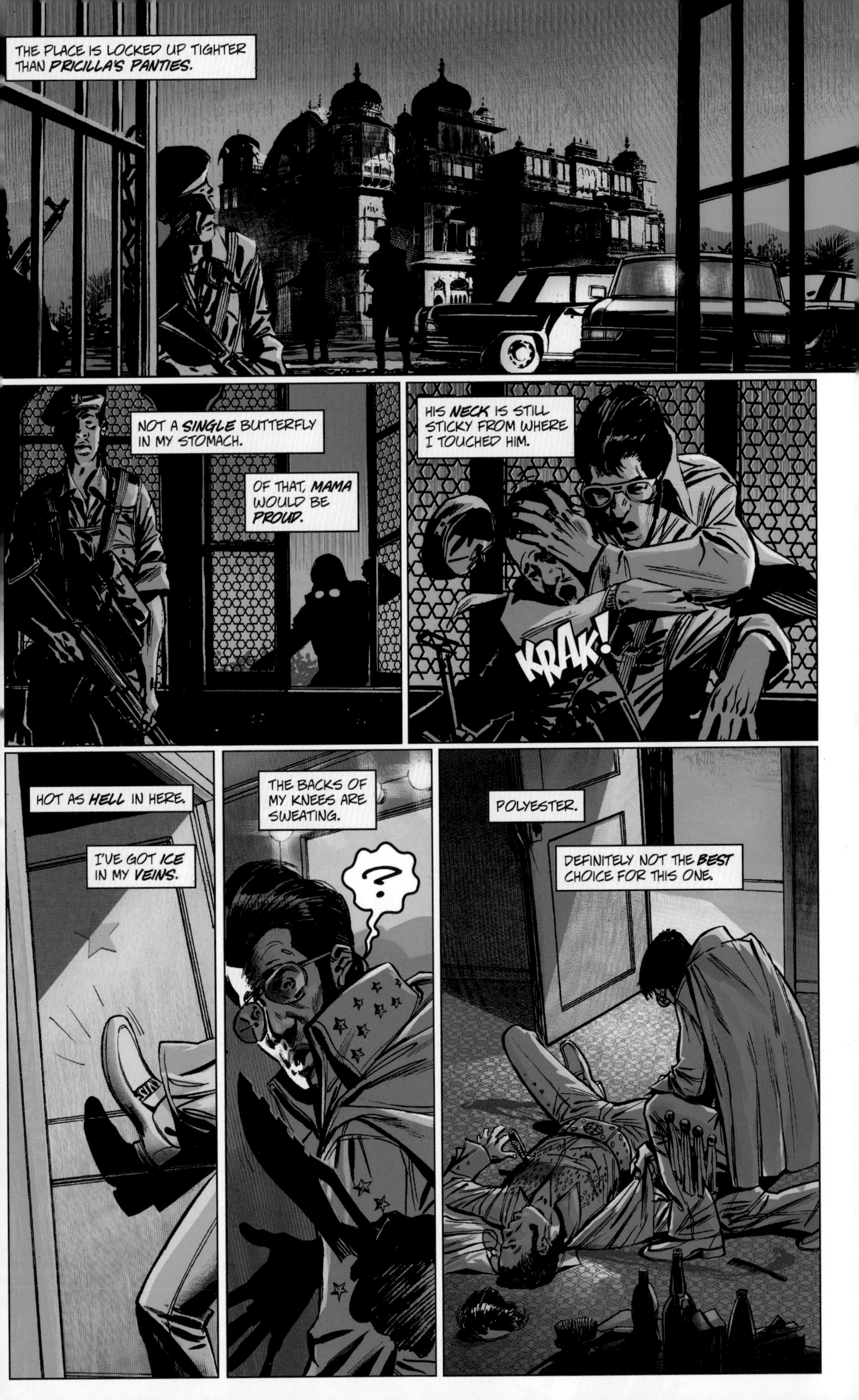
THE PLACE IS LOCKED UP TIGHTER THAN PRICILLA'S PANTIES.
NOT A SINGLE BUTTERFLY IN MY STOMACH.
OF THAT, MAMA WOULD BE PROUD.
HIS NECK IS STILL STICKY FROM WHERE I TOUCHED HIM.
KRAK!
HOT AS HELL IN HERE.
I'VE GOT ICE IN MY VEINS.
THE BACKS OF MY KNEES ARE SWEATING.
?
POLYESTER.
DEFINITELY NOT THE BEST CHOICE FOR THIS ONE.

I HEAR THE AUDIENCE.

WHISPERS.

LAUGHTER.

AN OCCASIONAL COUGH.

THEN SILENCE.

THE CROWD GOES WILD.

THEIR KING IS IN THE HOUSE.

ELVIS OP/ RATE:3322 3 10-11-1977 Targ... ...ham al-Hamdi

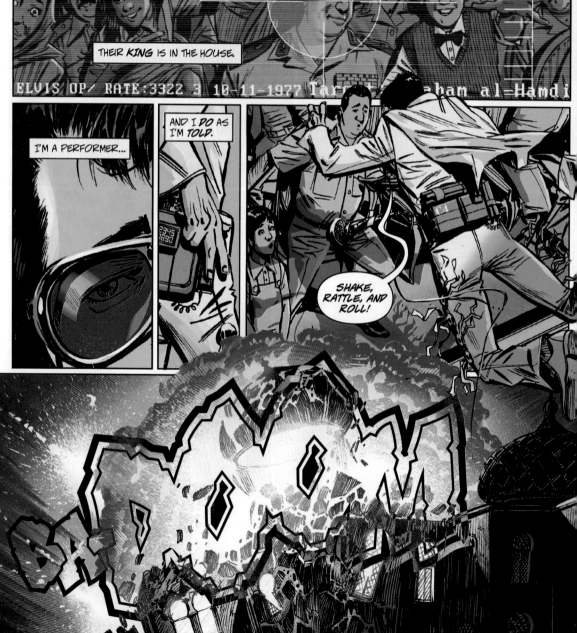

I'M A PERFORMER...

AND I DO AS I'M TOLD.

SHAKE, RATTLE, AND ROLL!

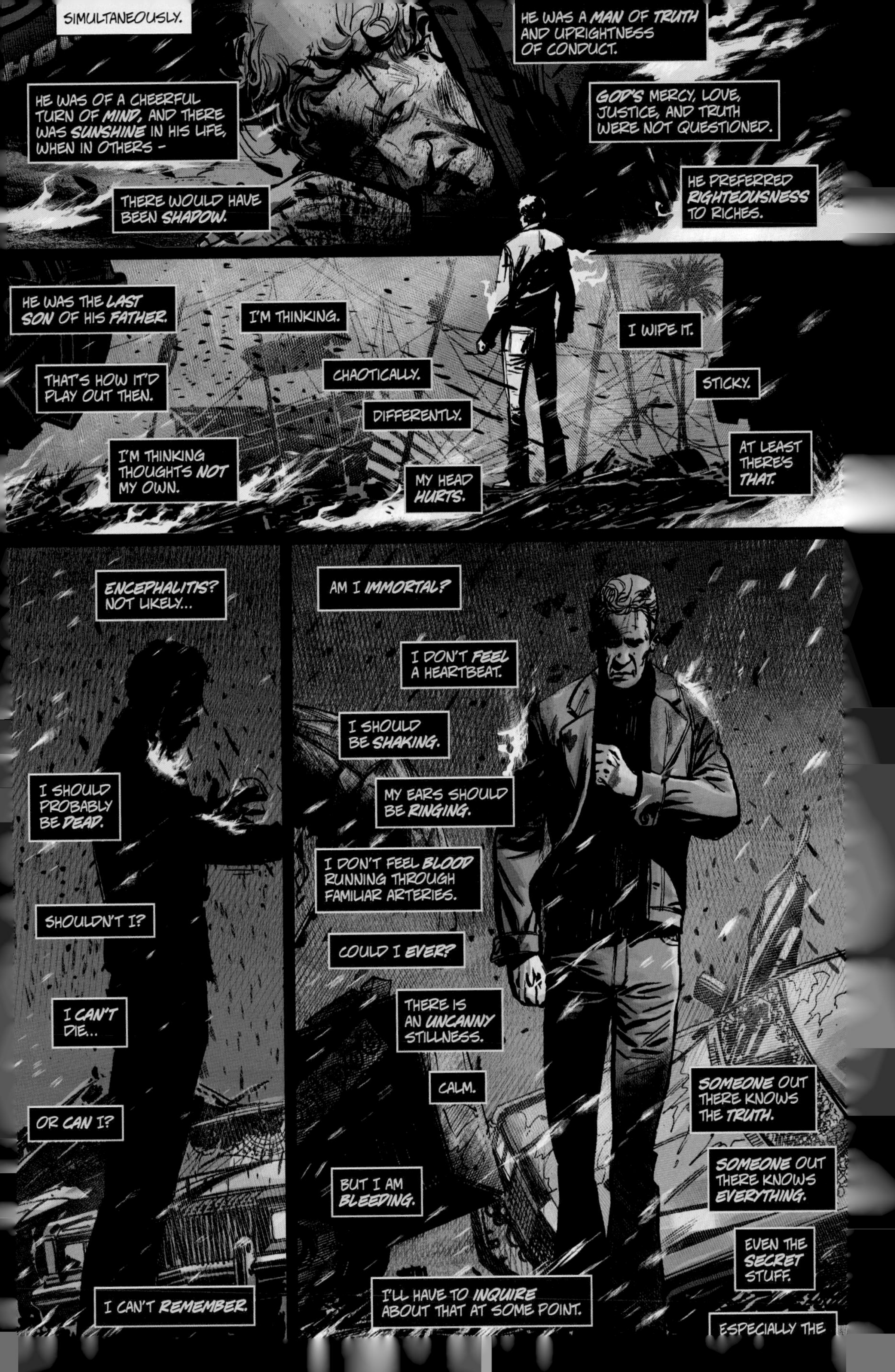
SIMULTANEOUSLY.
HE WAS OF A CHEERFUL TURN OF MIND, AND THERE WAS SUNSHINE IN HIS LIFE, WHEN IN OTHERS -
THERE WOULD HAVE BEEN SHADOW.
HE WAS A MAN OF TRUTH AND UPRIGHTNESS OF CONDUCT.
GOD'S MERCY, LOVE, JUSTICE, AND TRUTH WERE NOT QUESTIONED.
HE PREFERRED RIGHTEOUSNESS TO RICHES.
HE WAS THE LAST SON OF HIS FATHER.
THAT'S HOW IT'D PLAY OUT THEN.
I'M THINKING THOUGHTS NOT MY OWN.
I'M THINKING.
CHAOTICALLY.
DIFFERENTLY.
MY HEAD HURTS.
I WIPE IT.
STICKY.
AT LEAST THERE'S THAT.
ENCEPHALITIS? NOT LIKELY...
I SHOULD PROBABLY BE DEAD.
SHOULDN'T I?
I CAN'T DIE...
OR CAN I?
I CAN'T REMEMBER.
AM I IMMORTAL?
I DON'T FEEL A HEARTBEAT.
I SHOULD BE SHAKING.
MY EARS SHOULD BE RINGING.
I DON'T FEEL BLOOD RUNNING THROUGH FAMILIAR ARTERIES.
COULD I EVER?
THERE IS AN UNCANNY STILLNESS.
CALM.
BUT I AM BLEEDING.
SOMEONE OUT THERE KNOWS THE TRUTH.
SOMEONE OUT THERE KNOWS EVERYTHING.
EVEN THE SECRET STUFF.
I'LL HAVE TO INQUIRE ABOUT THAT AT SOME POINT.
ESPECIALLY THE

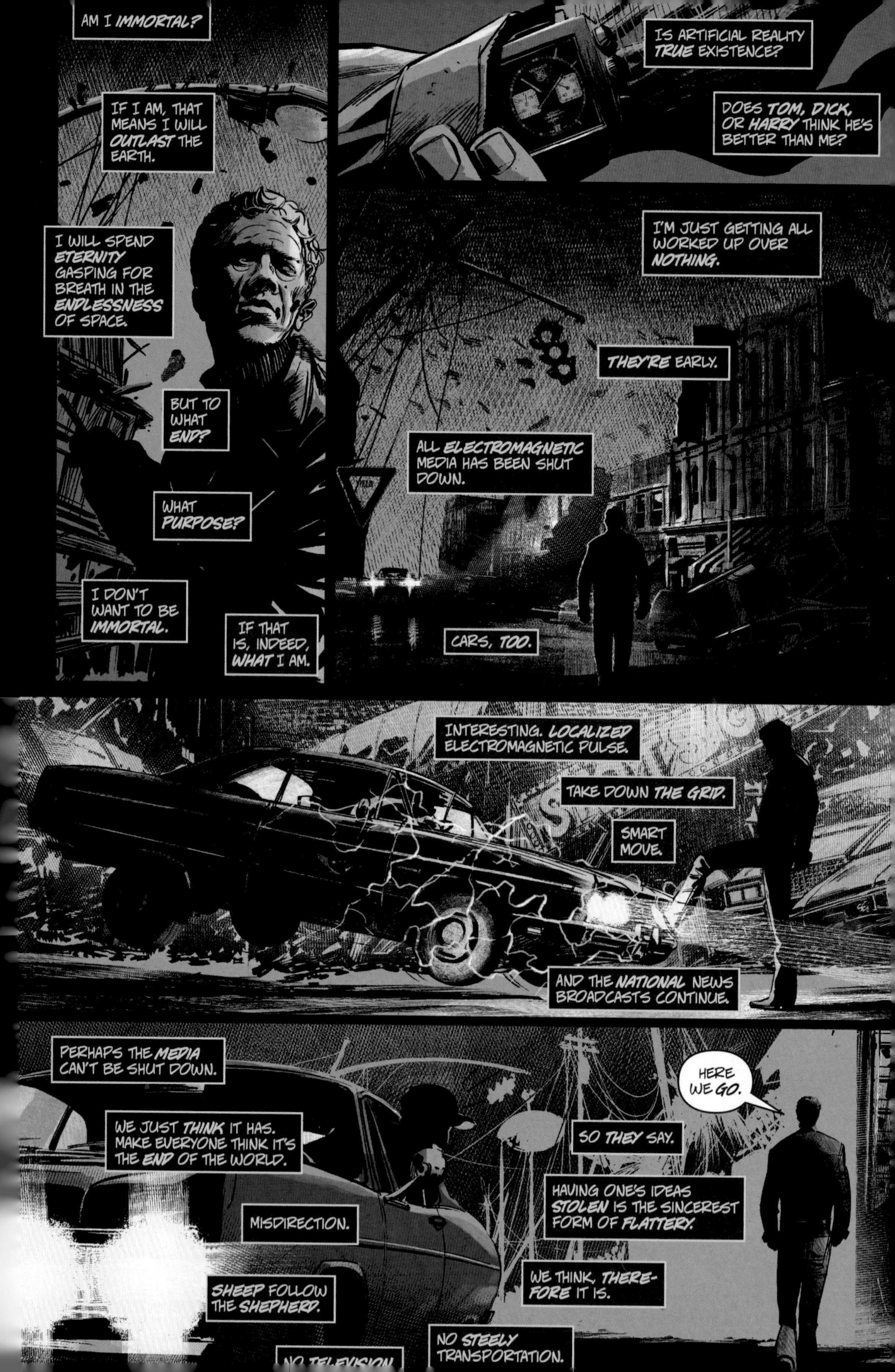
AM I IMMORTAL?
IF I AM, THAT MEANS I WILL OUTLAST THE EARTH.
I WILL SPEND ETERNITY GASPING FOR BREATH IN THE ENDLESSNESS OF SPACE.
BUT TO WHAT END?
WHAT PURPOSE?
I DON'T WANT TO BE IMMORTAL.
IF THAT IS, INDEED, WHAT I AM.
IS ARTIFICIAL REALITY TRUE EXISTENCE?
DOES TOM, DICK, OR HARRY THINK HE'S BETTER THAN ME?
I'M JUST GETTING ALL WORKED UP OVER NOTHING.
THEY'RE EARLY.
ALL ELECTROMAGNETIC MEDIA HAS BEEN SHUT DOWN.
CARS, TOO.
INTERESTING. LOCALIZED ELECTROMAGNETIC PULSE.
TAKE DOWN THE GRID.
SMART MOVE.
AND THE NATIONAL NEWS BROADCASTS CONTINUE.
PERHAPS THE MEDIA CAN'T BE SHUT DOWN.
WE JUST THINK IT HAS. MAKE EVERYONE THINK IT'S THE END OF THE WORLD.
MISDIRECTION.
SHEEP FOLLOW THE SHEPHERD.
HERE WE GO.
SO THEY SAY.
HAVING ONE'S IDEAS STOLEN IS THE SINCEREST FORM OF FLATTERY.
WE THINK, THEREFORE IT IS.
NO STEELY TRANSPORTATION.

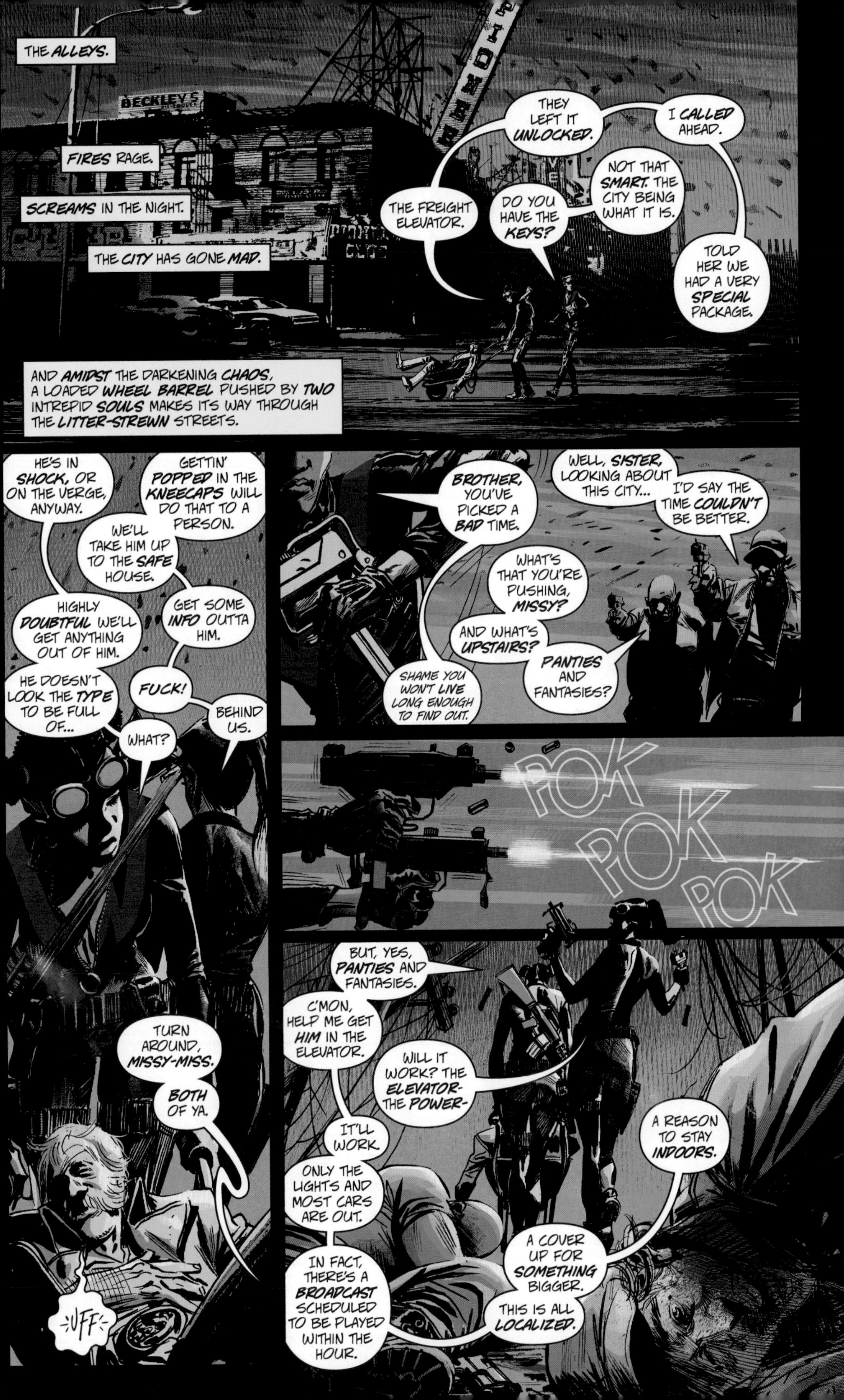
THE ALLEYS.
FIRES RAGE.
SCREAMS IN THE NIGHT.
THE CITY HAS GONE MAD.
THE FREIGHT ELEVATOR.
THEY LEFT IT UNLOCKED.
I CALLED AHEAD.
DO YOU HAVE THE KEYS?
NOT THAT SMART. THE CITY BEING WHAT IT IS.
TOLD HER WE HAD A VERY SPECIAL PACKAGE.
AND AMIDST THE DARKENING CHAOS, A LOADED WHEEL BARREL PUSHED BY TWO INTREPID SOULS MAKES ITS WAY THROUGH THE LITTER-STREWN STREETS.
HE'S IN SHOCK, OR ON THE VERGE, ANYWAY.
GETTIN' POPPED IN THE KNEECAPS WILL DO THAT TO A PERSON.
WE'LL TAKE HIM UP TO THE SAFE HOUSE.
GET SOME INFO OUTTA HIM.
HIGHLY DOUBTFUL WE'LL GET ANYTHING OUT OF HIM.
HE DOESN'T LOOK THE TYPE TO BE FULL OF...
FUCK!
WHAT?
BEHIND US.
TURN AROUND, MISSY-MISS.
BOTH OF YA.
UFF
BROTHER, YOU'VE PICKED A BAD TIME.
WELL, SISTER, LOOKING ABOUT THIS CITY...
I'D SAY THE TIME COULDN'T BE BETTER.
WHAT'S THAT YOU'RE PUSHING, MISSY?
AND WHAT'S UPSTAIRS?
PANTIES AND FANTASIES?
SHAME YOU WON'T LIVE LONG ENOUGH TO FIND OUT.
POK
POK
POK
BUT, YES, PANTIES AND FANTASIES.
C'MON, HELP ME GET HIM IN THE ELEVATOR.
WILL IT WORK? THE ELEVATOR- THE POWER-
IT'LL WORK.
ONLY THE LIGHTS AND MOST CARS ARE OUT.
IN FACT, THERE'S A BROADCAST SCHEDULED TO BE PLAYED WITHIN THE HOUR.
A REASON TO STAY INDOORS.
A COVER UP FOR SOMETHING BIGGER.
THIS IS ALL LOCALIZED.

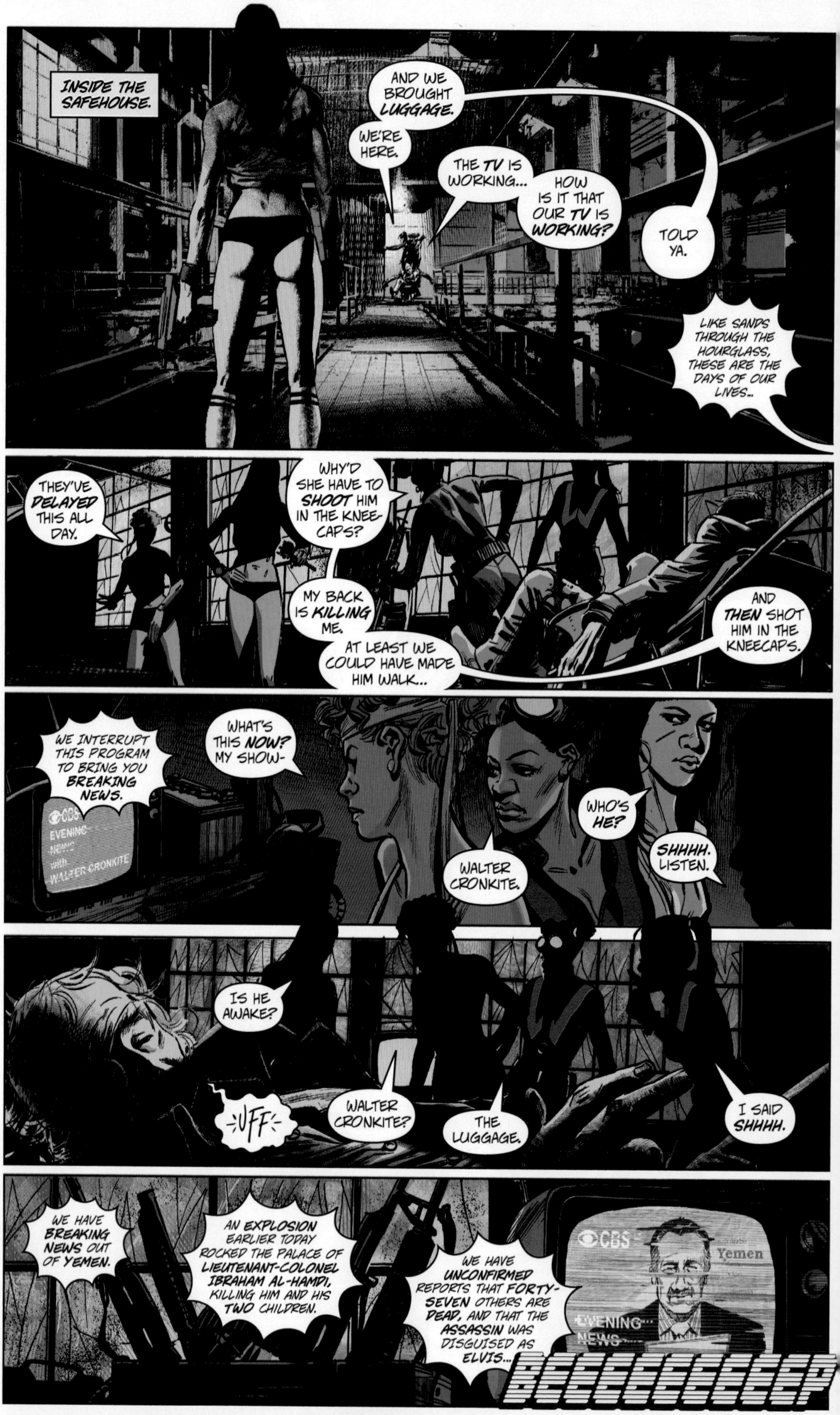
INSIDE THE SAFEHOUSE.
AND WE BROUGHT LUGGAGE.
WE'RE HERE.
THE TV IS WORKING...
HOW IS IT THAT OUR TV IS WORKING?
TOLD YA.
LIKE SANDS THROUGH THE HOURGLASS, THESE ARE THE DAYS OF OUR LIVES...
THEY'VE DELAYED THIS ALL DAY.
WHY'D SHE HAVE TO SHOOT HIM IN THE KNEE-CAPS?
MY BACK IS KILLING ME.
AT LEAST WE COULD HAVE MADE HIM WALK...
AND THEN SHOT HIM IN THE KNEECAPS.
WE INTERRUPT THIS PROGRAM TO BRING YOU BREAKING NEWS.
CBS EVENING NEWS with WALTER CRONKITE
WHAT'S THIS NOW? MY SHOW-
WHO'S HE?
WALTER CRONKITE.
SHHHH. LISTEN.
IS HE AWAKE?
UFF
WALTER CRONKITE?
THE LUGGAGE.
I SAID SHHHH.
WE HAVE BREAKING NEWS OUT OF YEMEN.
AN EXPLOSION EARLIER TODAY ROCKED THE PALACE OF LIEUTENANT-COLONEL IBRAHAM AL-HAMDI, KILLING HIM AND HIS TWO CHILDREN.
WE HAVE UNCONFIRMED REPORTS THAT FORTY-SEVEN OTHERS ARE DEAD, AND THAT THE ASSASSIN WAS DISGUISED AS ELVIS...
CBS
Yemen
EVENING NEWS
BEEEEEEEEEEP

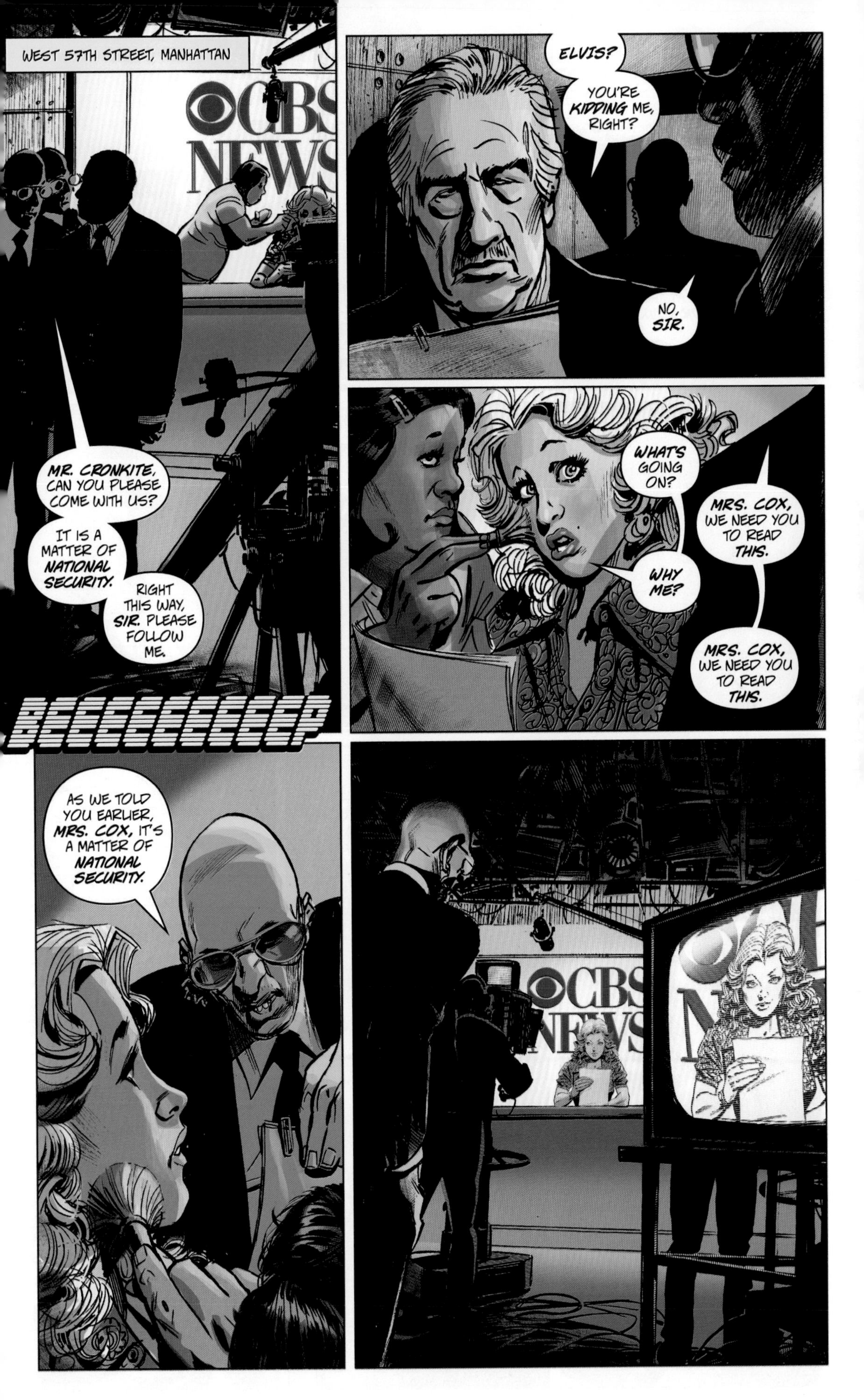
WEST 57TH STREET, MANHATTAN
CBS NEWS
MR. CRONKITE, CAN YOU PLEASE COME WITH US?
IT IS A MATTER OF NATIONAL SECURITY.
RIGHT THIS WAY, SIR. PLEASE FOLLOW ME.
ELVIS?
YOU'RE KIDDING ME, RIGHT?
NO, SIR.
BEEEEEEEEEEEP
WHAT'S GOING ON?
MRS. COX, WE NEED YOU TO READ THIS.
WHY ME?
MRS. COX, WE NEED YOU TO READ THIS.
AS WE TOLD YOU EARLIER, MRS. COX, IT'S A MATTER OF NATIONAL SECURITY.
CBS NEWS

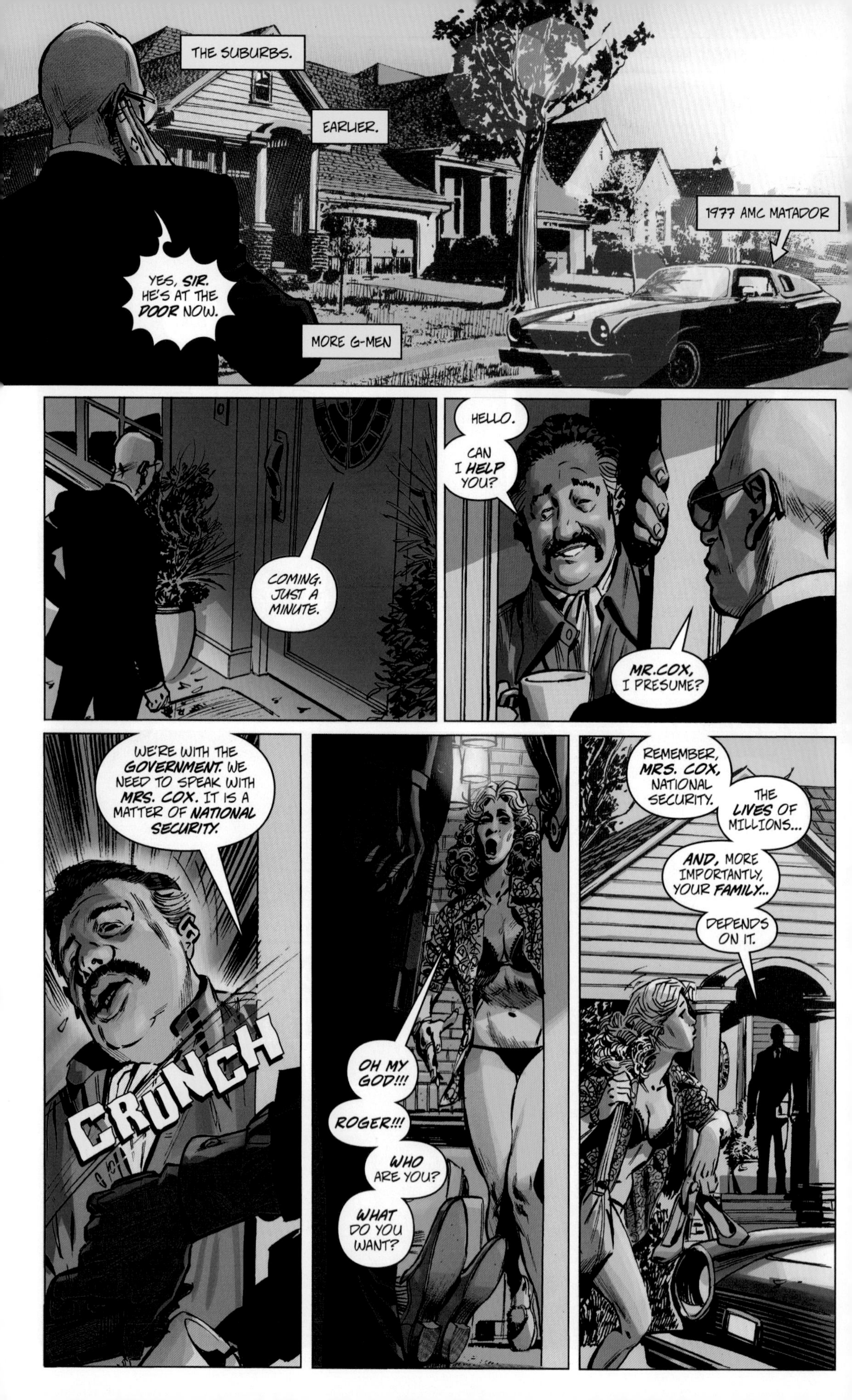
THE SUBURBS.
EARLIER.
1977 AMC MATADOR
YES, SIR. HE'S AT THE DOOR NOW.
MORE G-MEN
COMING. JUST A MINUTE.
HELLO.
CAN I HELP YOU?
MR.COX, I PRESUME?
WE'RE WITH THE GOVERNMENT. WE NEED TO SPEAK WITH MRS. COX. IT IS A MATTER OF NATIONAL SECURITY.
CRUNCH
OH MY GOD!!!
ROGER!!!
WHO ARE YOU?
WHAT DO YOU WANT?
REMEMBER, MRS. COX, NATIONAL SECURITY.
THE LIVES OF MILLIONS...
AND, MORE IMPORTANTLY, YOUR FAMILY...
DEPENDS ON IT.

YOU WALK THROUGH *LIFE*, AND YOU DO YOUR *BEST* TO CONFIDENTLY LOOK *PEOPLE* IN THE *EYE*. LOOKING PEOPLE IN THE EYE, *ONE* SOMETIMES WONDERS WHAT *DARK SECRETS* ARE THEY HIDING. THEIR STOIC *FACADE* PLAYING OUT *DAILY* TO PLACATE *SOCIETAL NORMS*. WHAT BROUGHT THEM TO THAT *PLACE* IN TIME? THAT VERY *MOMENT*? YOU SEE AN *ATTRACTIVE WOMAN* STOPPED AT A LIGHT IN *RUSH HOUR* TRAFFIC, FRANTICALLY PUTTING ON *MAKEUP* IN HER REAR VIEW MIRROR...

YOU THINK TO YOURSELF... WHAT *CIRCUMSTANCES* PUT HER IN THAT POSITION? WHAT'S HER *SECRET*, AND IS IT WORTH IT JUST TO KEEP UP *APPEARANCES*?

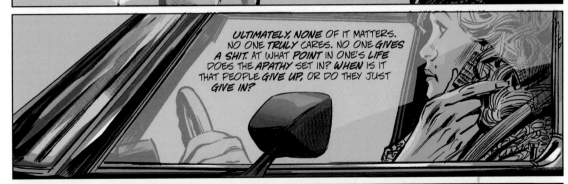

ULTIMATELY, NONE OF IT MATTERS. NO ONE *TRULY* CARES. NO ONE GIVES A *SHIT*. AT WHAT *POINT* IN ONE'S *LIFE* DOES THE *APATHY* SET IN? WHEN IS IT THAT PEOPLE *GIVE UP*, OR DO THEY JUST *GIVE IN*?

HOOONK HOOONK

THE *LIGHT* AIN'T GETTIN' ANY GREENER, *TOOTS*!!! *MOVE YOUR ASS*!!!

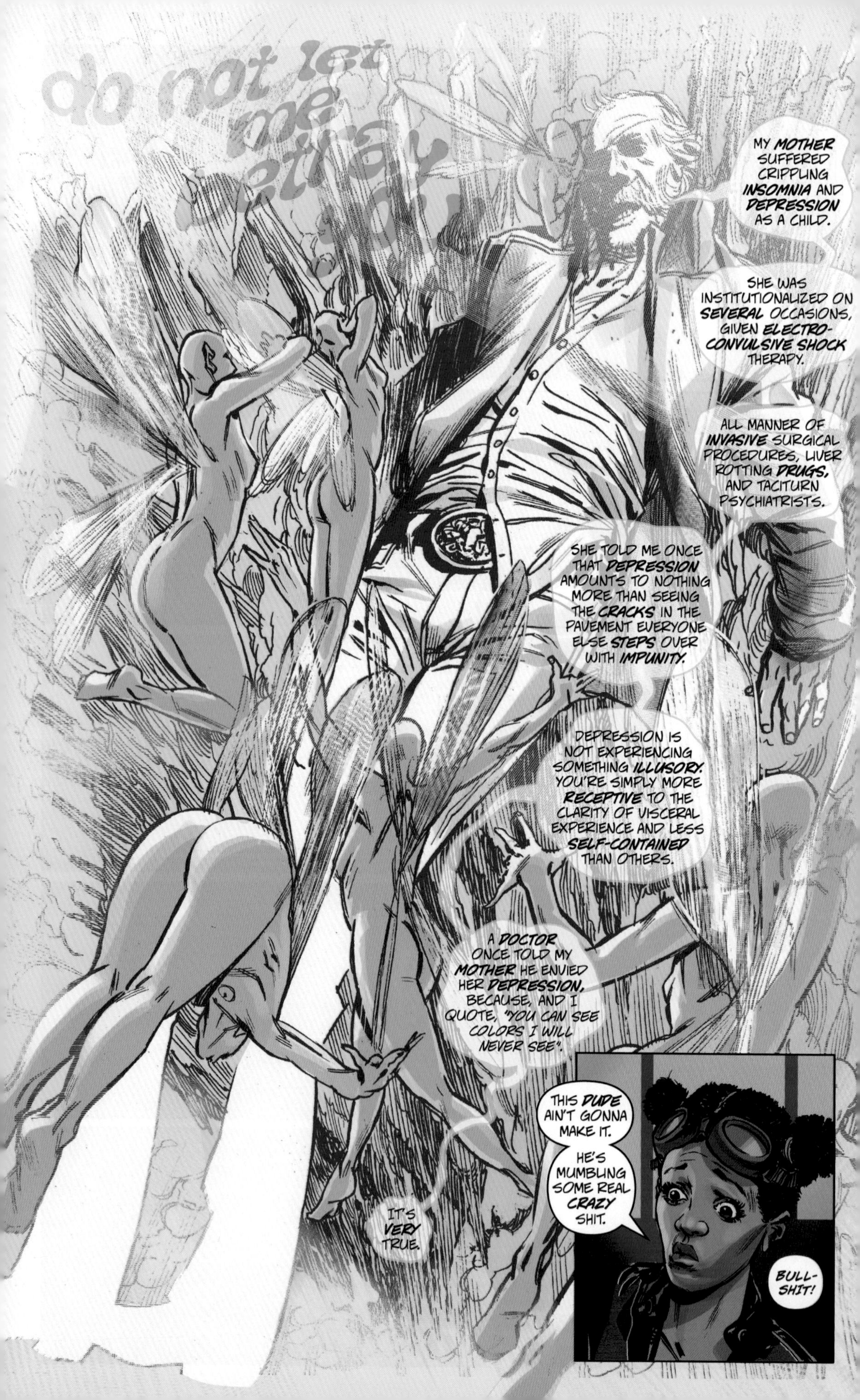
do not let me
MY MOTHER SUFFERED CRIPPLING INSOMNIA AND DEPRESSION AS A CHILD.
SHE WAS INSTITUTIONALIZED ON SEVERAL OCCASIONS, GIVEN ELECTRO-CONVULSIVE SHOCK THERAPY.
ALL MANNER OF INVASIVE SURGICAL PROCEDURES, LIVER ROTTING DRUGS, AND TACITURN PSYCHIATRISTS.
SHE TOLD ME ONCE THAT DEPRESSION AMOUNTS TO NOTHING MORE THAN SEEING THE CRACKS IN THE PAVEMENT EVERYONE ELSE STEPS OVER WITH IMPUNITY.
DEPRESSION IS NOT EXPERIENCING SOMETHING ILLUSORY. YOU'RE SIMPLY MORE RECEPTIVE TO THE CLARITY OF VISCERAL EXPERIENCE AND LESS SELF-CONTAINED THAN OTHERS.
A DOCTOR ONCE TOLD MY MOTHER HE ENVIED HER DEPRESSION, BECAUSE, AND I QUOTE, "YOU CAN SEE COLORS I WILL NEVER SEE".
IT'S VERY TRUE.
THIS DUDE AIN'T GONNA MAKE IT.
HE'S MUMBLING SOME REAL CRAZY SHIT.
BULL-SHIT!

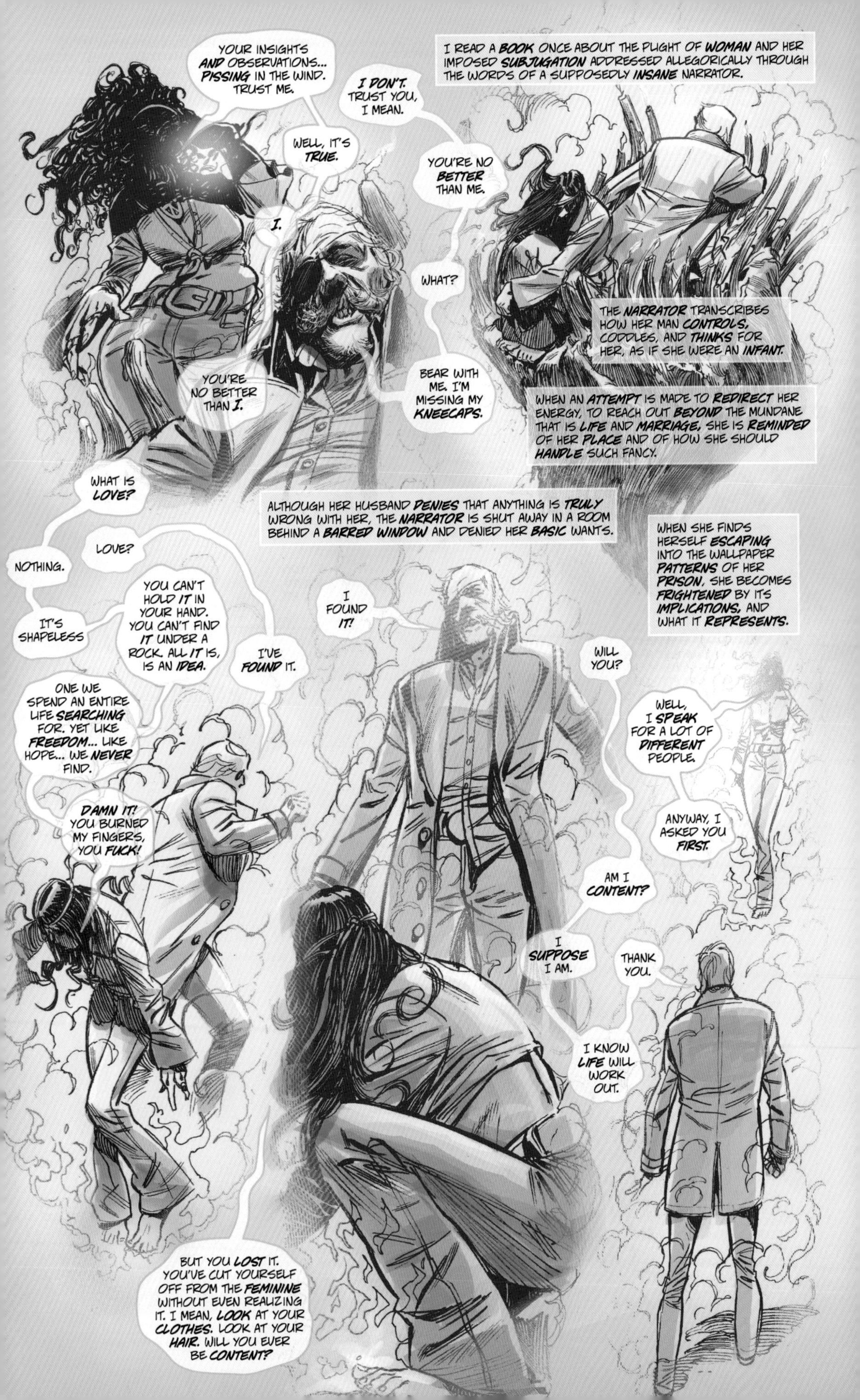
YOUR INSIGHTS AND OBSERVATIONS... PISSING IN THE WIND. TRUST ME.
I DON'T. TRUST YOU, I MEAN.
WELL, IT'S TRUE.
YOU'RE NO BETTER THAN ME.
I.
WHAT?
YOU'RE NO BETTER THAN I.
BEAR WITH ME. I'M MISSING MY KNEECAPS.
I READ A BOOK ONCE ABOUT THE PLIGHT OF WOMAN AND HER IMPOSED SUBJUGATION ADDRESSED ALLEGORICALLY THROUGH THE WORDS OF A SUPPOSEDLY INSANE NARRATOR.
THE NARRATOR TRANSCRIBES HOW HER MAN CONTROLS, CODDLES, AND THINKS FOR HER, AS IF SHE WERE AN INFANT.
WHEN AN ATTEMPT IS MADE TO REDIRECT HER ENERGY, TO REACH OUT BEYOND THE MUNDANE THAT IS LIFE AND MARRIAGE, SHE IS REMINDED OF HER PLACE AND OF HOW SHE SHOULD HANDLE SUCH FANCY.
WHAT IS LOVE?
NOTHING.
LOVE?
IT'S SHAPELESS
YOU CAN'T HOLD IT IN YOUR HAND. YOU CAN'T FIND IT UNDER A ROCK. ALL IT IS, IS AN IDEA.
ONE WE SPEND AN ENTIRE LIFE SEARCHING FOR. YET LIKE FREEDOM... LIKE HOPE... WE NEVER FIND.
I'VE FOUND IT.
DAMN IT! YOU BURNED MY FINGERS, YOU FUCK!
ALTHOUGH HER HUSBAND DENIES THAT ANYTHING IS TRULY WRONG WITH HER, THE NARRATOR IS SHUT AWAY IN A ROOM BEHIND A BARRED WINDOW AND DENIED HER BASIC WANTS.
I FOUND IT!
BUT YOU LOST IT. YOU'VE CUT YOURSELF OFF FROM THE FEMININE WITHOUT EVEN REALIZING IT. I MEAN, LOOK AT YOUR CLOTHES. LOOK AT YOUR HAIR. WILL YOU EVER BE CONTENT?
WHEN SHE FINDS HERSELF ESCAPING INTO THE WALLPAPER PATTERNS OF HER PRISON, SHE BECOMES FRIGHTENED BY ITS IMPLICATIONS, AND WHAT IT REPRESENTS.
WILL YOU?
WELL, I SPEAK FOR A LOT OF DIFFERENT PEOPLE.
ANYWAY, I ASKED YOU FIRST.
AM I CONTENT?
I SUPPOSE I AM.
THANK YOU.
I KNOW LIFE WILL WORK OUT.

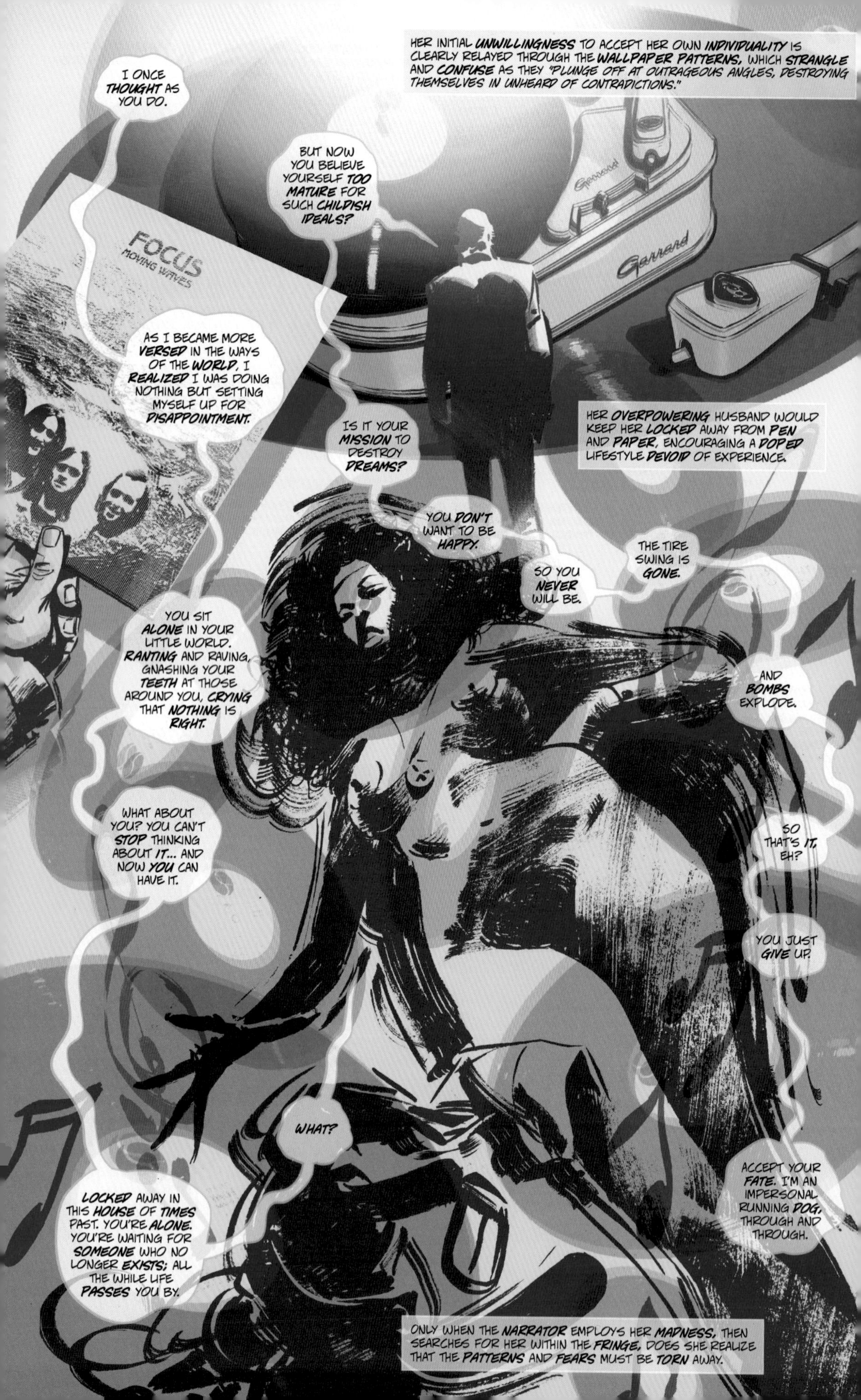
HER INITIAL UNWILLINGNESS TO ACCEPT HER OWN INDIVIDUALITY IS CLEARLY RELAYED THROUGH THE WALLPAPER PATTERNS, WHICH STRANGLE AND CONFUSE AS THEY "PLUNGE OFF AT OUTRAGEOUS ANGLES, DESTROYING THEMSELVES IN UNHEARD OF CONTRADICTIONS."
I ONCE THOUGHT AS YOU DO.
BUT NOW YOU BELIEVE YOURSELF TOO MATURE FOR SUCH CHILDISH IDEALS?
FOCUS
MOVING WAVES
Garrard
Garrard
AS I BECAME MORE VERSED IN THE WAYS OF THE WORLD, I REALIZED I WAS DOING NOTHING BUT SETTING MYSELF UP FOR DISAPPOINTMENT.
IS IT YOUR MISSION TO DESTROY DREAMS?
HER OVERPOWERING HUSBAND WOULD KEEP HER LOCKED AWAY FROM PEN AND PAPER, ENCOURAGING A DOPED LIFESTYLE DEVOID OF EXPERIENCE.
YOU DON'T WANT TO BE HAPPY.
SO YOU NEVER WILL BE.
THE TIRE SWING IS GONE.
YOU SIT ALONE IN YOUR LITTLE WORLD. RANTING AND RAVING, GNASHING YOUR TEETH AT THOSE AROUND YOU, CRYING THAT NOTHING IS RIGHT.
AND BOMBS EXPLODE.
WHAT ABOUT YOU? YOU CAN'T STOP THINKING ABOUT IT... AND NOW YOU CAN HAVE IT.
SO THAT'S IT, EH?
YOU JUST GIVE UP.
WHAT?
LOCKED AWAY IN THIS HOUSE OF TIMES PAST. YOU'RE ALONE. YOU'RE WAITING FOR SOMEONE WHO NO LONGER EXISTS; ALL THE WHILE LIFE PASSES YOU BY.
ACCEPT YOUR FATE. I'M AN IMPERSONAL RUNNING DOG, THROUGH AND THROUGH.
ONLY WHEN THE NARRATOR EMPLOYS HER MADNESS, THEN SEARCHES FOR HER WITHIN THE FRINGE, DOES SHE REALIZE THAT THE PATTERNS AND FEARS MUST BE TORN AWAY.

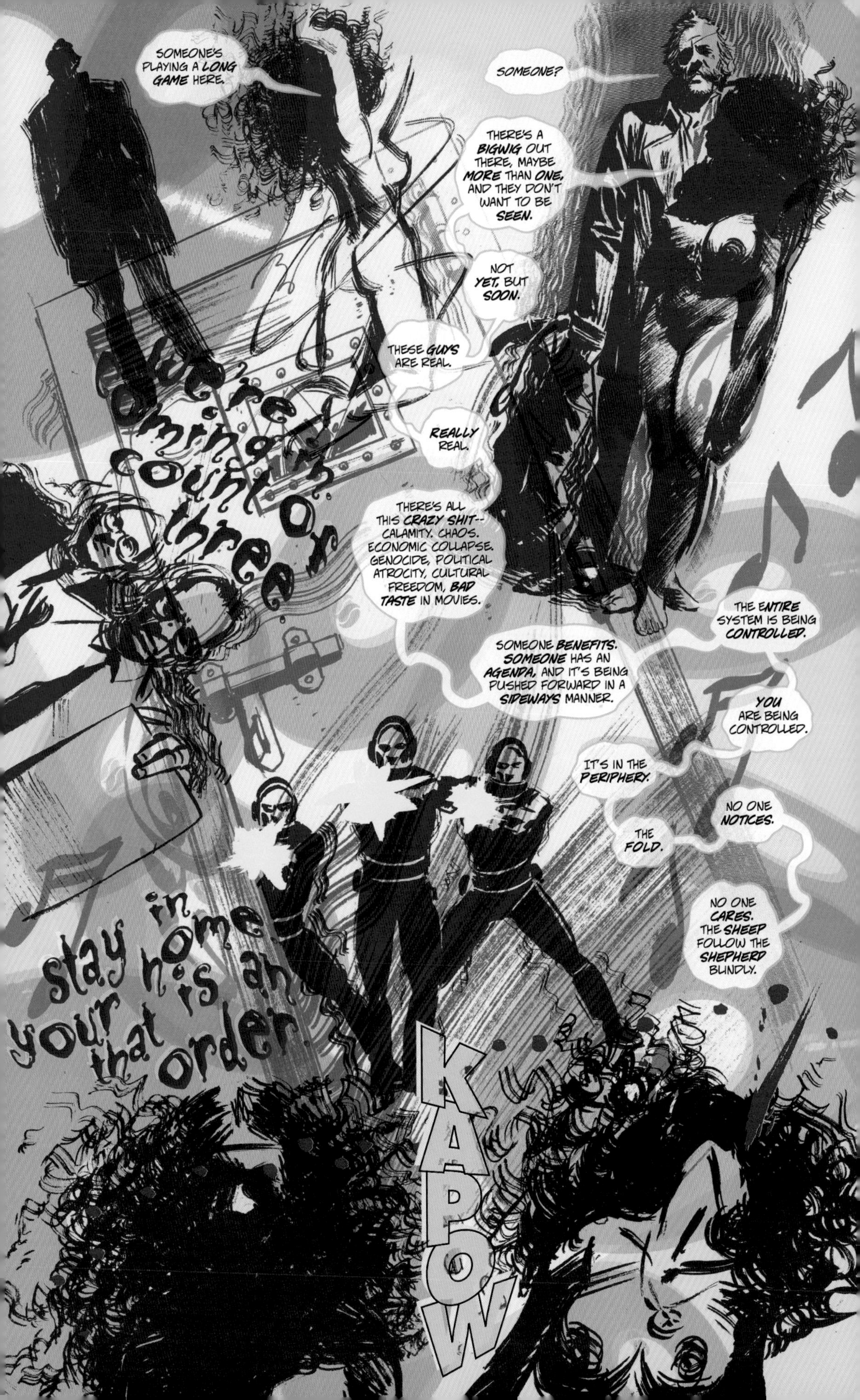
SOMEONE'S PLAYING A LONG GAME HERE.
SOMEONE?
THERE'S A BIGWIG OUT THERE, MAYBE MORE THAN ONE, AND THEY DON'T WANT TO BE SEEN.
NOT YET, BUT SOON.
THESE GUYS ARE REAL.
REALLY REAL.
THERE'S ALL THIS CRAZY SHIT-- CALAMITY. CHAOS. ECONOMIC COLLAPSE. GENOCIDE, POLITICAL ATROCITY, CULTURAL FREEDOM, BAD TASTE IN MOVIES.
SOMEONE BENEFITS. SOMEONE HAS AN AGENDA, AND IT'S BEING PUSHED FORWARD IN A SIDEWAYS MANNER.
THE ENTIRE SYSTEM IS BEING CONTROLLED.
YOU ARE BEING CONTROLLED.
IT'S IN THE PERIPHERY.
THE FOLD.
NO ONE NOTICES.
NO ONE CARES. THE SHEEP FOLLOW THE SHEPHERD BLINDLY.
count of three
stay in your home that is an order
KAPOW

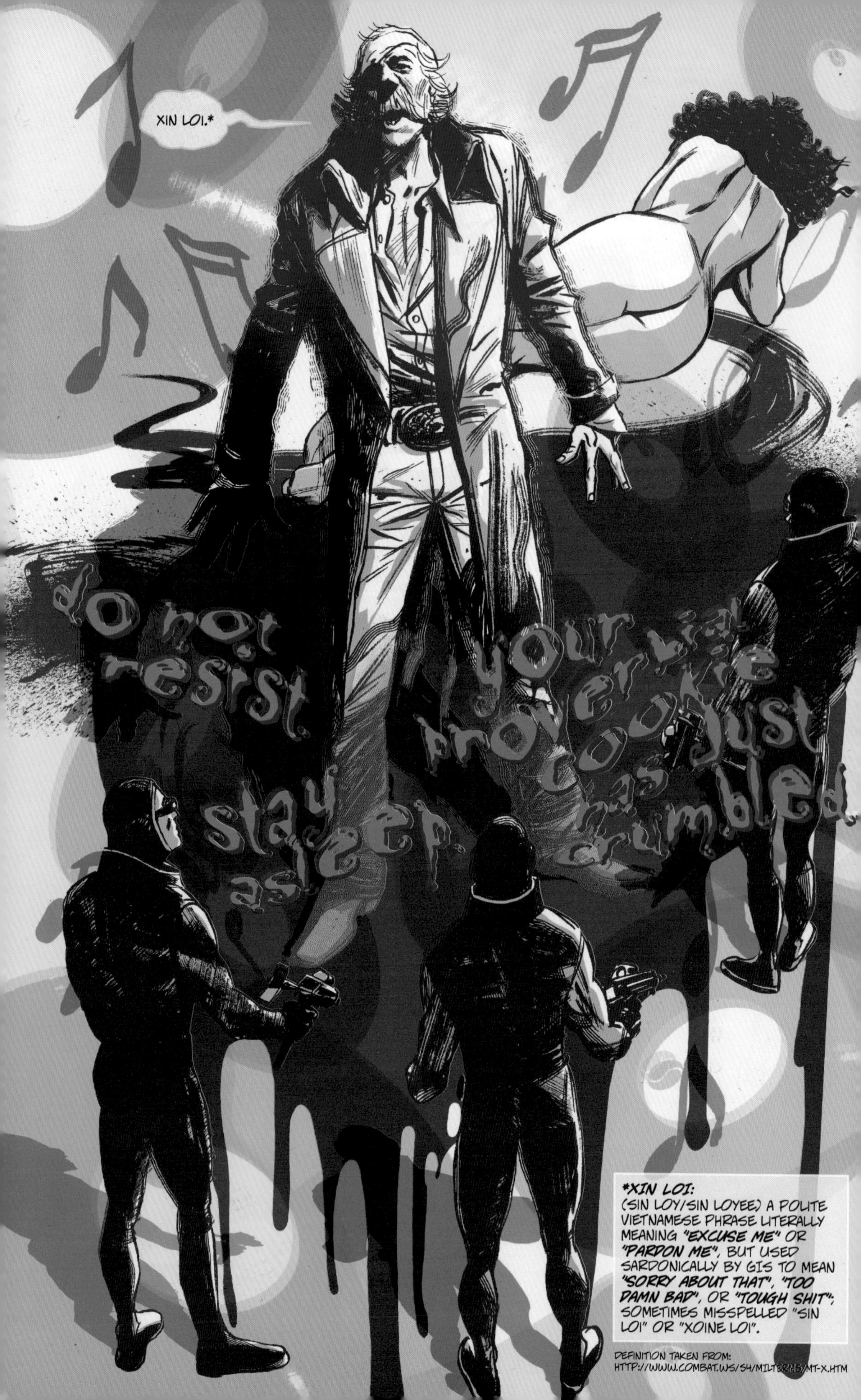
XIN LOI.*
do not resist.
stay asleep.
your will power
has just crumbled.
*XIN LOI:
(SIN LOY/SIN LOYEE) A POLITE VIETNAMESE PHRASE LITERALLY MEANING **"EXCUSE ME"** OR **"PARDON ME"**, BUT USED SARDONICALLY BY GIS TO MEAN **"SORRY ABOUT THAT"**, **"TOO DAMN BAD"**, OR **"TOUGH SHIT"**; SOMETIMES MISSPELLED "SIN LOI" OR "XOINE LOI".
DEFINITION TAKEN FROM:
HTTP://WWW.COMBAT.WS/S4/MILTERMS/MT-X.HTM

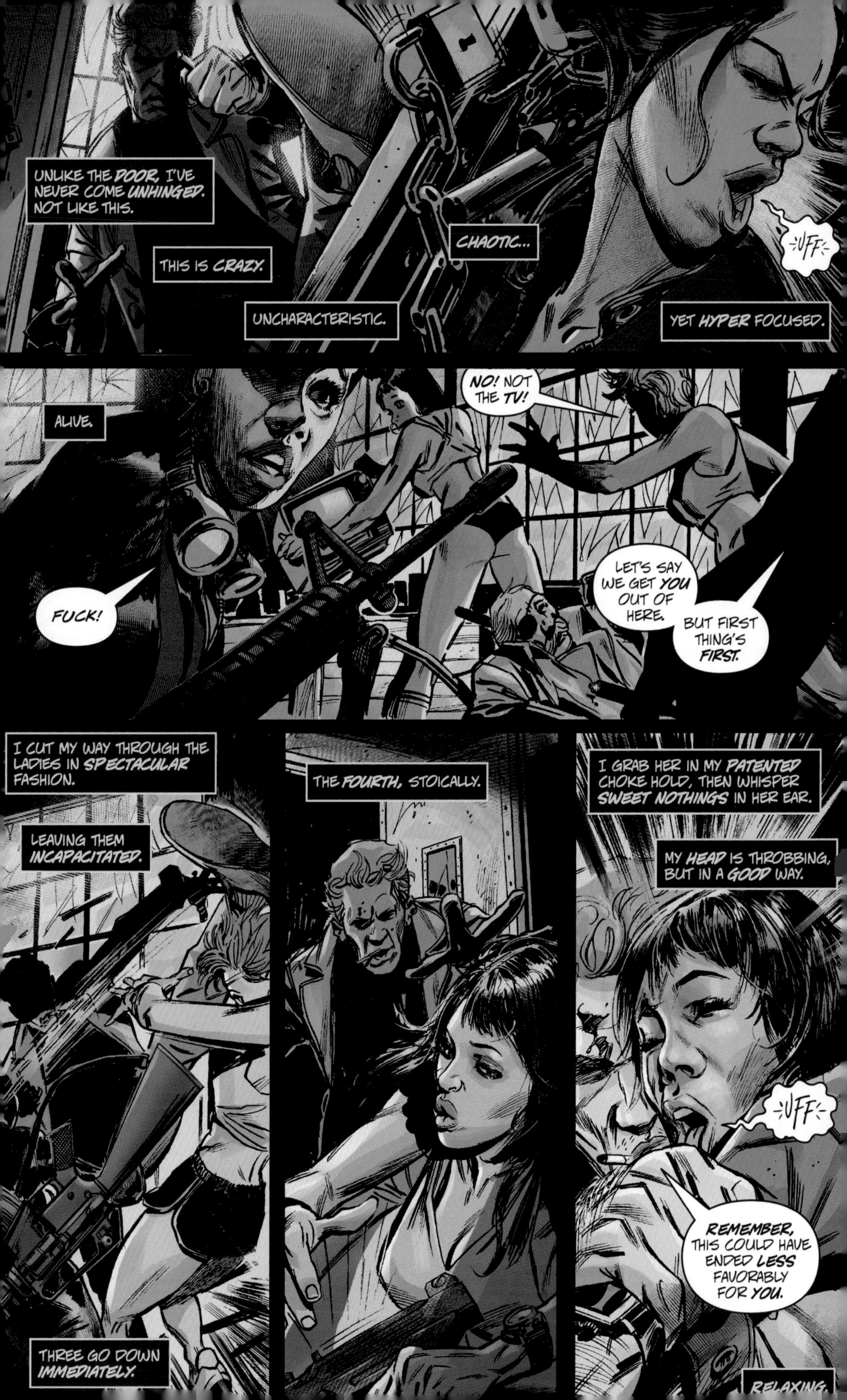
UNLIKE THE DOOR, I'VE NEVER COME UNHINGED. NOT LIKE THIS.
THIS IS CRAZY.
UNCHARACTERISTIC.
CHAOTIC...
UFF
YET HYPER FOCUSED.
ALIVE.
NO! NOT THE TV!
FUCK!
LET'S SAY WE GET YOU OUT OF HERE.
BUT FIRST THING'S FIRST.
I CUT MY WAY THROUGH THE LADIES IN SPECTACULAR FASHION.
LEAVING THEM INCAPACITATED.
THREE GO DOWN IMMEDIATELY.
THE FOURTH, STOICALLY.
I GRAB HER IN MY PATENTED CHOKE HOLD, THEN WHISPER SWEET NOTHINGS IN HER EAR.
MY HEAD IS THROBBING, BUT IN A GOOD WAY.
UFF
REMEMBER, THIS COULD HAVE ENDED LESS FAVORABLY FOR YOU.
RELAXING.

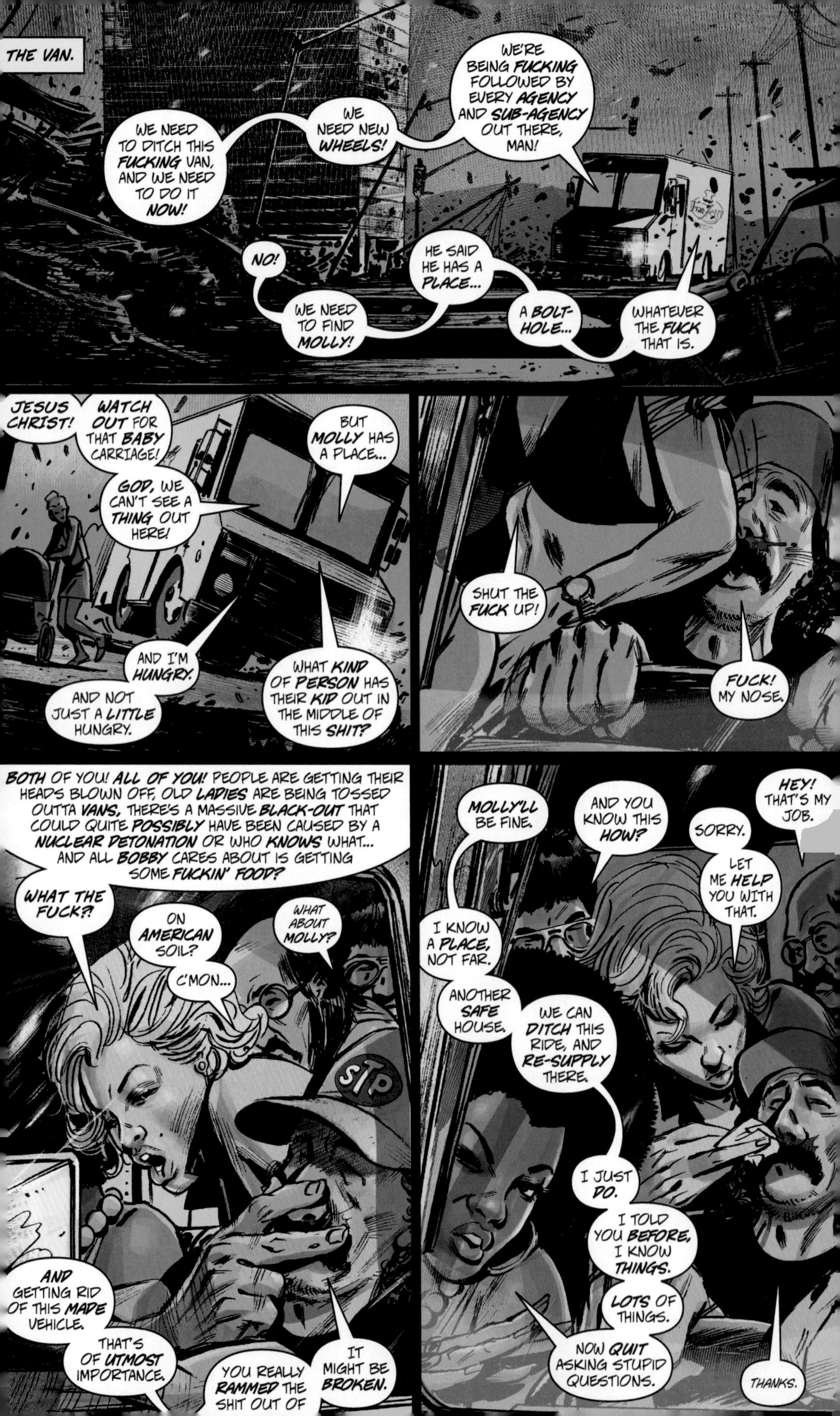
THE VAN.
WE NEED TO DITCH THIS FUCKING VAN, AND WE NEED TO DO IT NOW!
WE NEED NEW WHEELS!
WE'RE BEING FUCKING FOLLOWED BY EVERY AGENCY AND SUB-AGENCY OUT THERE, MAN!
NO!
WE NEED TO FIND MOLLY!
HE SAID HE HAS A PLACE...
A BOLT-HOLE...
WHATEVER THE FUCK THAT IS.
JESUS CHRIST!
WATCH OUT FOR THAT BABY CARRIAGE!
GOD, WE CAN'T SEE A THING OUT HERE!
BUT MOLLY HAS A PLACE...
AND I'M HUNGRY.
AND NOT JUST A LITTLE HUNGRY.
WHAT KIND OF PERSON HAS THEIR KID OUT IN THE MIDDLE OF THIS SHIT?
SHUT THE FUCK UP!
FUCK! MY NOSE.
BOTH OF YOU! ALL OF YOU! PEOPLE ARE GETTING THEIR HEADS BLOWN OFF, OLD LADIES ARE BEING TOSSED OUTTA VANS, THERE'S A MASSIVE BLACK-OUT THAT COULD QUITE POSSIBLY HAVE BEEN CAUSED BY A NUCLEAR DETONATION OR WHO KNOWS WHAT... AND ALL BOBBY CARES ABOUT IS GETTING SOME FUCKIN' FOOD?
WHAT THE FUCK?!
ON AMERICAN SOIL?
C'MON...
WHAT ABOUT MOLLY?
AND GETTING RID OF THIS MADE VEHICLE.
THAT'S OF UTMOST IMPORTANCE.
YOU REALLY RAMMED THE SHIT OUT OF
IT MIGHT BE BROKEN.
MOLLY'LL BE FINE.
AND YOU KNOW THIS HOW?
I KNOW A PLACE, NOT FAR.
ANOTHER SAFE HOUSE.
WE CAN DITCH THIS RIDE, AND RE-SUPPLY THERE.
I JUST DO.
I TOLD YOU BEFORE, I KNOW THINGS.
LOTS OF THINGS.
NOW QUIT ASKING STUPID QUESTIONS.
HEY! THAT'S MY JOB.
SORRY.
LET ME HELP YOU WITH THAT.
THANKS.

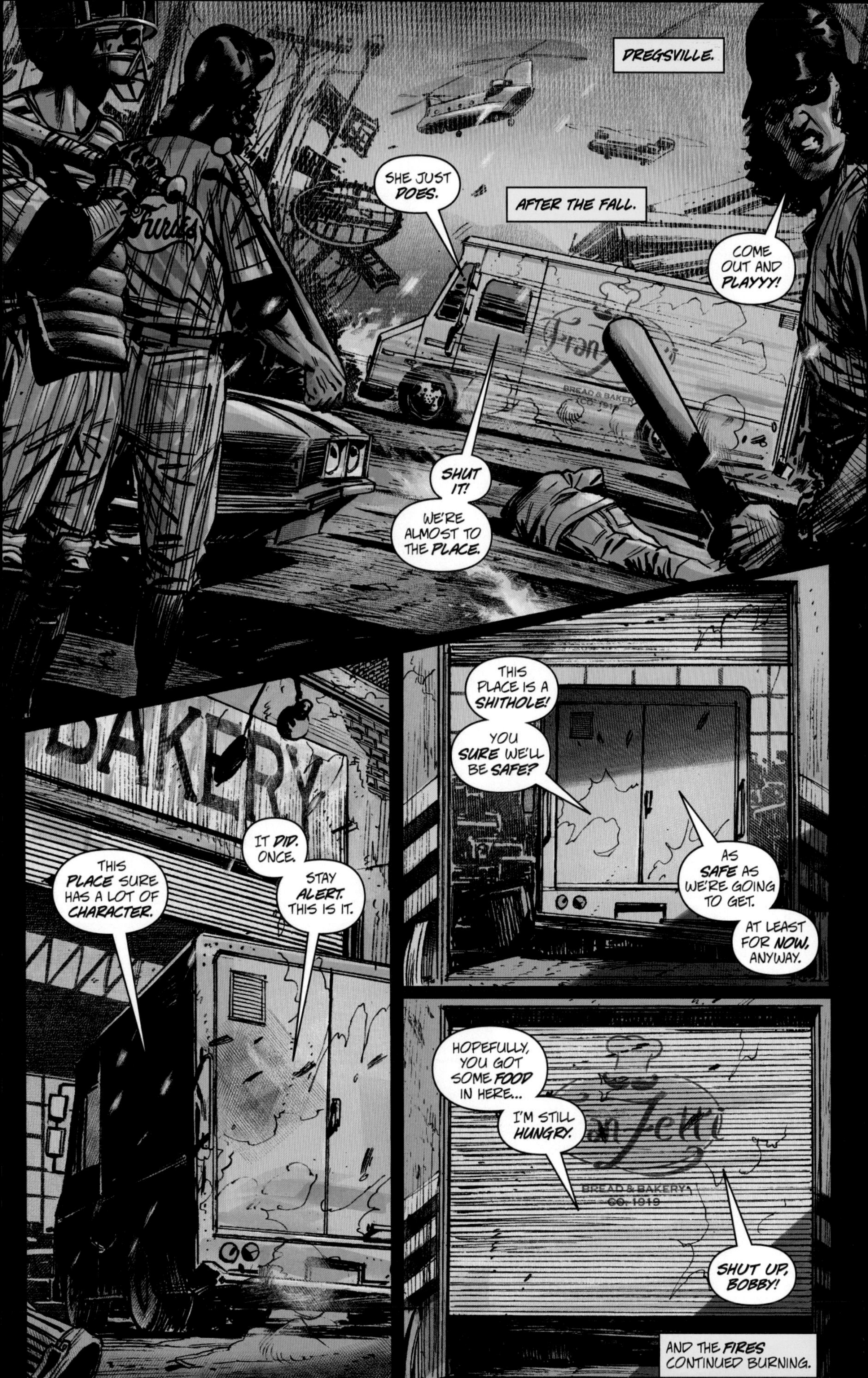
DREGSVILLE.
Furies
AFTER THE FALL.
SHE JUST DOES.
COME OUT AND PLAYYY!
SHUT IT!
WE'RE ALMOST TO THE PLACE.
BAKERY
THIS PLACE SURE HAS A LOT OF CHARACTER.
IT DID. ONCE.
STAY ALERT. THIS IS IT.
THIS PLACE IS A SHITHOLE!
YOU SURE WE'LL BE SAFE?
AS SAFE AS WE'RE GOING TO GET.
AT LEAST FOR NOW, ANYWAY.
HOPEFULLY, YOU GOT SOME FOOD IN HERE...
I'M STILL HUNGRY.
BREAD & BAKERY
CO. 1919
SHUT UP, BOBBY!
AND THE FIRES CONTINUED BURNING.

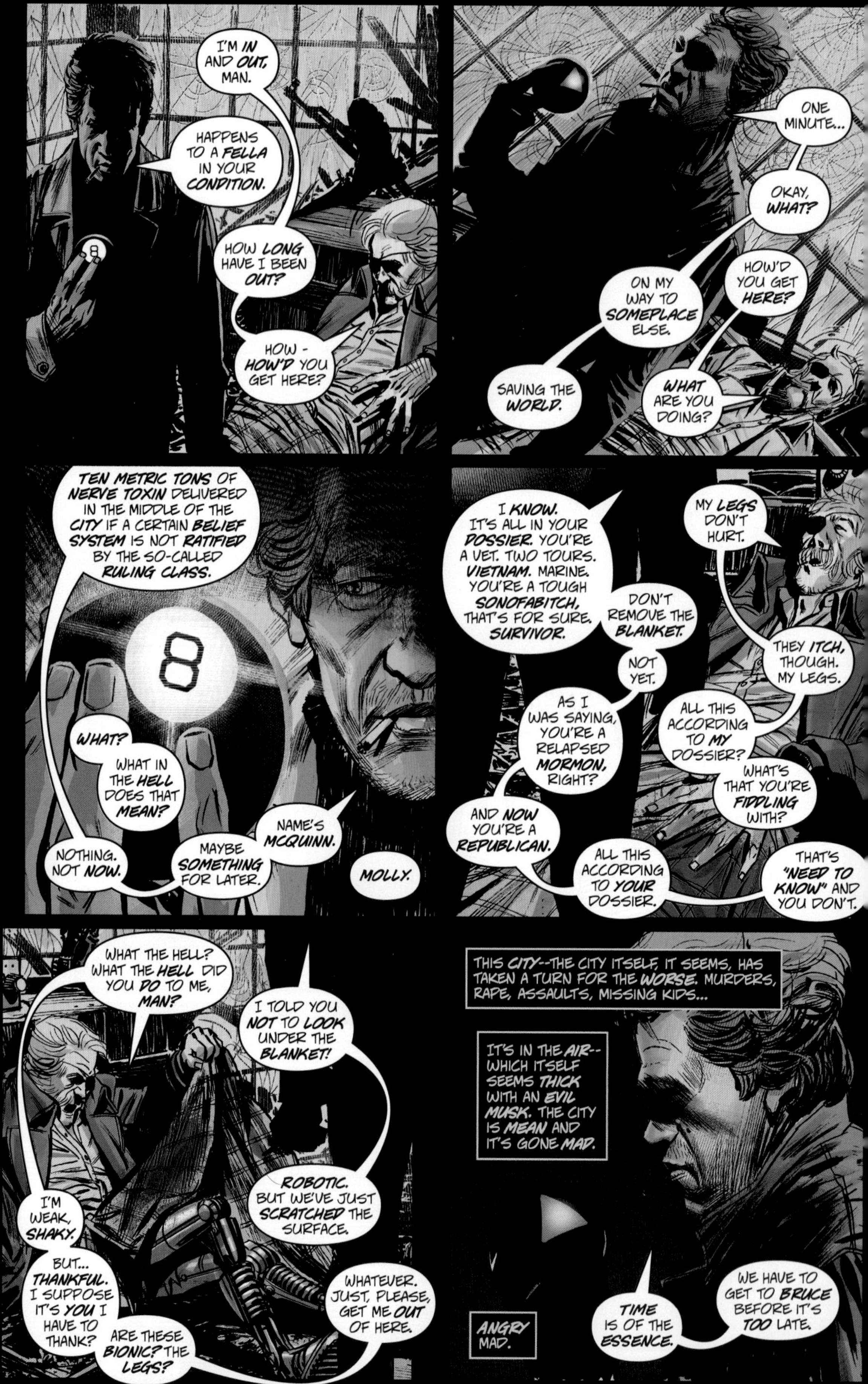

I'M IN AND OUT, MAN.
HAPPENS TO A FELLA IN YOUR CONDITION.
HOW LONG HAVE I BEEN OUT?
HOW - HOW'D YOU GET HERE?
ONE MINUTE...
OKAY, WHAT?
HOW'D YOU GET HERE?
ON MY WAY TO SOMEPLACE ELSE.
SAVING THE WORLD.
WHAT ARE YOU DOING?
TEN METRIC TONS OF NERVE TOXIN DELIVERED IN THE MIDDLE OF THE CITY IF A CERTAIN BELIEF SYSTEM IS NOT RATIFIED BY THE SO-CALLED RULING CLASS.
WHAT?
WHAT IN THE HELL DOES THAT MEAN?
NOTHING. NOT NOW.
MAYBE SOMETHING FOR LATER.
NAME'S MCQUINN.
MOLLY.
I KNOW. IT'S ALL IN YOUR DOSSIER. YOU'RE A VET. TWO TOURS. VIETNAM. MARINE. YOU'RE A TOUGH SONOFABITCH, THAT'S FOR SURE. SURVIVOR.
MY LEGS DON'T HURT.
DON'T REMOVE THE BLANKET.
NOT YET.
THEY ITCH, THOUGH. MY LEGS.
AS I WAS SAYING, YOU'RE A RELAPSED MORMON, RIGHT?
ALL THIS ACCORDING TO MY DOSSIER?
WHAT'S THAT YOU'RE FIDDLING WITH?
AND NOW YOU'RE A REPUBLICAN.
ALL THIS ACCORDING TO YOUR DOSSIER.
THAT'S "NEED TO KNOW" AND YOU DON'T.
WHAT THE HELL? WHAT THE HELL DID YOU DO TO ME, MAN?
I TOLD YOU NOT TO LOOK UNDER THE BLANKET!
I'M WEAK, SHAKY.
ROBOTIC. BUT WE'VE JUST SCRATCHED THE SURFACE.
BUT... THANKFUL. I SUPPOSE IT'S YOU I HAVE TO THANK?
ARE THESE BIONIC? THE LEGS?
WHATEVER. JUST, PLEASE, GET ME OUT OF HERE.
THIS CITY--THE CITY ITSELF, IT SEEMS, HAS TAKEN A TURN FOR THE WORSE. MURDERS, RAPE, ASSAULTS, MISSING KIDS...
IT'S IN THE AIR--WHICH ITSELF SEEMS THICK WITH AN EVIL MUSK. THE CITY IS MEAN AND IT'S GONE MAD.
ANGRY MAD.
TIME IS OF THE ESSENCE.
WE HAVE TO GET TO BRUCE BEFORE IT'S TOO LATE.

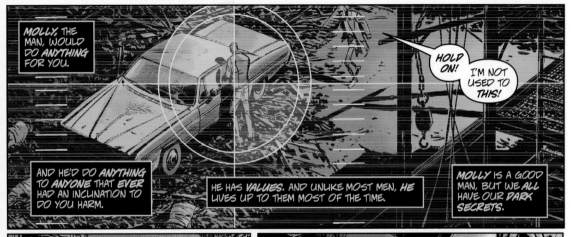

MOLLY, THE MAN, WOULD DO *ANYTHING* FOR YOU.

HOLD ON!

I'M NOT USED TO *THIS*!

AND HE'D DO *ANYTHING* TO *ANYONE* THAT *EVER* HAD AN INCLINATION TO DO YOU HARM.

HE HAS *VALUES*. AND UNLIKE MOST MEN, *HE* LIVES UP TO THEM MOST OF THE TIME.

MOLLY IS A GOOD MAN, BUT WE *ALL* HAVE OUR *DARK* SECRETS.

YOU GOT YOURSELF *TWO* SHAKES OF A LAMB'S TAIL TO...

STRIKE THAT - MAKE THAT *ONE* SHAKE...

GET IN!

MOLLY IS THE COMBINATION OF ALL THOSE *DARK SECRETS* COLLECTED OVER THE YEARS.

THAT DOESN'T MEAN HE'S *EVIL*, NECESSARILY, BUT IT DOES MEAN HE TELLS *HIS* OWN TRUTH...

HOLD ON!

I'M NOT *IN* THE CAR YET.

I HAVEN'T *QUITE* GOTTEN THE HANG OF *THESE* YET.

AND ACTS OUT ON THAT TRUTH.

SMOKE?

NO.

THANKS.

I'M TRYING TO QUIT.

NO.

YA *KNOW*, *THOSE* THINGS WILL *KILL* YA?

NO, *THEY* WON'T.

I TRY TO MAKE IT A RULE TO NOT *BELIEVE* EVERYTHING I *READ* IN AN INDIVIDUAL'S *DOSSIER*...

ESPECIALLY *DATED* DOSSIERS... THAT HAVE BEEN *MADE UP*.

MOST THINGS WILL.

BUT LET'S NOT GET ALL *SENTIMENTAL*.

WE DON'T HAVE *TIME* FOR THIS *FLOWERY HORSE SHIT*!

HOLD ON.

HERE WE GO.

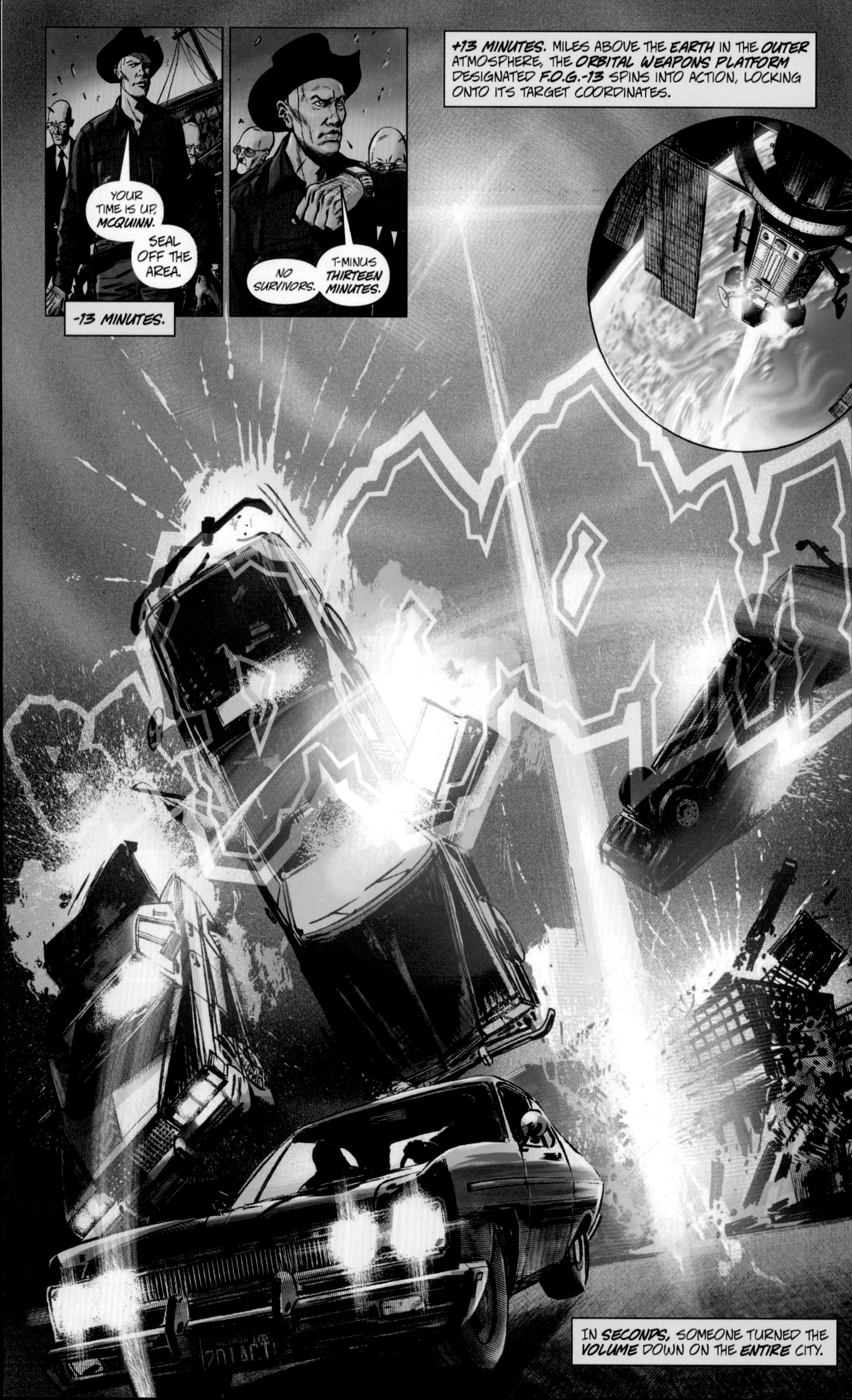

YOUR TIME IS UP, MCQUINN.
SEAL OFF THE AREA.
-13 MINUTES.
T-MINUS THIRTEEN MINUTES.
NO SURVIVORS.
+13 MINUTES. MILES ABOVE THE EARTH IN THE OUTER ATMOSPHERE, THE ORBITAL WEAPONS PLATFORM DESIGNATED F.O.G.-13 SPINS INTO ACTION, LOCKING ONTO ITS TARGET COORDINATES.
IN SECONDS, SOMEONE TURNED THE VOLUME DOWN ON THE ENTIRE CITY.

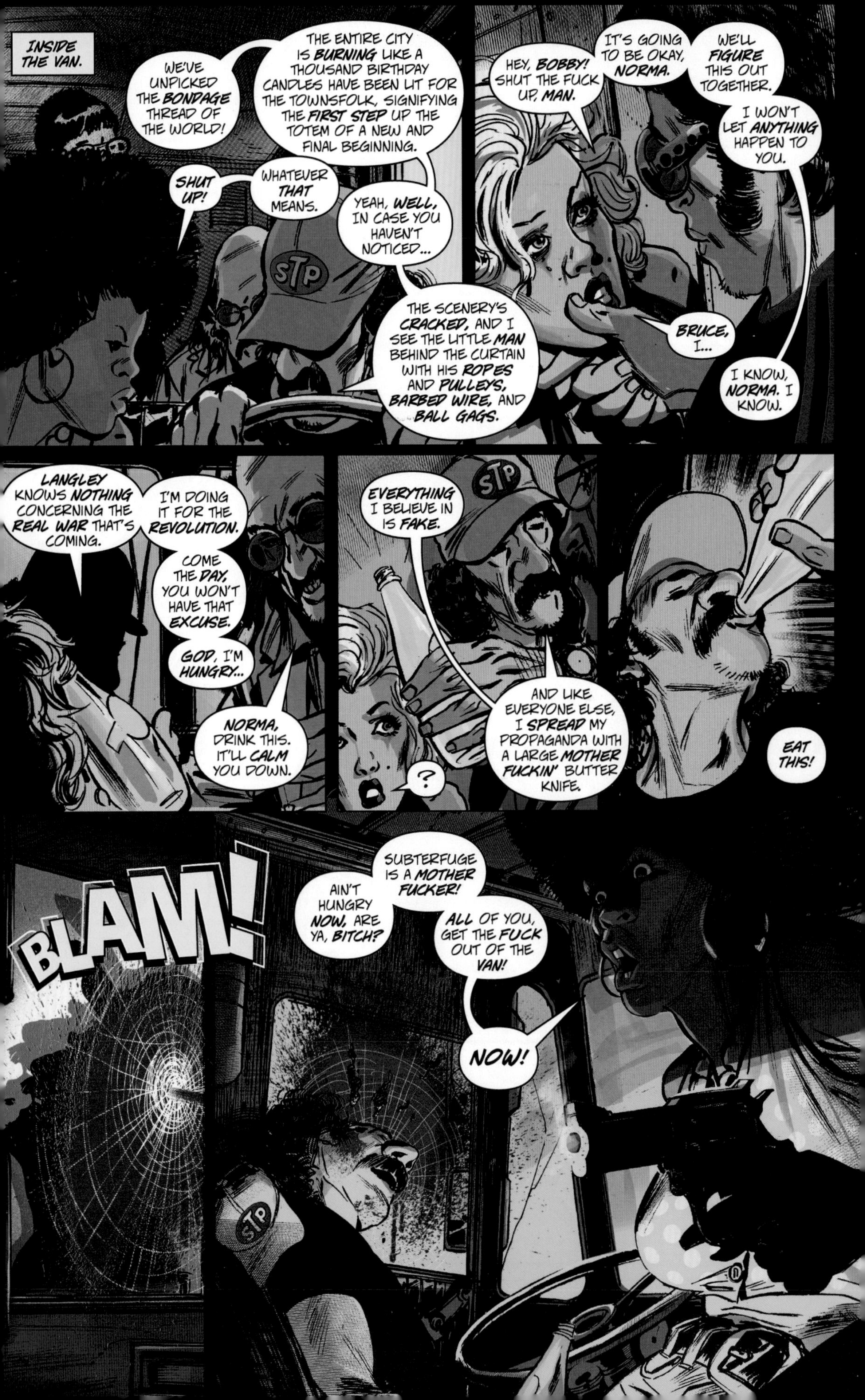
INSIDE THE VAN.
WE'VE UNPICKED THE BONDAGE THREAD OF THE WORLD!
THE ENTIRE CITY IS BURNING LIKE A THOUSAND BIRTHDAY CANDLES HAVE BEEN LIT FOR THE TOWNSFOLK, SIGNIFYING THE FIRST STEP UP THE TOTEM OF A NEW AND FINAL BEGINNING.
SHUT UP!
WHATEVER THAT MEANS.
YEAH, WELL, IN CASE YOU HAVEN'T NOTICED...
THE SCENERY'S CRACKED, AND I SEE THE LITTLE MAN BEHIND THE CURTAIN WITH HIS ROPES AND PULLEYS, BARBED WIRE, AND BALL GAGS.
HEY, BOBBY! SHUT THE FUCK UP, MAN.
IT'S GOING TO BE OKAY, NORMA.
WE'LL FIGURE THIS OUT TOGETHER.
I WON'T LET ANYTHING HAPPEN TO YOU.
BRUCE, I...
I KNOW, NORMA. I KNOW.
LANGLEY KNOWS NOTHING CONCERNING THE REAL WAR THAT'S COMING.
I'M DOING IT FOR THE REVOLUTION.
COME THE DAY, YOU WON'T HAVE THAT EXCUSE.
GOD, I'M HUNGRY...
NORMA, DRINK THIS. IT'LL CALM YOU DOWN.
?
EVERYTHING I BELIEVE IN IS FAKE.
AND LIKE EVERYONE ELSE, I SPREAD MY PROPAGANDA WITH A LARGE MOTHER FUCKIN' BUTTER KNIFE.
STP
EAT THIS!
BLAM!
AIN'T HUNGRY NOW, ARE YA, BITCH?
SUBTERFUGE IS A MOTHER FUCKER!
ALL OF YOU, GET THE FUCK OUT OF THE VAN!
NOW!

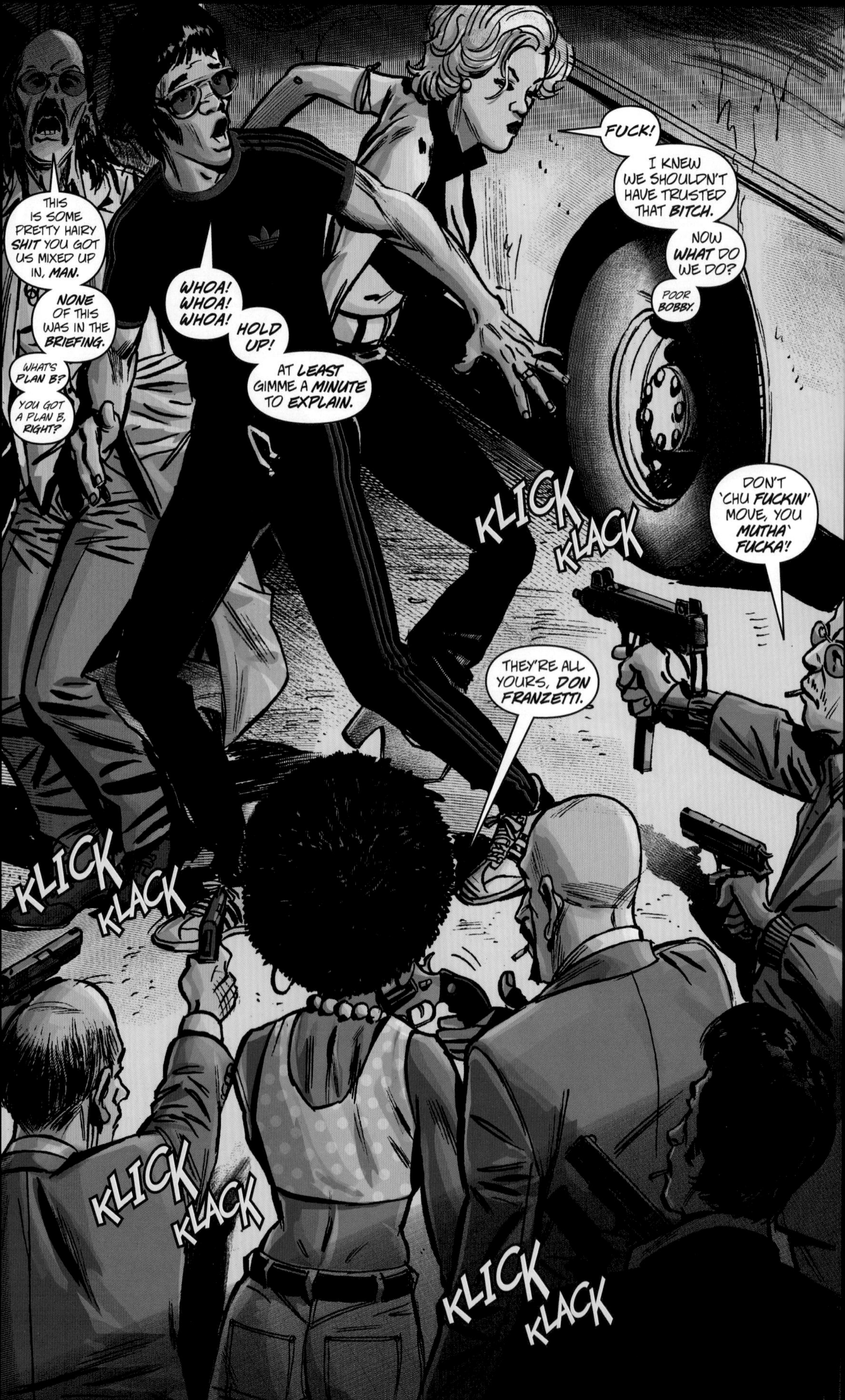
THIS IS SOME PRETTY HAIRY SHIT YOU GOT US MIXED UP IN, MAN.
NONE OF THIS WAS IN THE BRIEFING.
WHAT'S PLAN B?
YOU GOT A PLAN B, RIGHT?
WHOA! WHOA! WHOA!
HOLD UP!
AT LEAST GIMME A MINUTE TO EXPLAIN.
FUCK!
I KNEW WE SHOULDN'T HAVE TRUSTED THAT BITCH.
NOW WHAT DO WE DO?
POOR BOBBY.
KLICK KLACK
DON'T 'CHU FUCKIN' MOVE, YOU MUTHA' FUCKA'!
THEY'RE ALL YOURS, DON FRANZETTI.
KLICK KLACK
KLICK KLACK
KLICK KLACK

CHAPTER FOUR

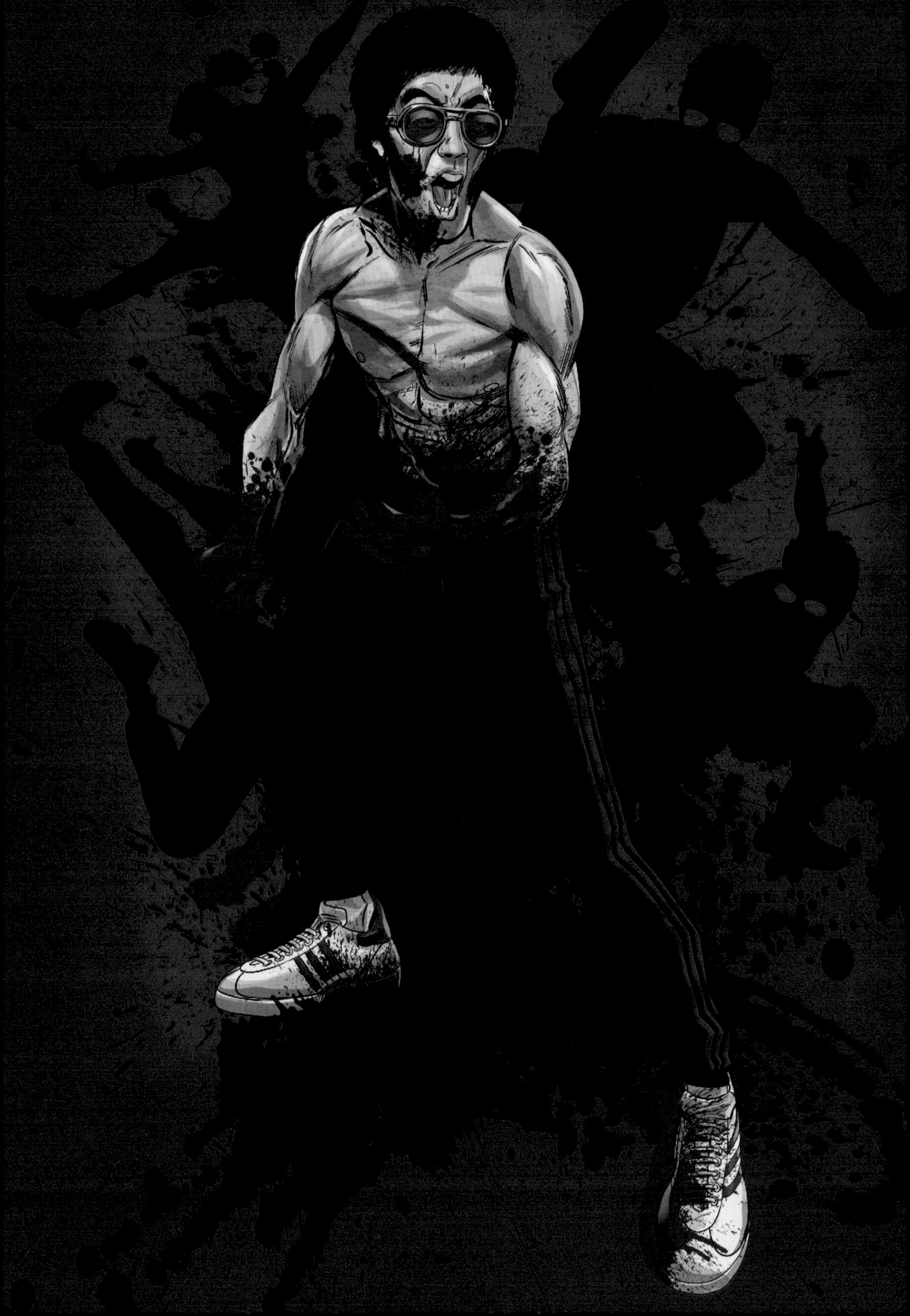

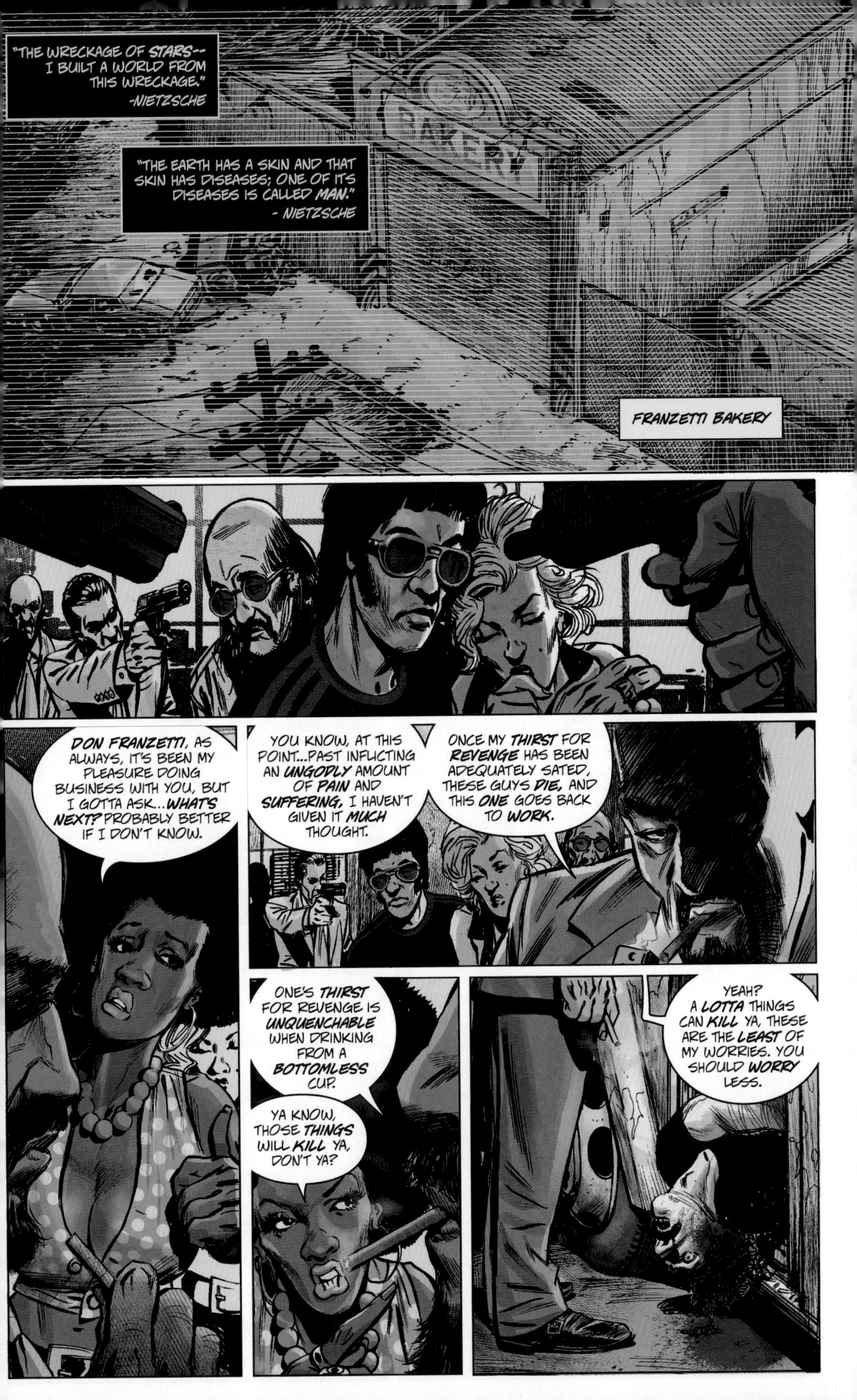
"THE WRECKAGE OF STARS-- I BUILT A WORLD FROM THIS WRECKAGE." -NIETZSCHE
"THE EARTH HAS A SKIN AND THAT SKIN HAS DISEASES; ONE OF ITS DISEASES IS CALLED MAN." - NIETZSCHE
BAKERY
FRANZETTI BAKERY
DON FRANZETTI, AS ALWAYS, IT'S BEEN MY PLEASURE DOING BUSINESS WITH YOU, BUT I GOTTA ASK...WHAT'S NEXT? PROBABLY BETTER IF I DON'T KNOW.
YOU KNOW, AT THIS POINT...PAST INFLICTING AN UNGODLY AMOUNT OF PAIN AND SUFFERING, I HAVEN'T GIVEN IT MUCH THOUGHT.
ONCE MY THIRST FOR REVENGE HAS BEEN ADEQUATELY SATED, THESE GUYS DIE, AND THIS ONE GOES BACK TO WORK.
ONE'S THIRST FOR REVENGE IS UNQUENCHABLE WHEN DRINKING FROM A BOTTOMLESS CUP.
YA KNOW, THOSE THINGS WILL KILL YA, DON'T YA?
YEAH? A LOTTA THINGS CAN KILL YA, THESE ARE THE LEAST OF MY WORRIES. YOU SHOULD WORRY LESS.

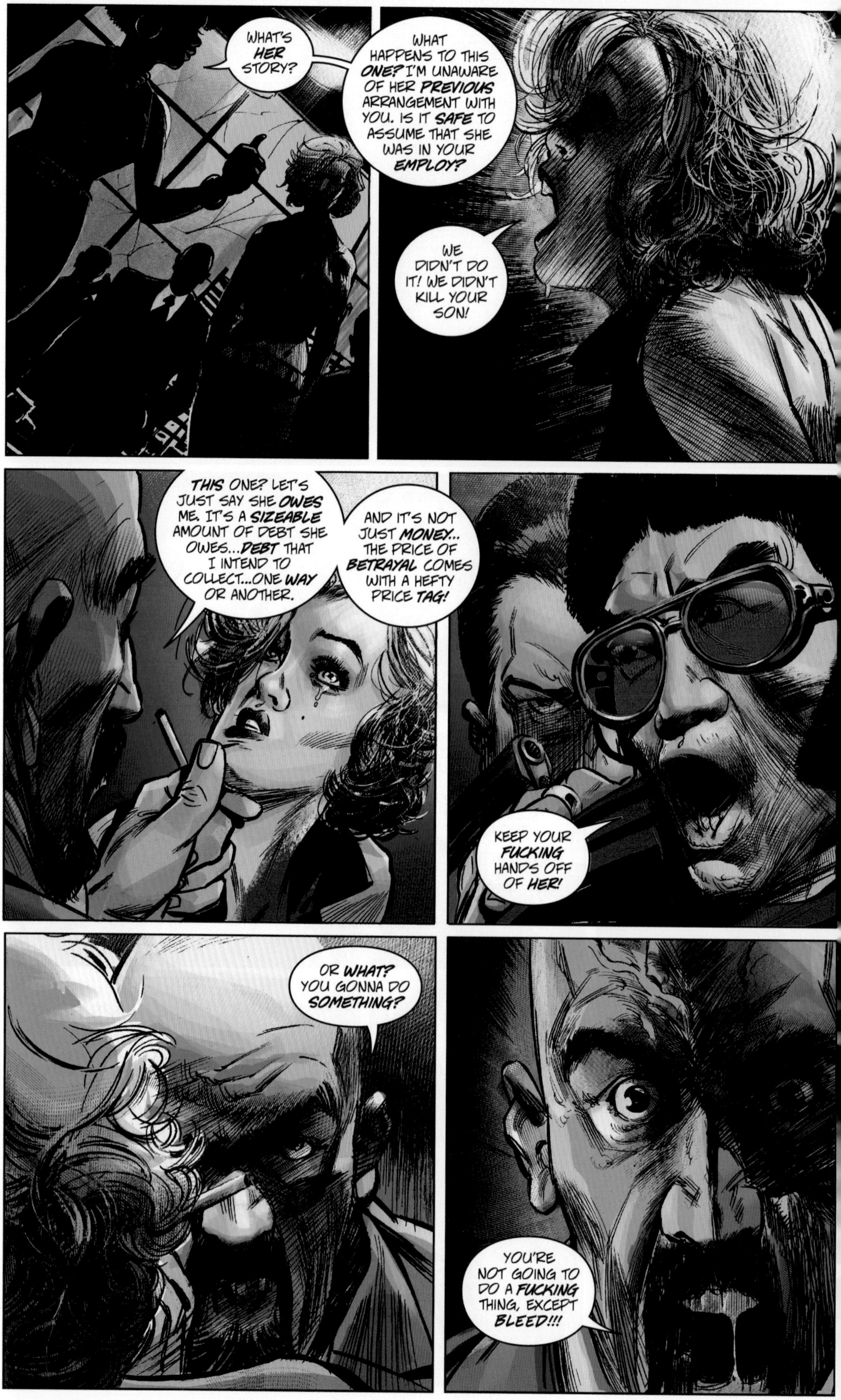
WHAT'S HER STORY?
WHAT HAPPENS TO THIS ONE? I'M UNAWARE OF HER PREVIOUS ARRANGEMENT WITH YOU. IS IT SAFE TO ASSUME THAT SHE WAS IN YOUR EMPLOY?
WE DIDN'T DO IT! WE DIDN'T KILL YOUR SON!
THIS ONE? LET'S JUST SAY SHE OWES ME. IT'S A SIZEABLE AMOUNT OF DEBT SHE OWES...DEBT THAT I INTEND TO COLLECT...ONE WAY OR ANOTHER.
AND IT'S NOT JUST MONEY... THE PRICE OF BETRAYAL COMES WITH A HEFTY PRICE TAG!
KEEP YOUR FUCKING HANDS OFF OF HER!
OR WHAT? YOU GONNA DO SOMETHING?
YOU'RE NOT GOING TO DO A FUCKING THING, EXCEPT BLEED!!!

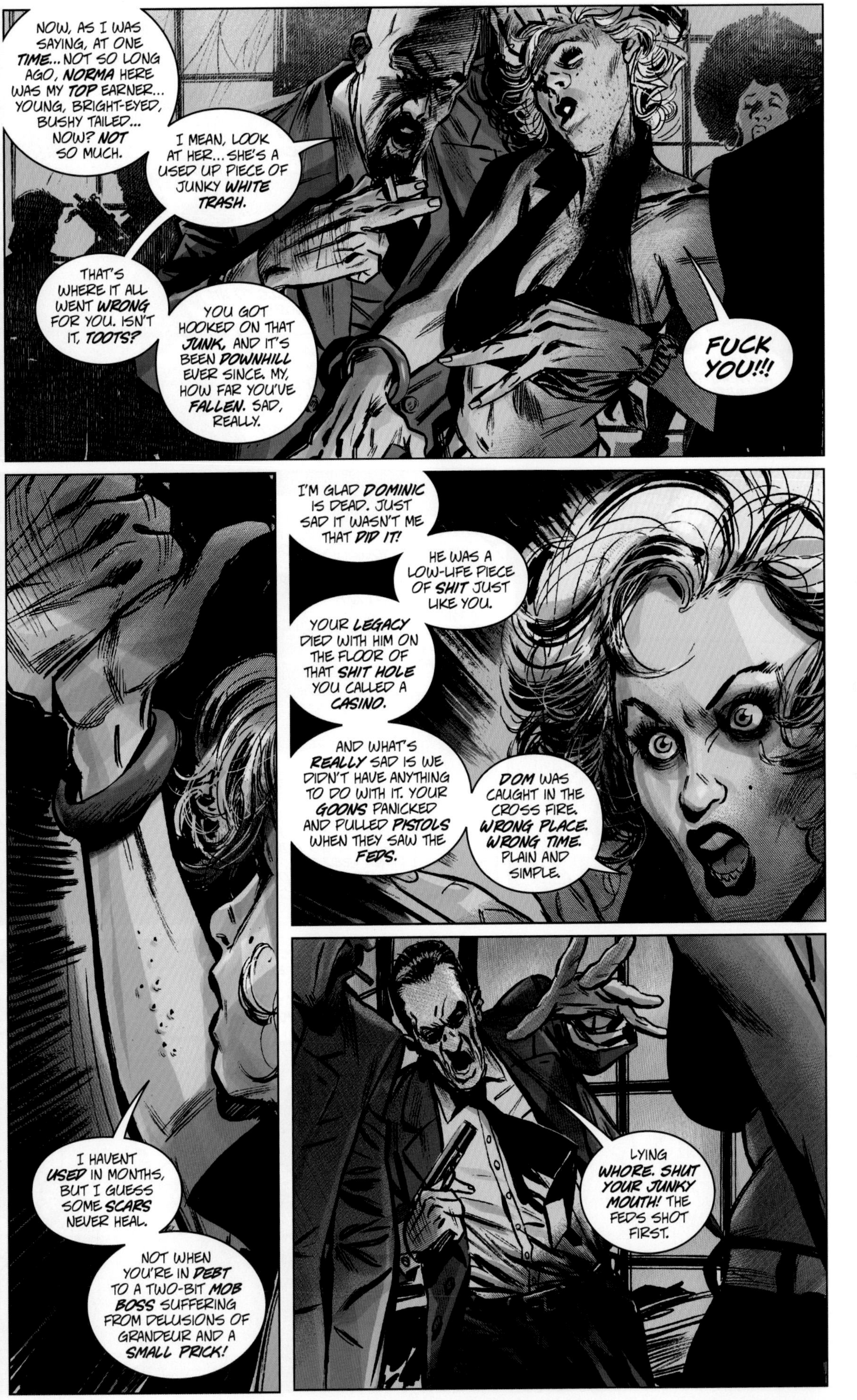
NOW, AS I WAS SAYING, AT ONE TIME... NOT SO LONG AGO, NORMA HERE WAS MY TOP EARNER... YOUNG, BRIGHT-EYED, BUSHY TAILED... NOW? NOT SO MUCH.
I MEAN, LOOK AT HER... SHE'S A USED UP PIECE OF JUNKY WHITE TRASH.
THAT'S WHERE IT ALL WENT WRONG FOR YOU. ISN'T IT, TOOTS?
YOU GOT HOOKED ON THAT JUNK, AND IT'S BEEN DOWNHILL EVER SINCE. MY, HOW FAR YOU'VE FALLEN. SAD, REALLY.
FUCK YOU!!!
I HAVENT USED IN MONTHS, BUT I GUESS SOME SCARS NEVER HEAL.
NOT WHEN YOU'RE IN DEBT TO A TWO-BIT MOB BOSS SUFFERING FROM DELUSIONS OF GRANDEUR AND A SMALL PRICK!
I'M GLAD DOMINIC IS DEAD. JUST SAD IT WASN'T ME THAT DID IT!
HE WAS A LOW-LIFE PIECE OF SHIT JUST LIKE YOU.
YOUR LEGACY DIED WITH HIM ON THE FLOOR OF THAT SHIT HOLE YOU CALLED A CASINO.
AND WHAT'S REALLY SAD IS WE DIDN'T HAVE ANYTHING TO DO WITH IT. YOUR GOONS PANICKED AND PULLED PISTOLS WHEN THEY SAW THE FEDS.
DOM WAS CAUGHT IN THE CROSS FIRE. WRONG PLACE. WRONG TIME. PLAIN AND SIMPLE.
LYING WHORE. SHUT YOUR JUNKY MOUTH! THE FEDS SHOT FIRST.

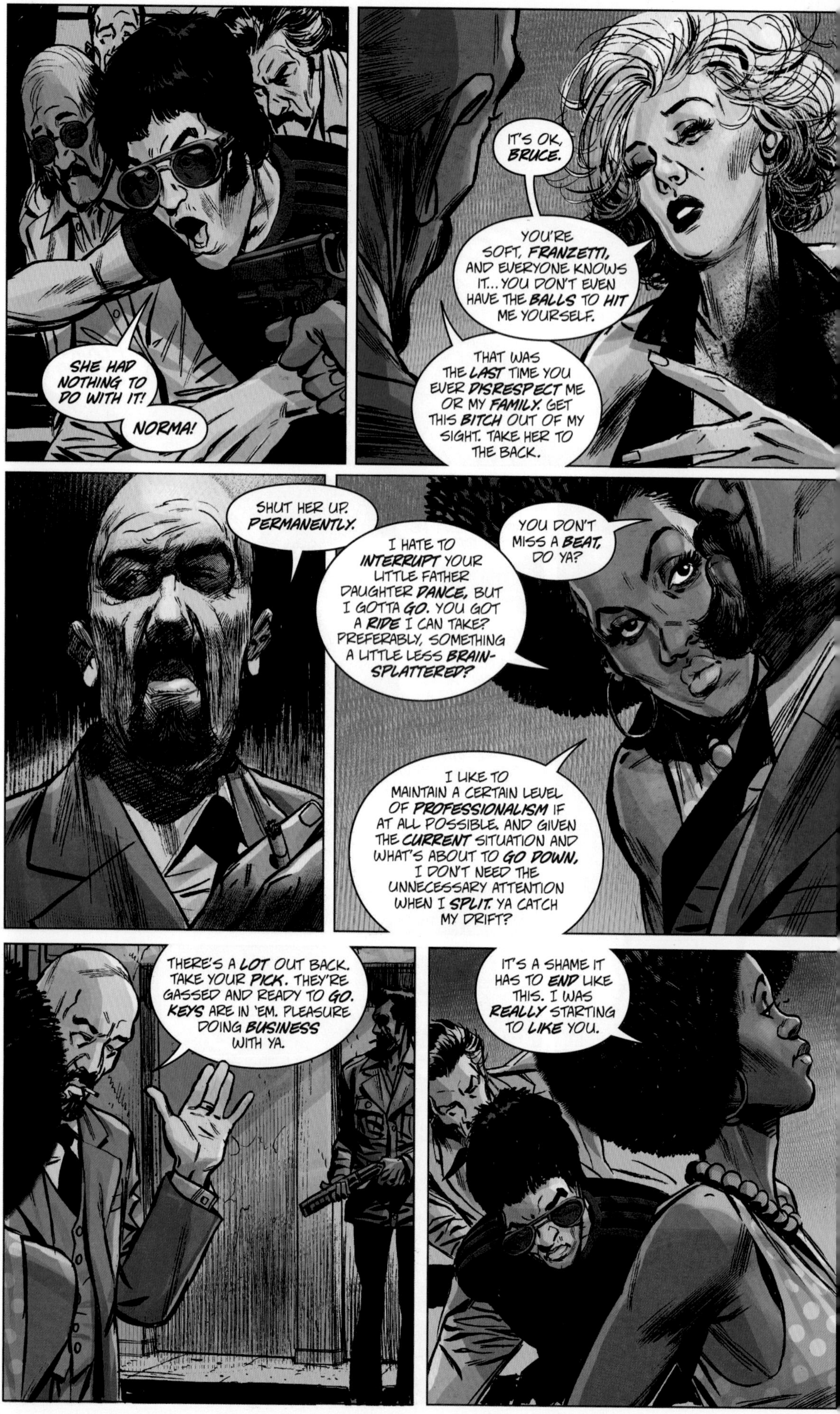
SHE HAD NOTHING TO DO WITH IT!
NORMA!
IT'S OK, BRUCE.
YOU'RE SOFT, FRANZETTI, AND EVERYONE KNOWS IT... YOU DON'T EVEN HAVE THE BALLS TO HIT ME YOURSELF.
THAT WAS THE LAST TIME YOU EVER DISRESPECT ME OR MY FAMILY. GET THIS BITCH OUT OF MY SIGHT. TAKE HER TO THE BACK.
SHUT HER UP. PERMANENTLY.
I HATE TO INTERRUPT YOUR LITTLE FATHER DAUGHTER DANCE, BUT I GOTTA GO. YOU GOT A RIDE I CAN TAKE? PREFERABLY, SOMETHING A LITTLE LESS BRAIN-SPLATTERED?
YOU DON'T MISS A BEAT, DO YA?
I LIKE TO MAINTAIN A CERTAIN LEVEL OF PROFESSIONALISM IF AT ALL POSSIBLE. AND GIVEN THE CURRENT SITUATION AND WHAT'S ABOUT TO GO DOWN, I DON'T NEED THE UNNECESSARY ATTENTION WHEN I SPLIT. YA CATCH MY DRIFT?
THERE'S A LOT OUT BACK. TAKE YOUR PICK. THEY'RE GASSED AND READY TO GO. KEYS ARE IN 'EM. PLEASURE DOING BUSINESS WITH YA.
IT'S A SHAME IT HAS TO END LIKE THIS. I WAS REALLY STARTING TO LIKE YOU.

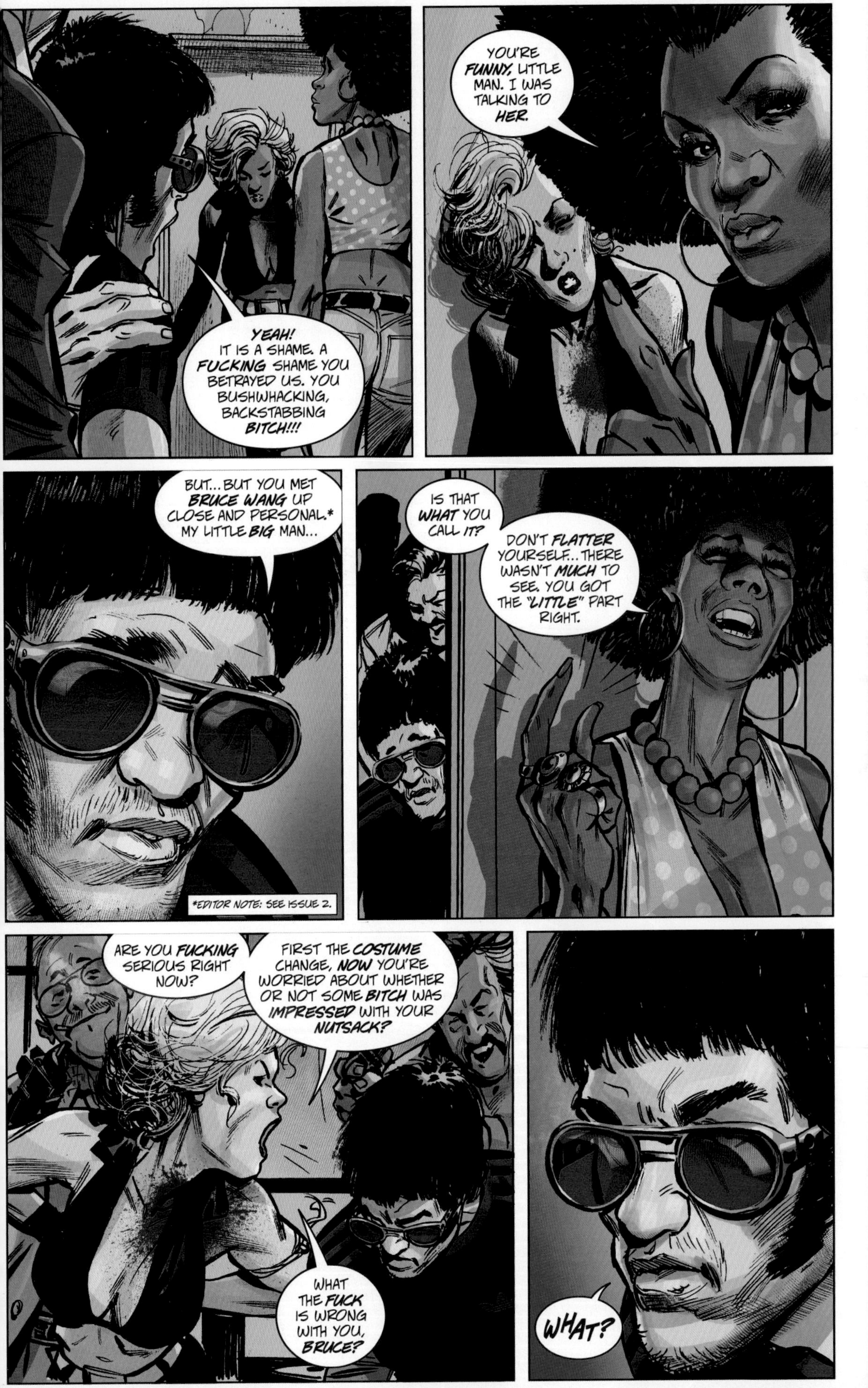
YEAH!
IT IS A SHAME. A FUCKING SHAME YOU BETRAYED US. YOU BUSHWHACKING, BACKSTABBING BITCH!!!
YOU'RE FUNNY, LITTLE MAN. I WAS TALKING TO HER.
BUT... BUT YOU MET BRUCE WANG UP CLOSE AND PERSONAL.* MY LITTLE BIG MAN...
*EDITOR NOTE: SEE ISSUE 2.
IS THAT WHAT YOU CALL IT?
DON'T FLATTER YOURSELF... THERE WASN'T MUCH TO SEE. YOU GOT THE "LITTLE" PART RIGHT.
ARE YOU FUCKING SERIOUS RIGHT NOW?
FIRST THE COSTUME CHANGE, NOW YOU'RE WORRIED ABOUT WHETHER OR NOT SOME BITCH WAS IMPRESSED WITH YOUR NUTSACK?
WHAT THE FUCK IS WRONG WITH YOU, BRUCE?
WHAT?

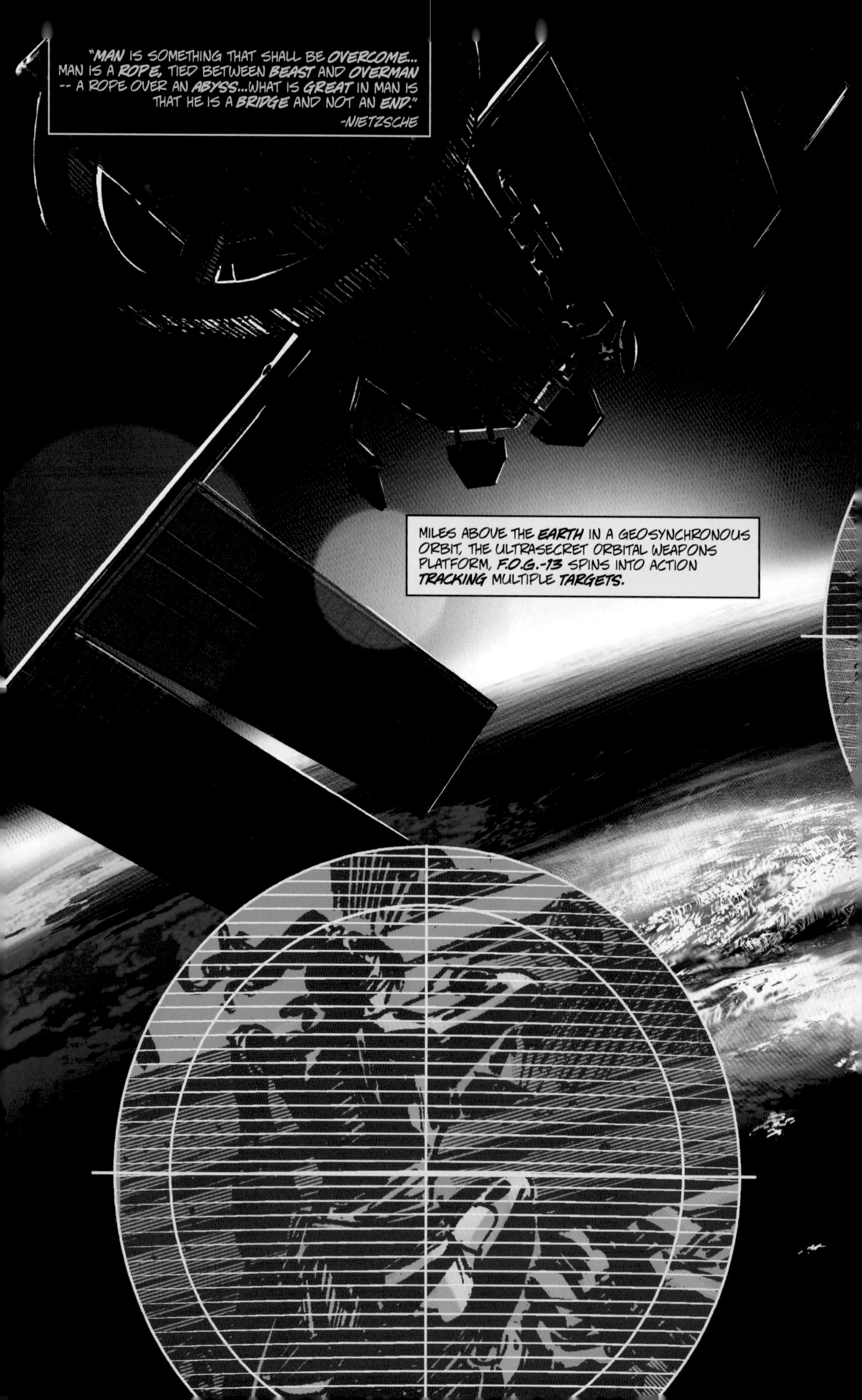
"MAN IS SOMETHING THAT SHALL BE OVERCOME... MAN IS A ROPE, TIED BETWEEN BEAST AND OVERMAN -- A ROPE OVER AN ABYSS...WHAT IS GREAT IN MAN IS THAT HE IS A BRIDGE AND NOT AN END."
-NIETZSCHE
MILES ABOVE THE EARTH IN A GEOSYNCHRONOUS ORBIT, THE ULTRASECRET ORBITAL WEAPONS PLATFORM, F.O.G.-13 SPINS INTO ACTION TRACKING MULTIPLE TARGETS.

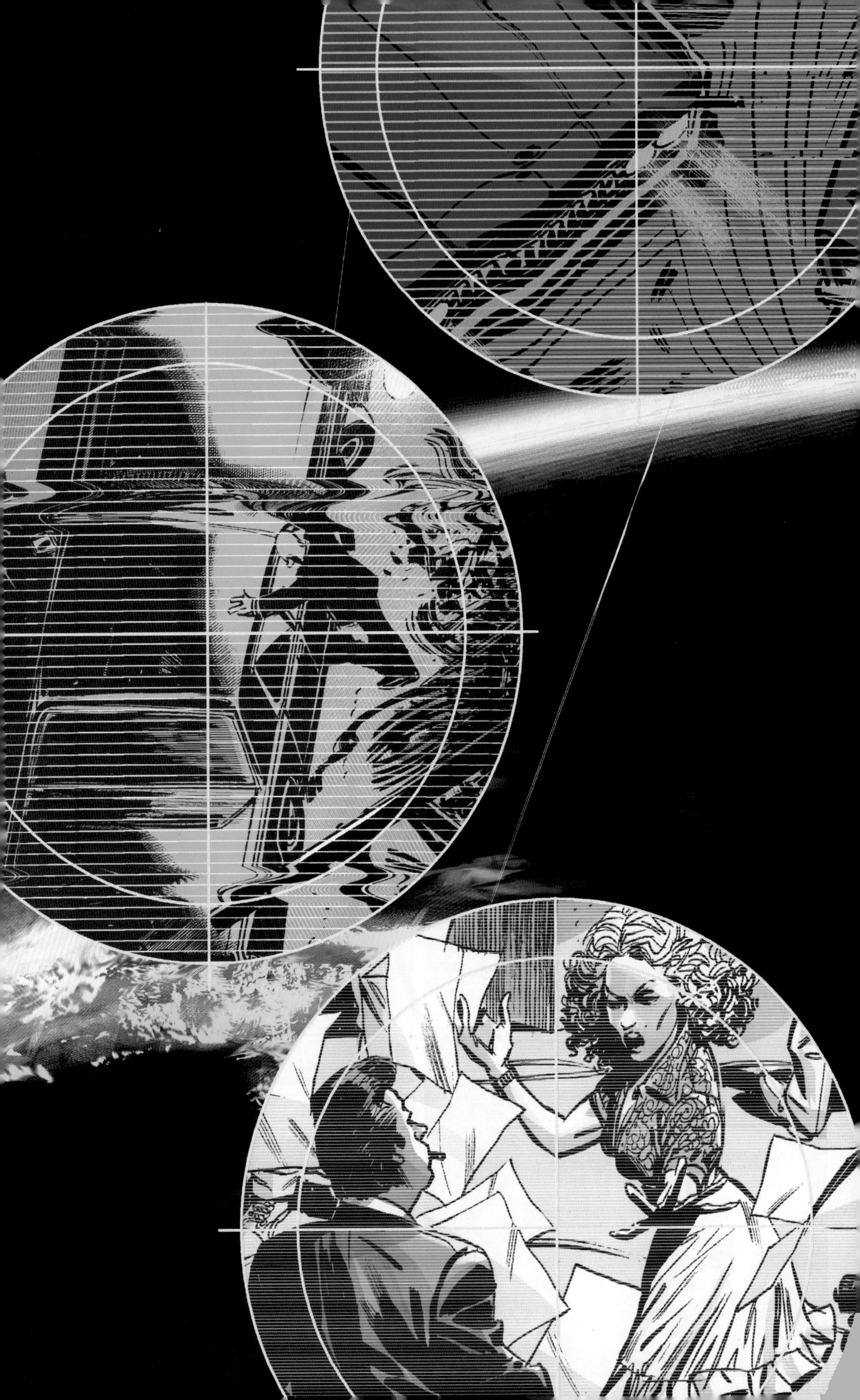

ELSEWHERE.

REQUEST SITE **CONTAINMENT** SCAN. TRACK COORDINATES ON MY **VECTOR**.

AFFIRMATIVE. WE'LL FIND **HIM**. DISEMBARKING NOW.

ORBITAL THERMAL SCAN IS **NEGATIVE**.

FOLLOW **CONTAINMENT** PROTOCOL.

SURVEY THE **DAMAGE**.

NO **SURVIVORS**.

7 MINUTES.

REPORT.

ALL CLEAR, SIR.

SAME HERE, SIR.

NOTHING.

NOTHING COULD HAVE SURVIVED THAT **LEVEL** OF DESTRUCTION. F.O.G.-13 DID WHAT IT WAS **DESIGNED** TO DO.

MAKES **QUICK** WORK OF THINGS, THAT'S FOR SURE. PERFORMED **BETTER** THAN EXPECTED.

WHERE IS **AGENT 3?**

HMMM... **WHAT DO** WE HAVE HERE?

HAHA, I HAVEN'T SEEN ONE OF THESE IN YEARS.

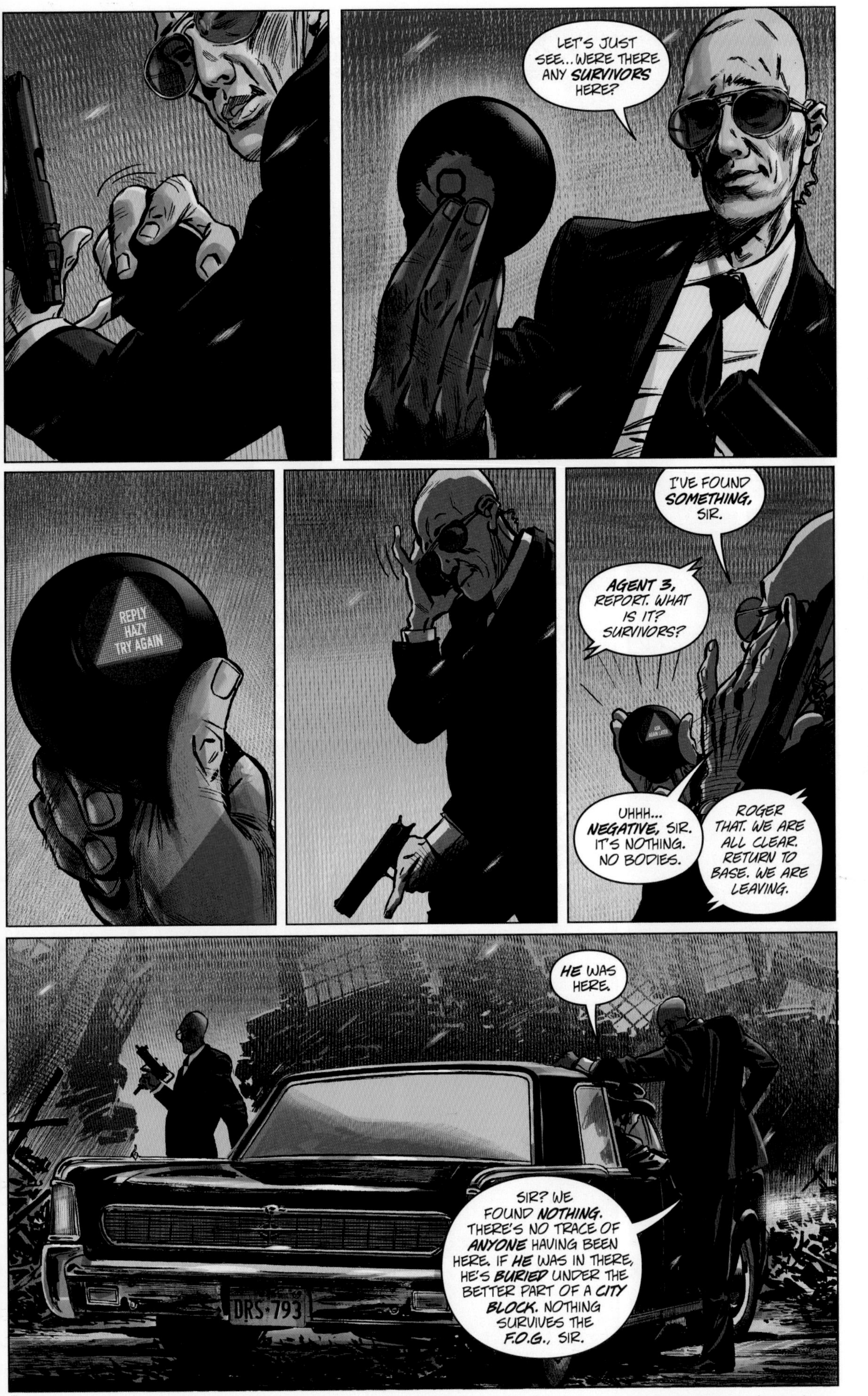
LET'S JUST SEE... WERE THERE ANY **SURVIVORS** HERE?
REPLY HAZY TRY AGAIN
I'VE FOUND **SOMETHING,** SIR.
AGENT 3, *REPORT. WHAT IS IT? SURVIVORS?*
UHHH... **NEGATIVE,** SIR. IT'S NOTHING. NO BODIES.
ROGER THAT. WE ARE ALL CLEAR. RETURN TO BASE. WE ARE LEAVING.
HE WAS HERE.
DRS 793
SIR? WE FOUND **NOTHING.** THERE'S NO TRACE OF **ANYONE** HAVING BEEN HERE. IF **HE** WAS IN THERE, HE'S **BURIED** UNDER THE BETTER PART OF A **CITY BLOCK.** NOTHING SURVIVES THE **F.O.G.,** SIR.

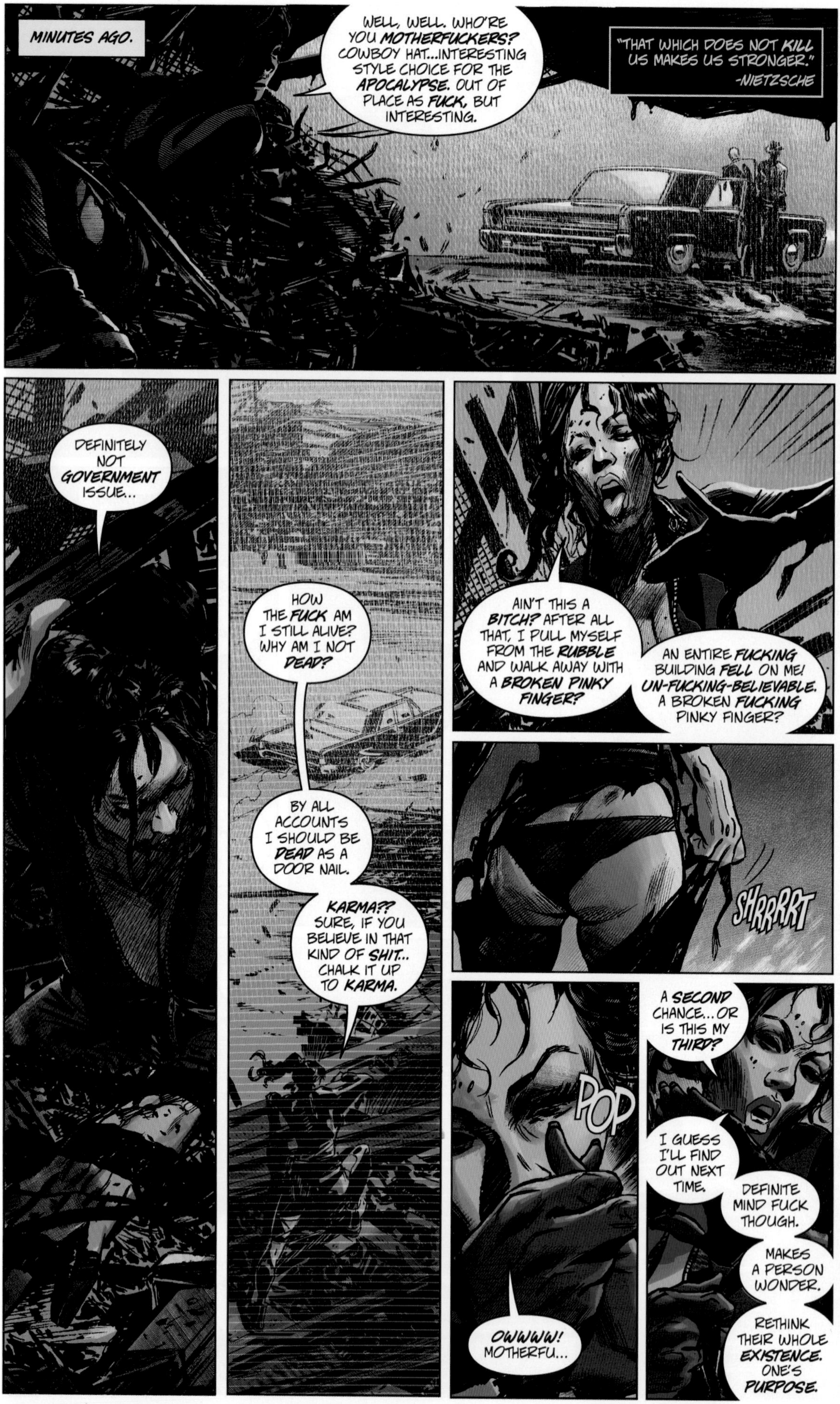

MINUTES AGO.
WELL, WELL. WHO'RE YOU MOTHERFUCKERS? COWBOY HAT...INTERESTING STYLE CHOICE FOR THE APOCALYPSE. OUT OF PLACE AS FUCK, BUT INTERESTING.
"THAT WHICH DOES NOT KILL US MAKES US STRONGER." -NIETZSCHE
DEFINITELY NOT GOVERNMENT ISSUE...
HOW THE FUCK AM I STILL ALIVE? WHY AM I NOT DEAD?
BY ALL ACCOUNTS I SHOULD BE DEAD AS A DOOR NAIL.
KARMA?? SURE, IF YOU BELIEVE IN THAT KIND OF SHIT... CHALK IT UP TO KARMA.
AIN'T THIS A BITCH? AFTER ALL THAT, I PULL MYSELF FROM THE RUBBLE AND WALK AWAY WITH A BROKEN PINKY FINGER?
AN ENTIRE FUCKING BUILDING FELL ON ME! UN-FUCKING-BELIEVABLE. A BROKEN FUCKING PINKY FINGER?
SHRRRRT
POP
OWWWW! MOTHERFU...
A SECOND CHANCE...OR IS THIS MY THIRD?
I GUESS I'LL FIND OUT NEXT TIME.
DEFINITE MIND FUCK THOUGH.
MAKES A PERSON WONDER.
RETHINK THEIR WHOLE EXISTENCE. ONE'S PURPOSE.

WHERE THE **HELL** ARE WE GOING?

TO SEE A **FRIEND**...AT LEAST HE **USED** TO BE THE LAST TIME I SAW HIM. YOU **SURE** YOU DON'T WANT A **SMOKE**?

YEAH, I'M SURE. LIKE I SAID EARLIER, THOSE **THINGS** WILL **KILL** YOU, MAN.

MOLLY, RIGHT?

LOOK, **MOLLY**, IF **THAT** WAS WHAT I THINK IT WAS BACK THERE-- AND I'M PRETTY **POSITIVE** IT WAS-- THEN WE'RE GOING TO NEED SOME **HELP** WITH THIS.

IT ALSO MEANS THEIR **TIMETABLE** HAS MOVED UP **EXPONENTIALLY.** THEY'RE GETTING CLOSE. **TOO** CLOSE. **TOO** FAST.

MY BEST ESTIMATE, THEY'RE **TWO TO THREE** MINUTES BEHIND US... GIVE OR TAKE ONE **TACTICAL EMP** THAT WASN'T 100% EFFECTIVE.

TACTICAL EMP? ROBOTIC LEGS? WHO EXACTLY ARE THE **THEY** YOU MYSTERIOUSLY KEEP REFERRING TO? AND WHAT DO **THEY** WANT EXACTLY? I **THOUGHT** I KNEW WHAT WAS GOING ON...

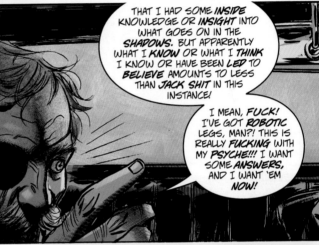

THAT I HAD SOME **INSIDE** KNOWLEDGE OR **INSIGHT** INTO WHAT GOES ON IN THE **SHADOWS.** BUT APPARENTLY WHAT I **KNOW** OR WHAT I **THINK** I KNOW OR HAVE BEEN **LED** TO **BELIEVE** AMOUNTS TO LESS THAN **JACK SHIT** IN THIS INSTANCE!

I MEAN, **FUCK!** I'VE GOT **ROBOTIC** LEGS, MAN?! THIS IS REALLY **FUCKING** WITH MY **PSYCHE!!!** I WANT SOME **ANSWERS,** AND I WANT 'EM **NOW!**

MY **MIND** IS SEETHING.

TOO MANY QUESTIONS, **MOLLY.** AND AT THE MOMENT, I'M **SHORT** ON ANSWERS. RIGHT NOW, ANYWAY.

MY **BRAIN** IS A BIT SCATTER-SHOT TODAY. IF MY **CALCULATIONS** ARE CORRECT, IN ABOUT **30 SECONDS** WE'LL HAVE **COMPANY.** AND **THEY'RE** GOING TO WANT ANSWERS, **TOO.**

HANG ON! WE'RE TURNING AROUND!

SCREEECH

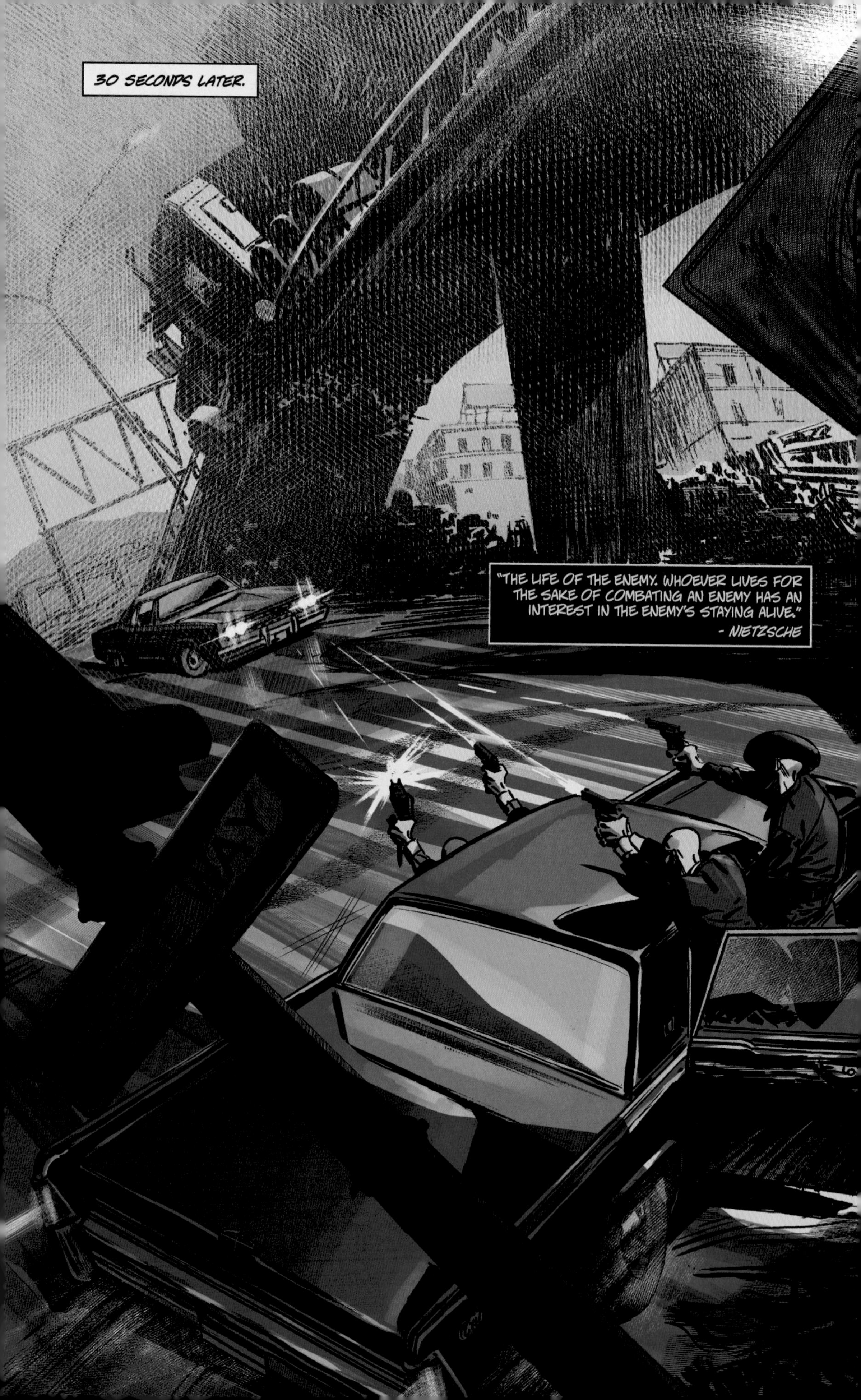
30 SECONDS LATER.
"THE LIFE OF THE ENEMY. WHOEVER LIVES FOR THE SAKE OF COMBATING AN ENEMY HAS AN INTEREST IN THE ENEMY'S STAYING ALIVE."
- NIETZSCHE

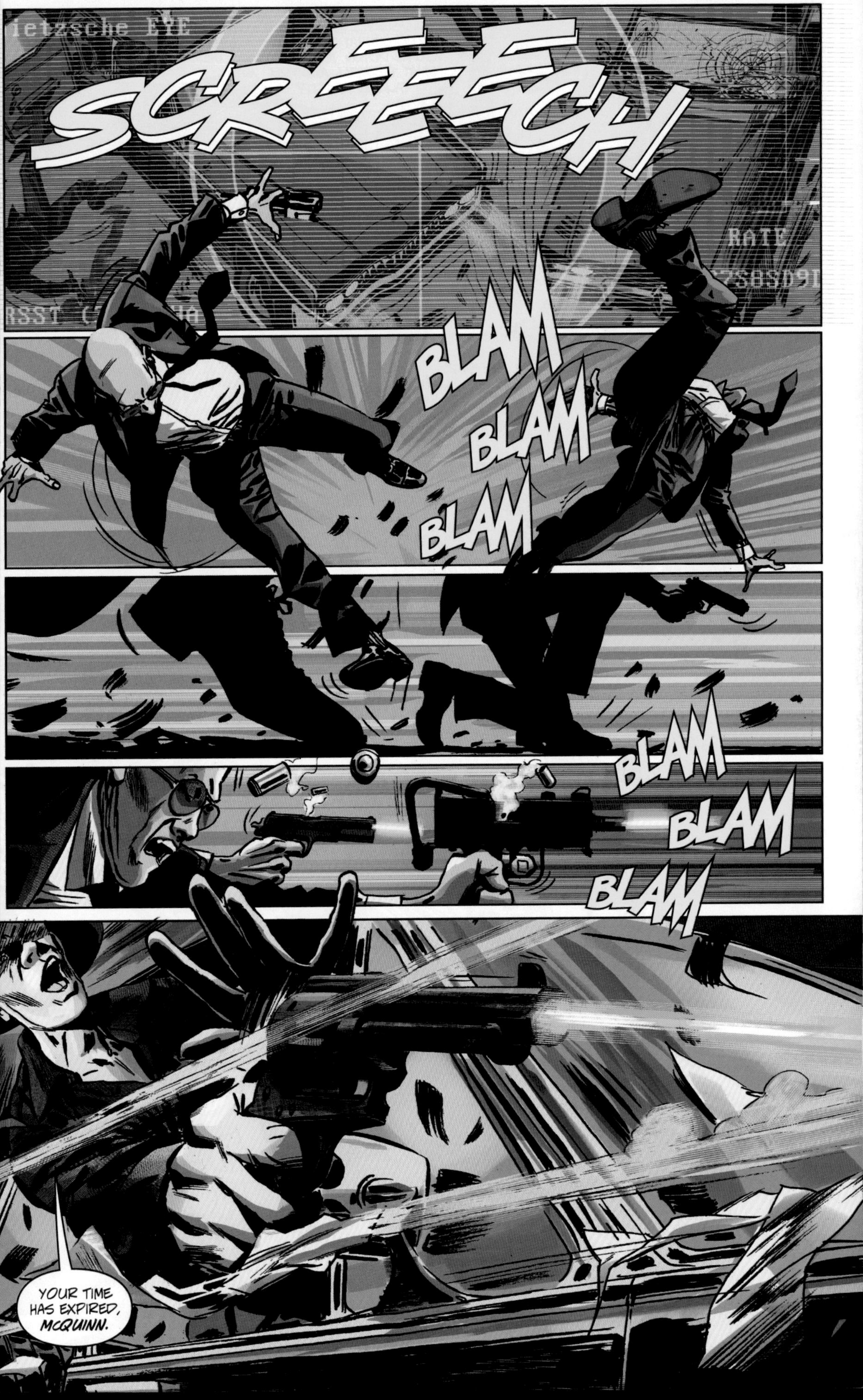
ietzsche EYE
SCREEECH
RATE
BLAM
BLAM
BLAM
BLAM
BLAM
BLAM
YOUR TIME HAS EXPIRED, MCQUINN.

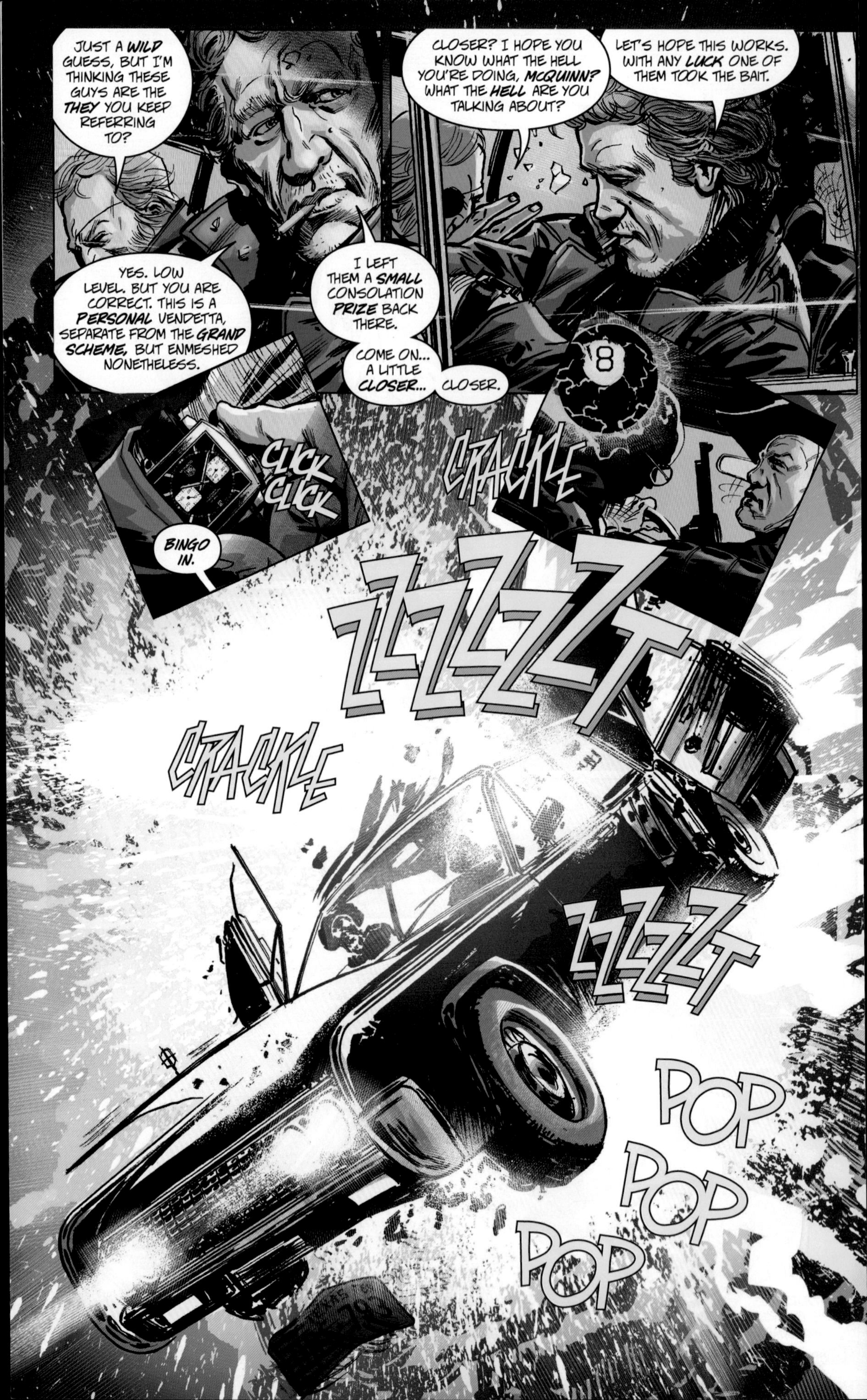
JUST A WILD GUESS, BUT I'M THINKING THESE GUYS ARE THE THEY YOU KEEP REFERRING TO?
YES. LOW LEVEL. BUT YOU ARE CORRECT. THIS IS A PERSONAL VENDETTA, SEPARATE FROM THE GRAND SCHEME, BUT ENMESHED NONETHELESS.
I LEFT THEM A SMALL CONSOLATION PRIZE BACK THERE.
CLOSER? I HOPE YOU KNOW WHAT THE HELL YOU'RE DOING, MCQUINN? WHAT THE HELL ARE YOU TALKING ABOUT?
LET'S HOPE THIS WORKS. WITH ANY LUCK ONE OF THEM TOOK THE BAIT.
COME ON... A LITTLE CLOSER...
CLOSER.
CLICK CLICK
BINGO IN.
8
CRACKLE
ZZZZZT
CRACKLE
ZZZZZT
POP
POP
POP

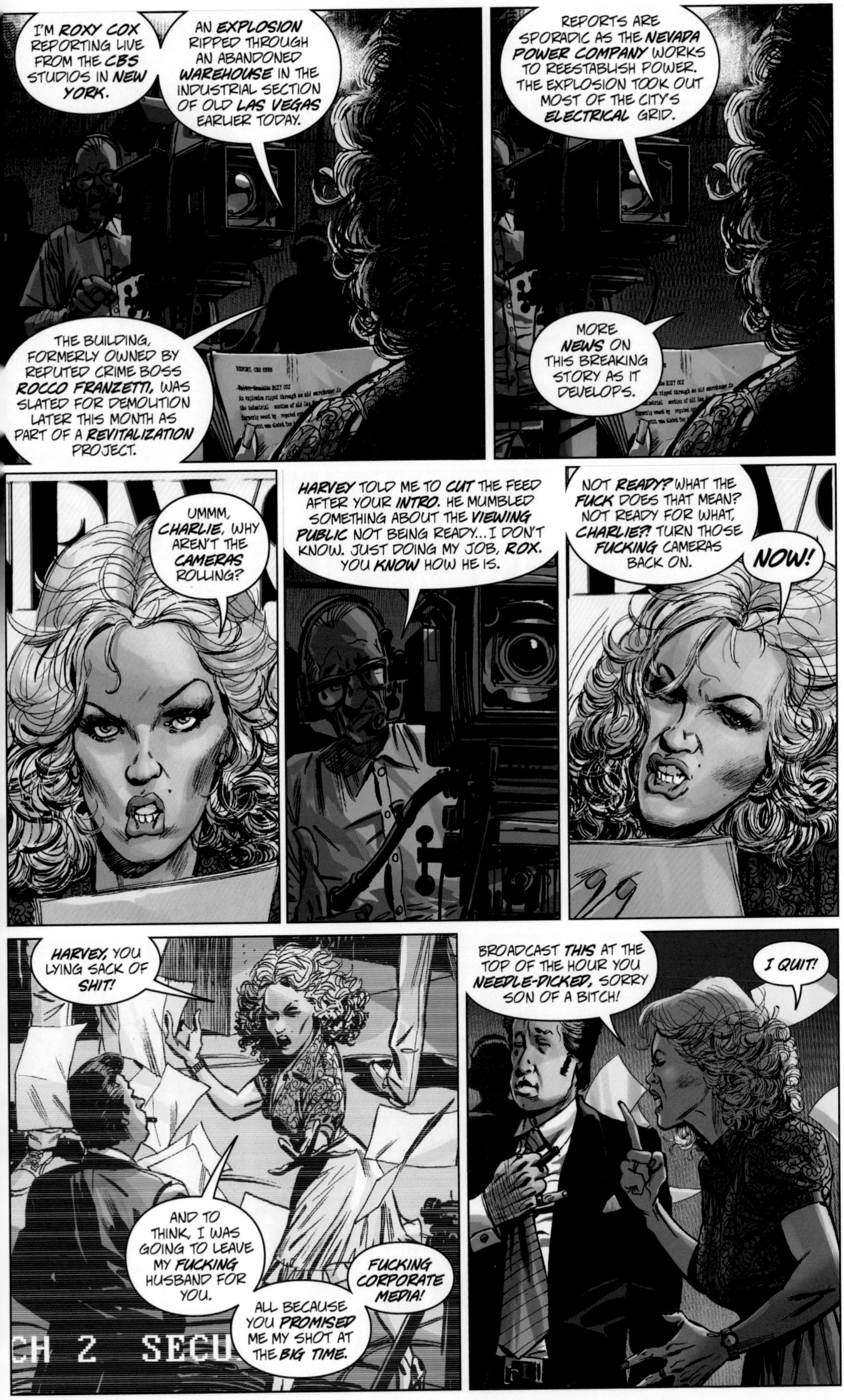
I'M ROXY COX REPORTING LIVE FROM THE CBS STUDIOS IN NEW YORK.
AN EXPLOSION RIPPED THROUGH AN ABANDONED WAREHOUSE IN THE INDUSTRIAL SECTION OF OLD LAS VEGAS EARLIER TODAY.
THE BUILDING, FORMERLY OWNED BY REPUTED CRIME BOSS ROCCO FRANZETTI, WAS SLATED FOR DEMOLITION LATER THIS MONTH AS PART OF A REVITALIZATION PROJECT.
REPORTS ARE SPORADIC AS THE NEVADA POWER COMPANY WORKS TO REESTABLISH POWER. THE EXPLOSION TOOK OUT MOST OF THE CITY'S ELECTRICAL GRID.
MORE NEWS ON THIS BREAKING STORY AS IT DEVELOPS.
UMMM, CHARLIE, WHY AREN'T THE CAMERAS ROLLING?
HARVEY TOLD ME TO CUT THE FEED AFTER YOUR INTRO. HE MUMBLED SOMETHING ABOUT THE VIEWING PUBLIC NOT BEING READY... I DON'T KNOW. JUST DOING MY JOB, ROX. YOU KNOW HOW HE IS.
NOT READY? WHAT THE FUCK DOES THAT MEAN? NOT READY FOR WHAT, CHARLIE?! TURN THOSE FUCKING CAMERAS BACK ON.
NOW!
HARVEY, YOU LYING SACK OF SHIT!
AND TO THINK, I WAS GOING TO LEAVE MY FUCKING HUSBAND FOR YOU.
ALL BECAUSE YOU PROMISED ME MY SHOT AT THE BIG TIME.
FUCKING CORPORATE MEDIA!
CH 2 SECU
BROADCAST THIS AT THE TOP OF THE HOUR YOU NEEDLE-DICKED, SORRY SON OF A BITCH!
I QUIT!

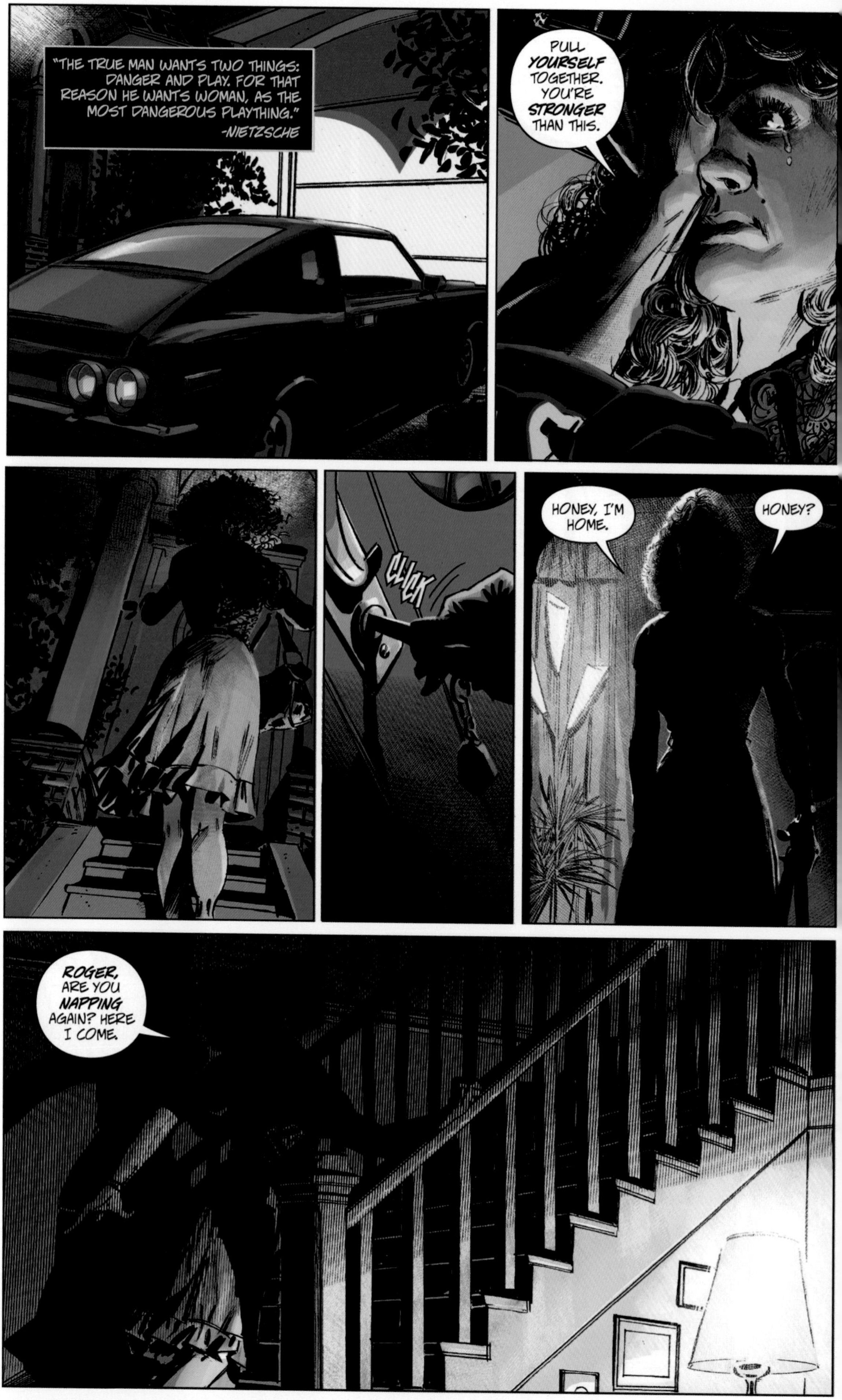
"THE TRUE MAN WANTS TWO THINGS: DANGER AND PLAY. FOR THAT REASON HE WANTS WOMAN, AS THE MOST DANGEROUS PLAYTHING."
-NIETZSCHE
PULL YOURSELF TOGETHER. YOU'RE STRONGER THAN THIS.
CLICK
HONEY, I'M HOME.
HONEY?
ROGER, ARE YOU NAPPING AGAIN? HERE I COME.

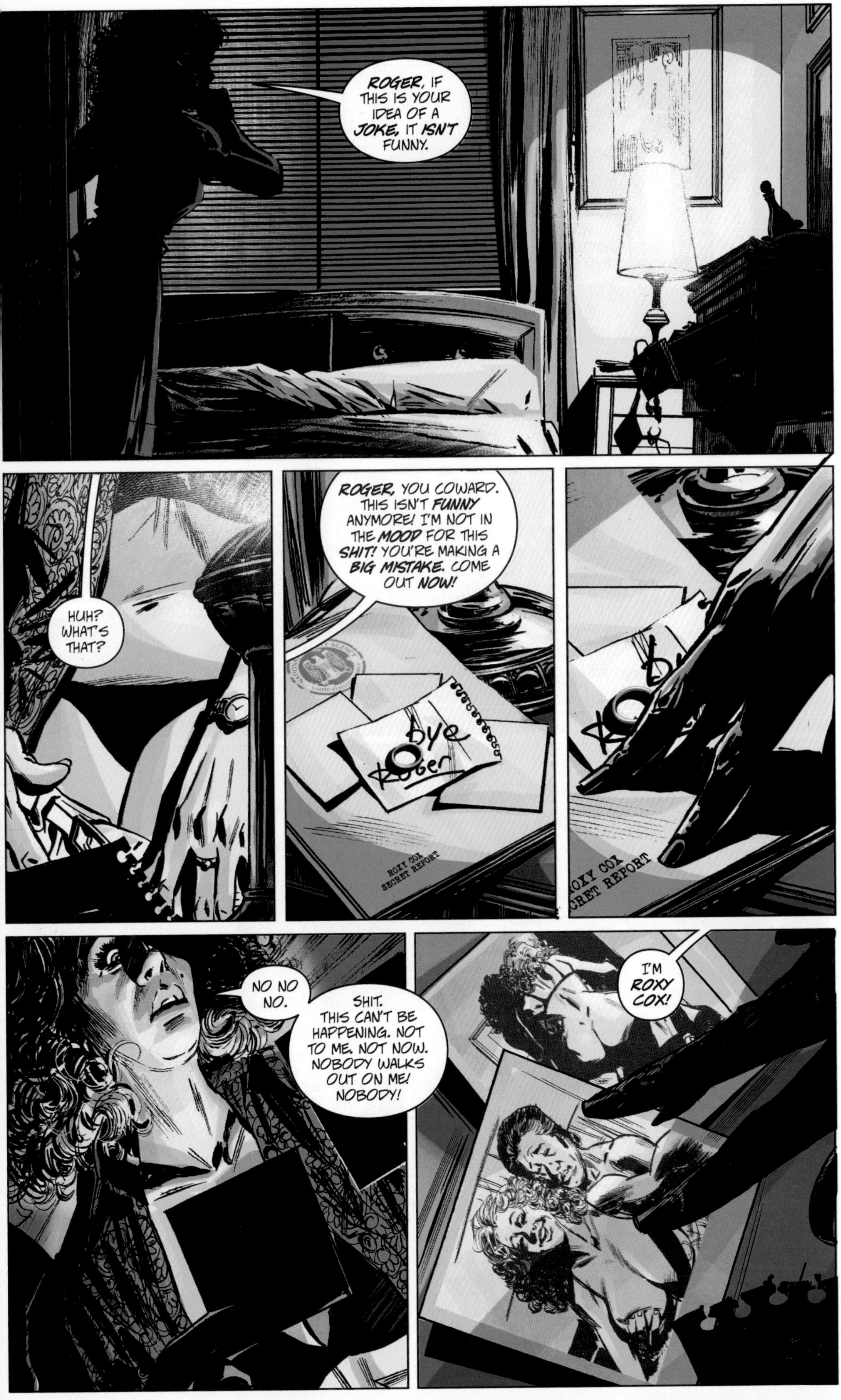
ROGER, IF THIS IS YOUR IDEA OF A JOKE, IT ISN'T FUNNY.
HUH? WHAT'S THAT?
ROGER, YOU COWARD. THIS ISN'T FUNNY ANYMORE! I'M NOT IN THE MOOD FOR THIS SHIT! YOU'RE MAKING A BIG MISTAKE. COME OUT NOW!
bye Roger
ROXY COX SECRET REPORT
ROXY COX SECRET REPORT
NO NO NO.
SHIT. THIS CAN'T BE HAPPENING. NOT TO ME. NOT NOW. NOBODY WALKS OUT ON ME! NOBODY!
I'M ROXY COX!

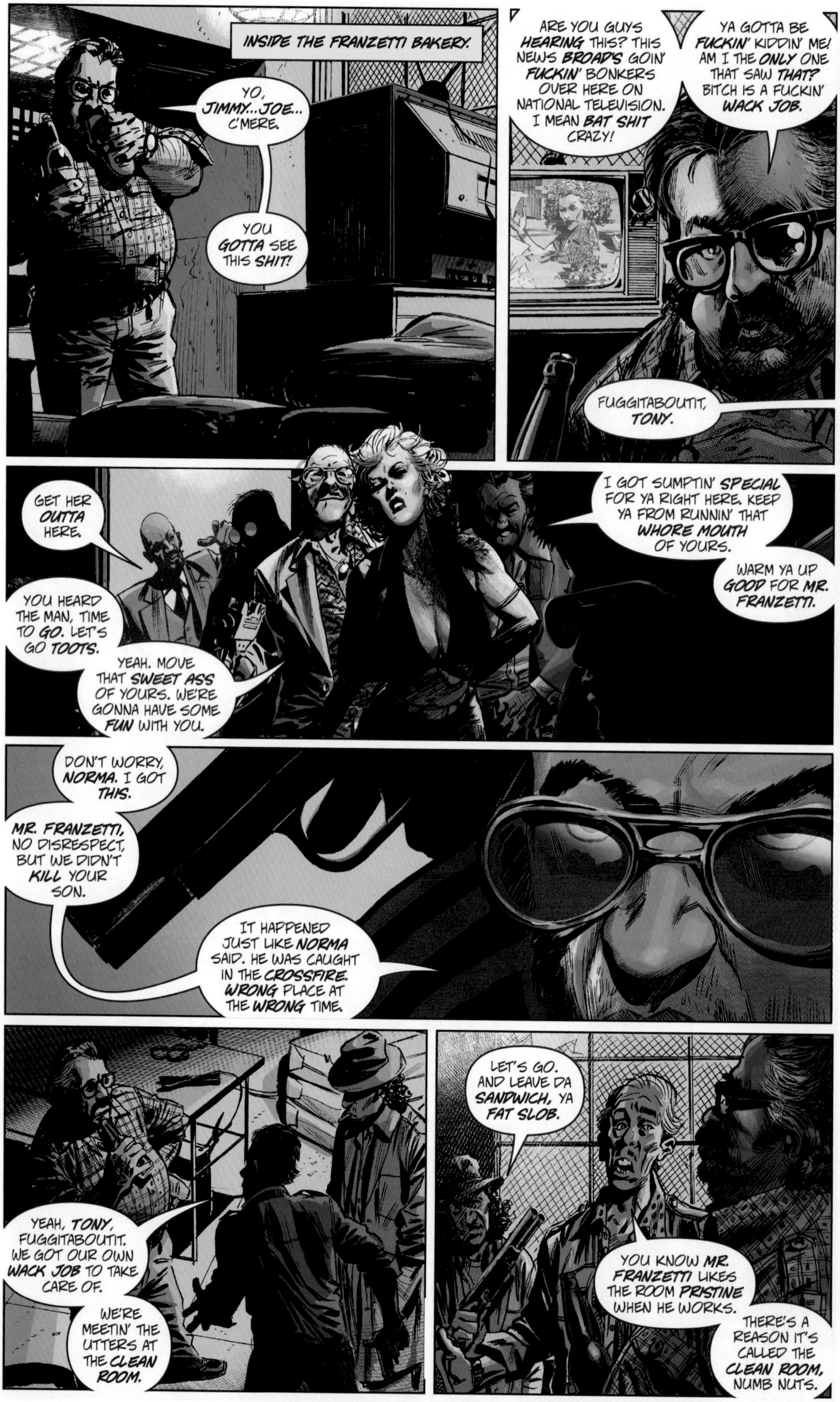
INSIDE THE FRANZETTI BAKERY.
YO, JIMMY...JOE... C'MERE.
YOU GOTTA SEE THIS SHIT!
ARE YOU GUYS HEARING THIS? THIS NEWS BROAD'S GOIN' FUCKIN' BONKERS OVER HERE ON NATIONAL TELEVISION. I MEAN BAT SHIT CRAZY!
YA GOTTA BE FUCKIN' KIDDIN' ME! AM I THE ONLY ONE THAT SAW THAT? BITCH IS A FUCKIN' WACK JOB.
FUGGITABOUTIT, TONY.
GET HER OUTTA HERE.
YOU HEARD THE MAN, TIME TO GO. LET'S GO TOOTS.
YEAH. MOVE THAT SWEET ASS OF YOURS. WE'RE GONNA HAVE SOME FUN WITH YOU.
I GOT SUMPTIN' SPECIAL FOR YA RIGHT HERE. KEEP YA FROM RUNNIN' THAT WHORE MOUTH OF YOURS.
WARM YA UP GOOD FOR MR. FRANZETTI.
DON'T WORRY, NORMA. I GOT THIS.
MR. FRANZETTI, NO DISRESPECT, BUT WE DIDN'T KILL YOUR SON.
IT HAPPENED JUST LIKE NORMA SAID. HE WAS CAUGHT IN THE CROSSFIRE. WRONG PLACE AT THE WRONG TIME.
YEAH, TONY, FUGGITABOUTIT. WE GOT OUR OWN WACK JOB TO TAKE CARE OF.
WE'RE MEETIN' THE UTTERS AT THE CLEAN ROOM.
LET'S GO. AND LEAVE DA SANDWICH, YA FAT SLOB.
YOU KNOW MR. FRANZETTI LIKES THE ROOM PRISTINE WHEN HE WORKS.
THERE'S A REASON IT'S CALLED THE CLEAN ROOM, NUMB NUTS.

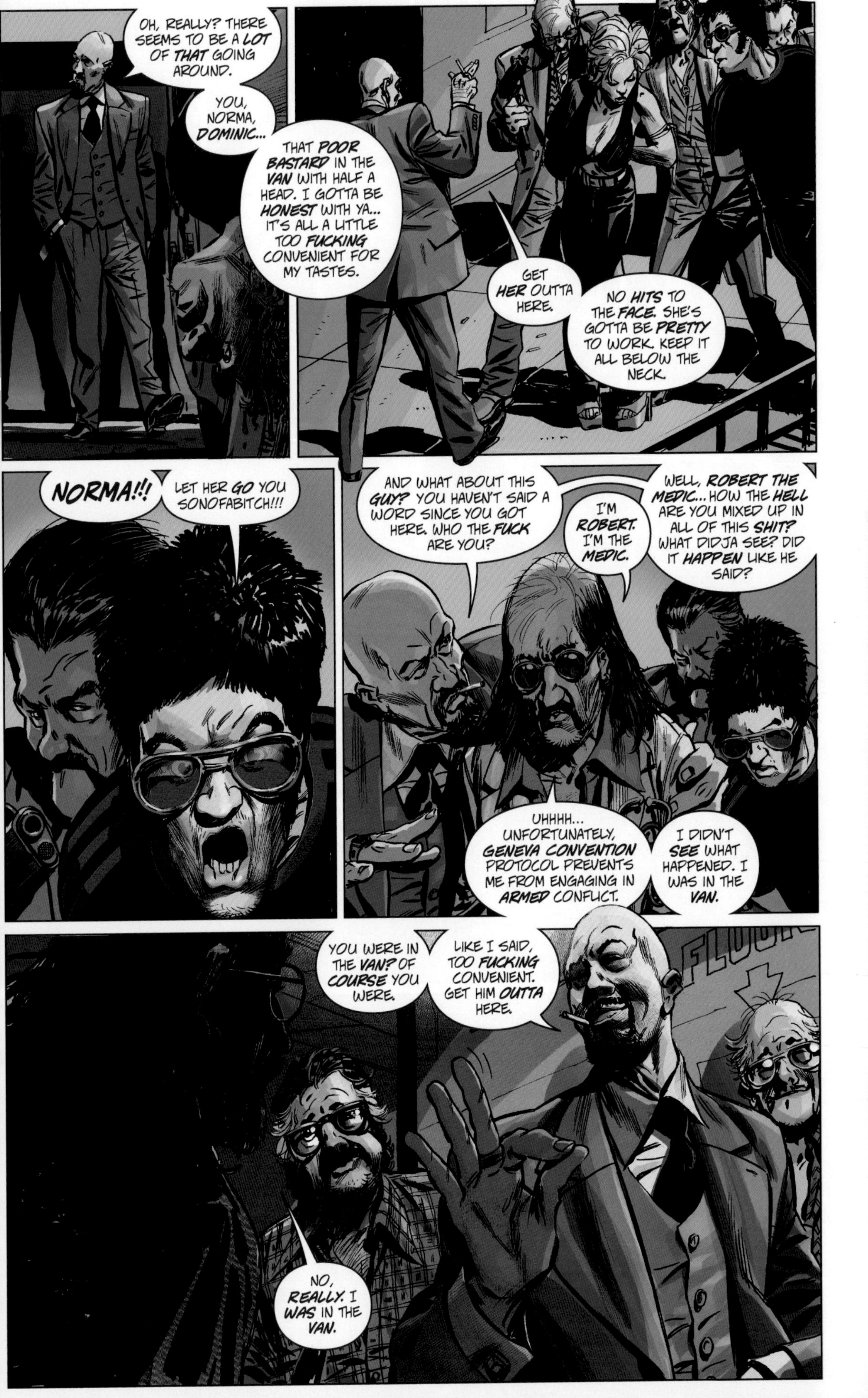
OH, REALLY? THERE SEEMS TO BE A LOT OF THAT GOING AROUND.
YOU, NORMA, DOMINIC...
THAT POOR BASTARD IN THE VAN WITH HALF A HEAD. I GOTTA BE HONEST WITH YA... IT'S ALL A LITTLE TOO FUCKING CONVENIENT FOR MY TASTES.
GET HER OUTTA HERE.
NO HITS TO THE FACE. SHE'S GOTTA BE PRETTY TO WORK. KEEP IT ALL BELOW THE NECK.
NORMA!!!
LET HER GO YOU SONOFABITCH!!!
AND WHAT ABOUT THIS GUY? YOU HAVEN'T SAID A WORD SINCE YOU GOT HERE. WHO THE FUCK ARE YOU?
I'M ROBERT. I'M THE MEDIC.
WELL, ROBERT THE MEDIC... HOW THE HELL ARE YOU MIXED UP IN ALL OF THIS SHIT? WHAT DIDJA SEE? DID IT HAPPEN LIKE HE SAID?
UHHHH... UNFORTUNATELY, GENEVA CONVENTION PROTOCOL PREVENTS ME FROM ENGAGING IN ARMED CONFLICT.
I DIDN'T SEE WHAT HAPPENED. I WAS IN THE VAN.
YOU WERE IN THE VAN? OF COURSE YOU WERE.
LIKE I SAID, TOO FUCKING CONVENIENT. GET HIM OUTTA HERE.
NO, REALLY. I WAS IN THE VAN.

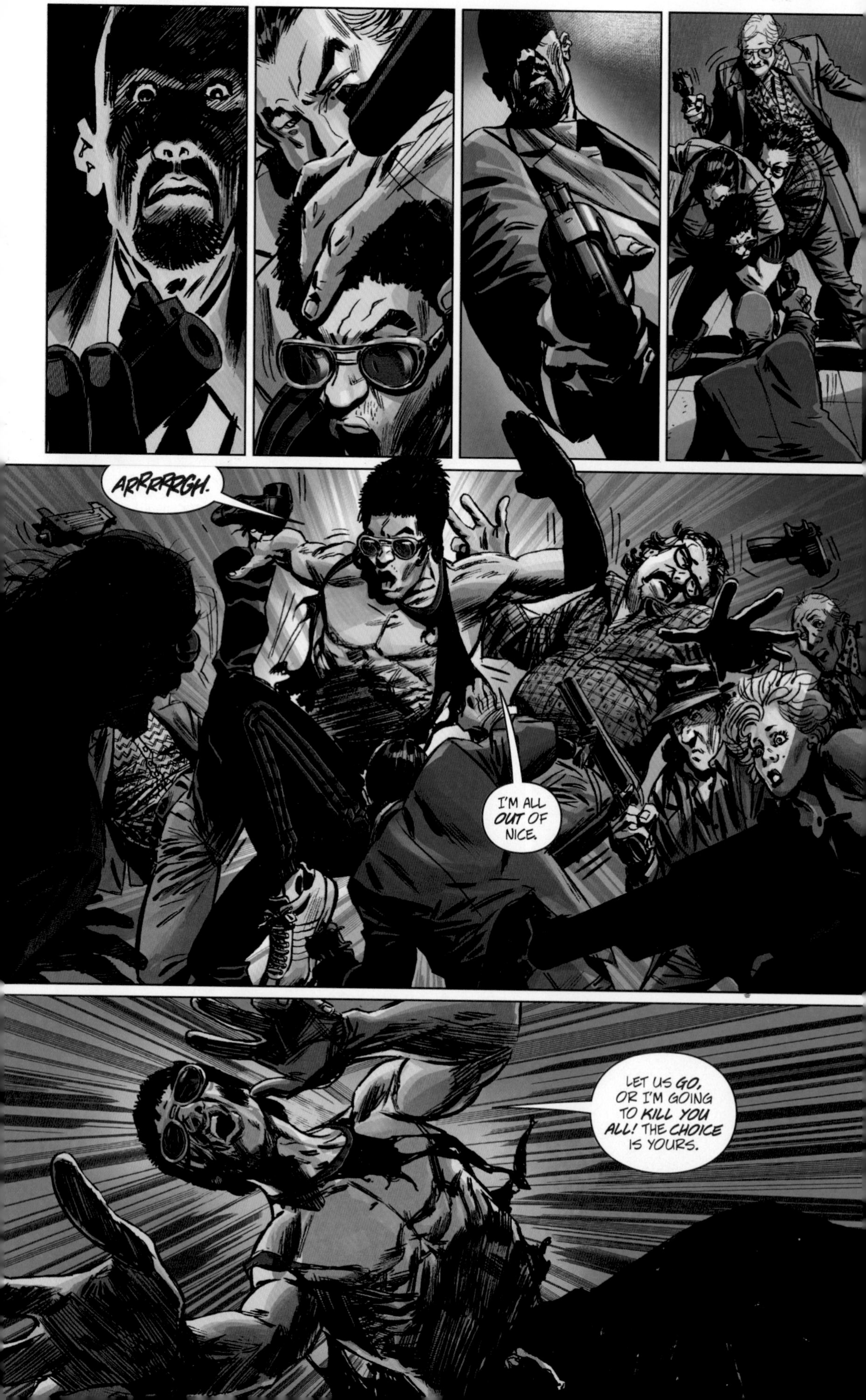
ARRRRRGH.
I'M ALL OUT OF NICE.
LET US GO, OR I'M GOING TO KILL YOU ALL! THE CHOICE IS YOURS.

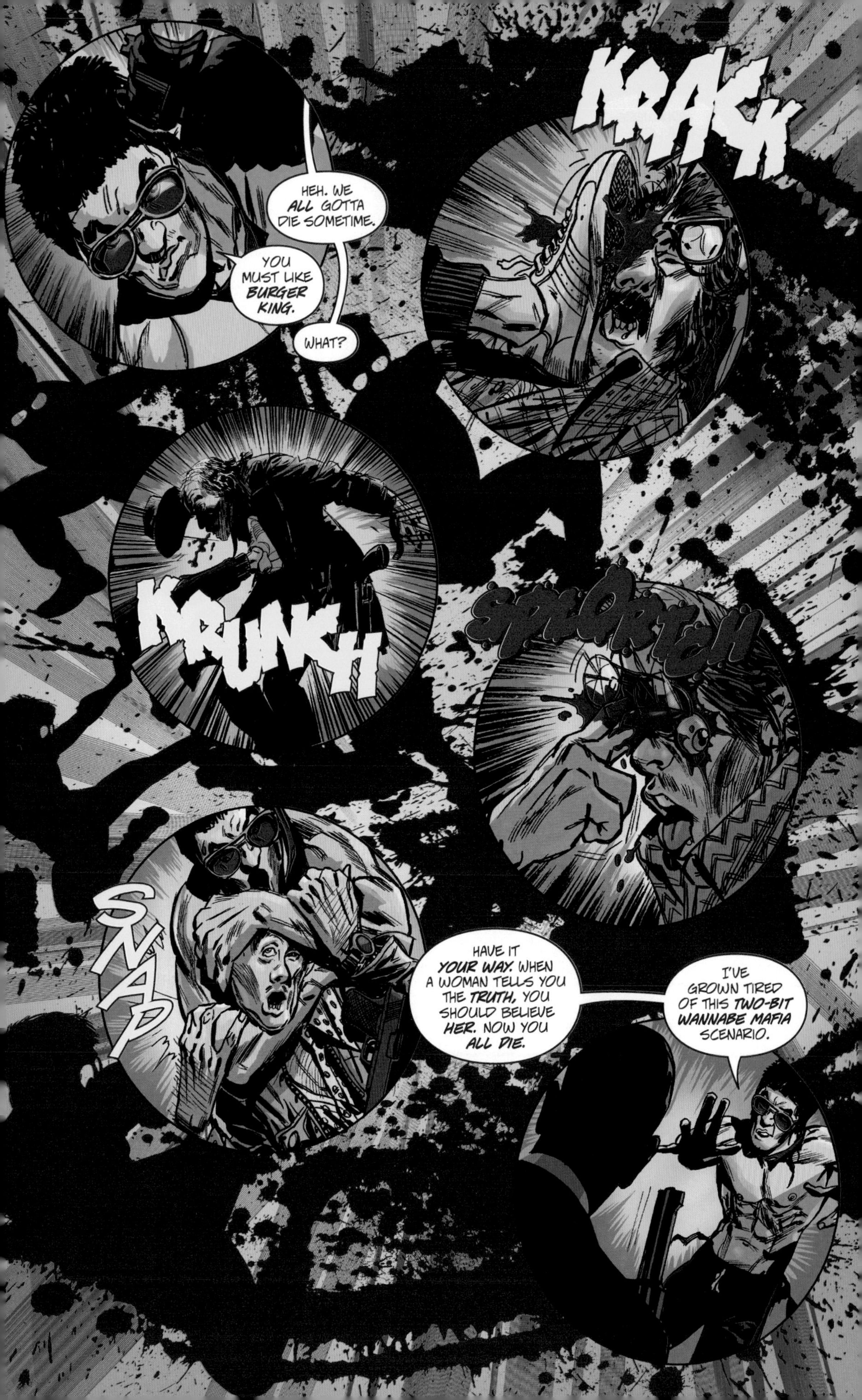
HEH. WE ALL GOTTA DIE SOMETIME.
YOU MUST LIKE BURGER KING.
WHAT?
KRACK
KRUNCH
SPLORTCH
SNAP
HAVE IT YOUR WAY. WHEN A WOMAN TELLS YOU THE TRUTH, YOU SHOULD BELIEVE HER. NOW YOU ALL DIE.
I'VE GROWN TIRED OF THIS TWO-BIT WANNABE MAFIA SCENARIO.

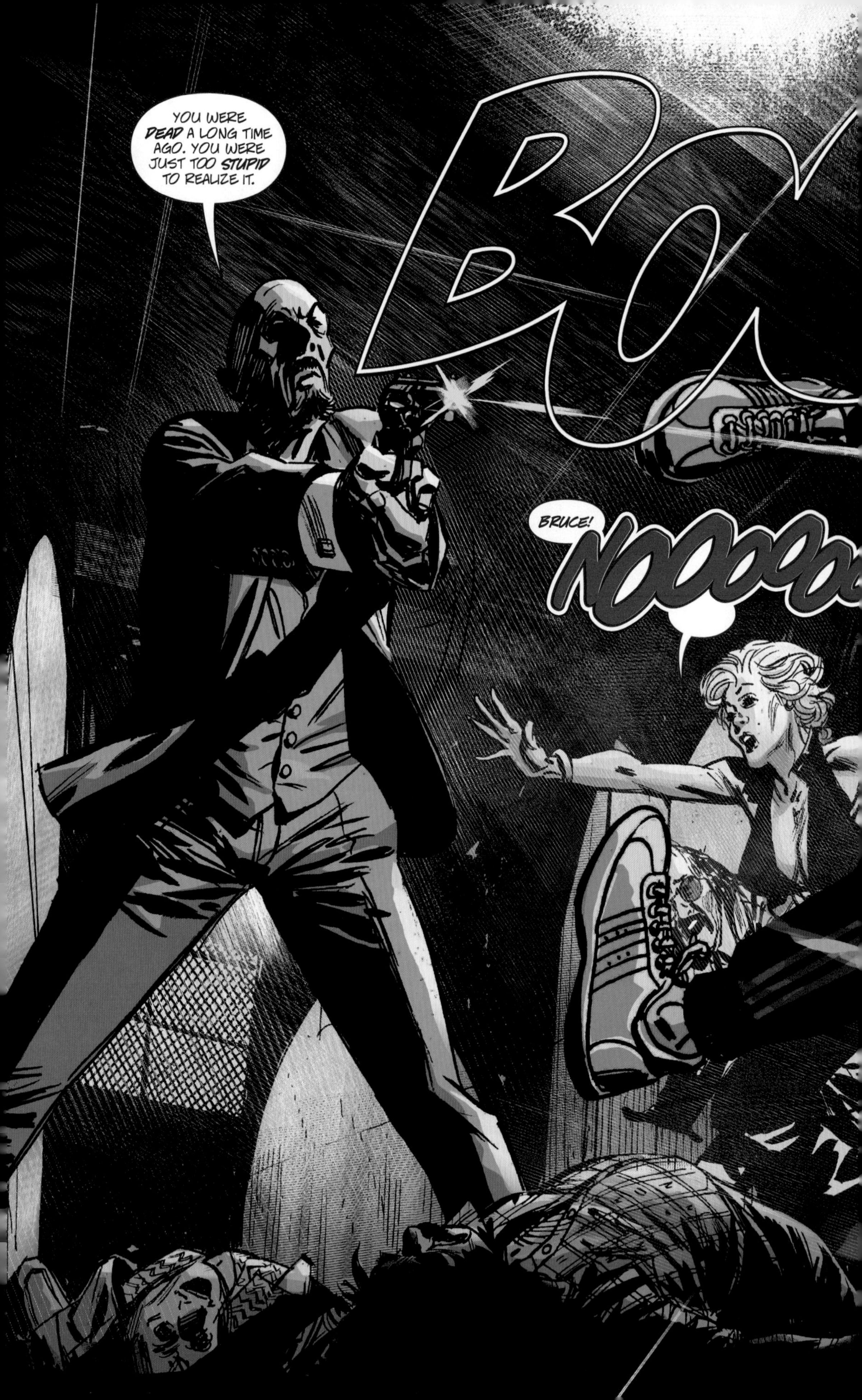
YOU WERE DEAD A LONG TIME AGO. YOU WERE JUST TOO STUPID TO REALIZE IT.
BRUCE!
NOOOOO

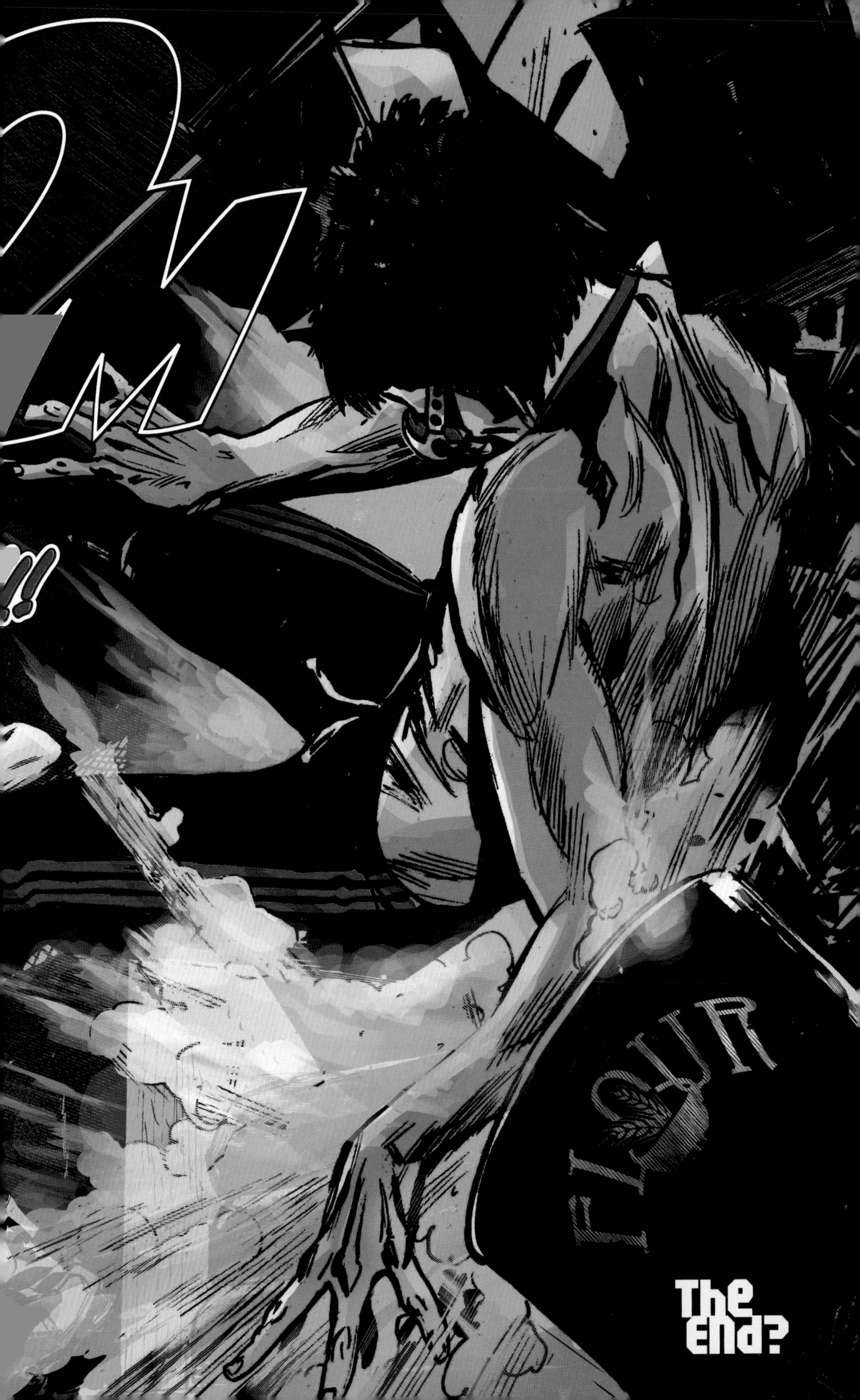
FLOUR
The End?

COVER GALLERY

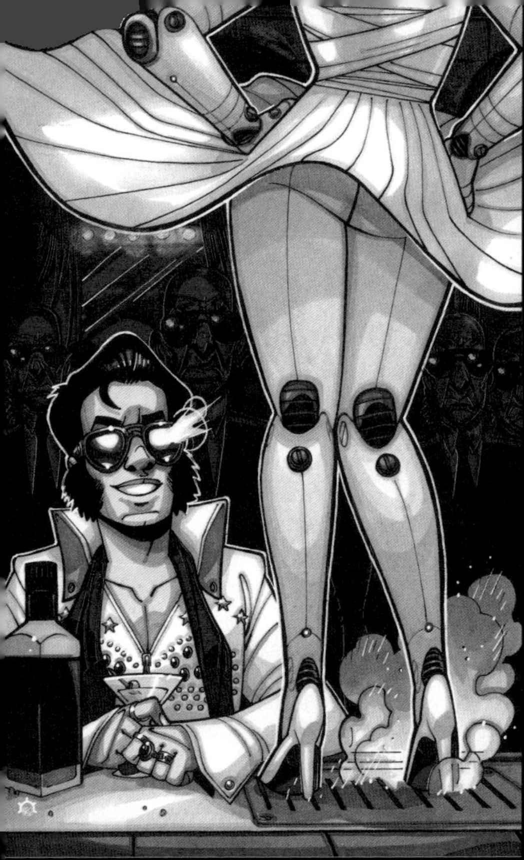

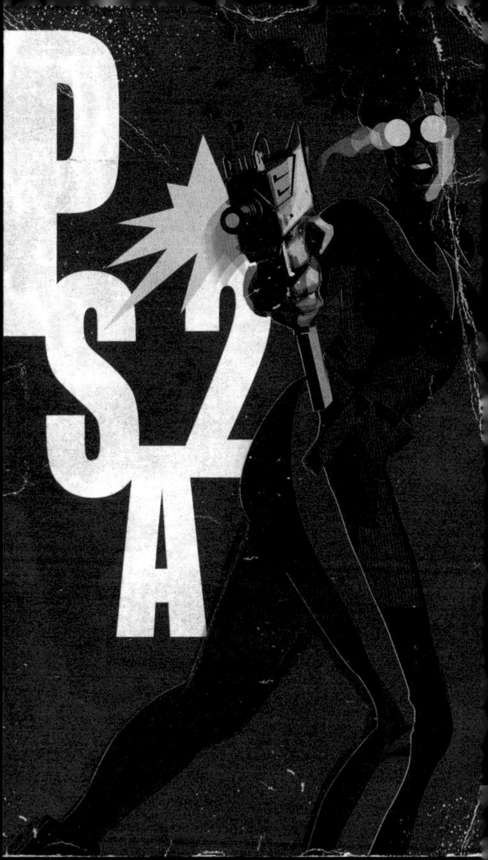
PSA
2

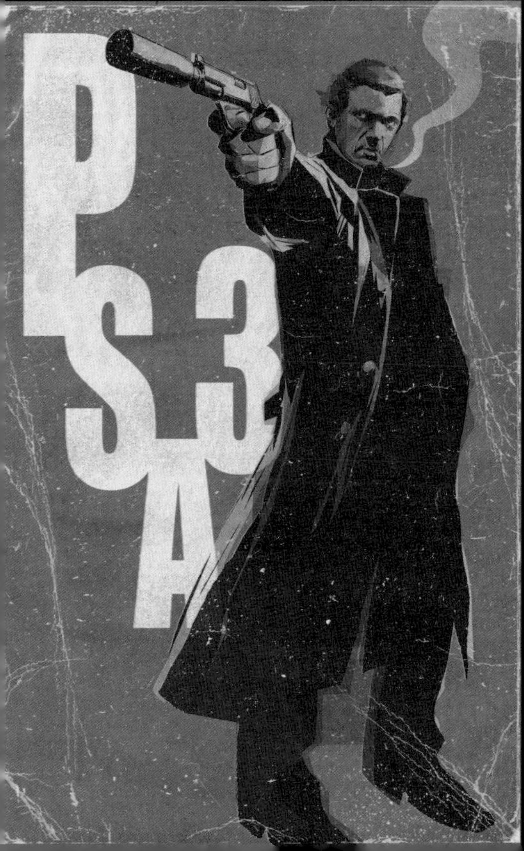
PSA
3

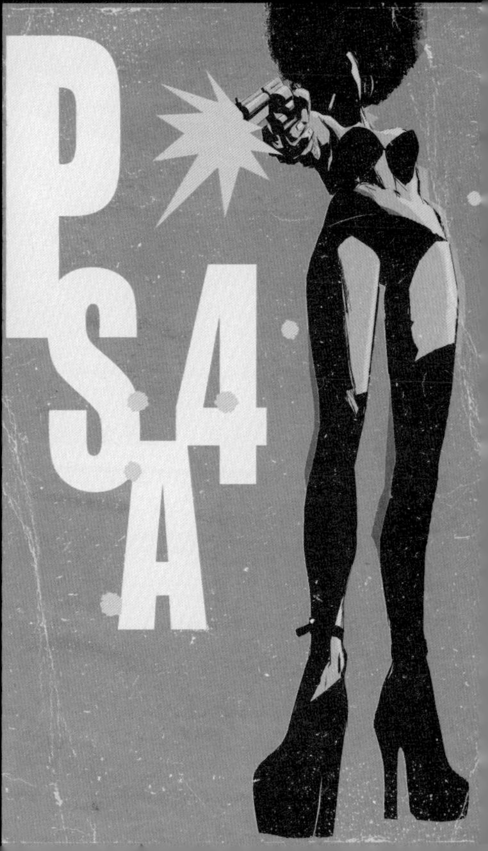
PSA
4

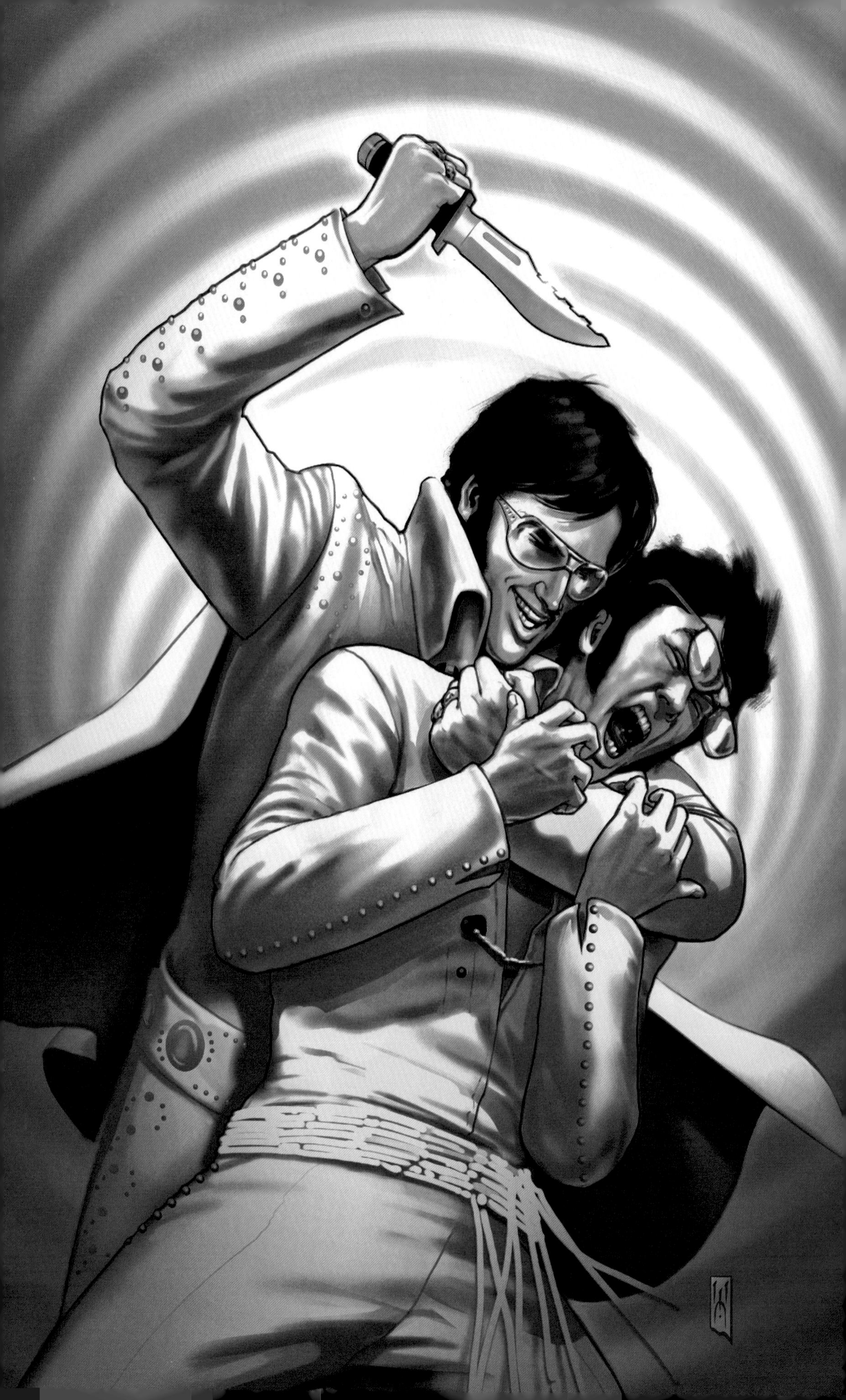

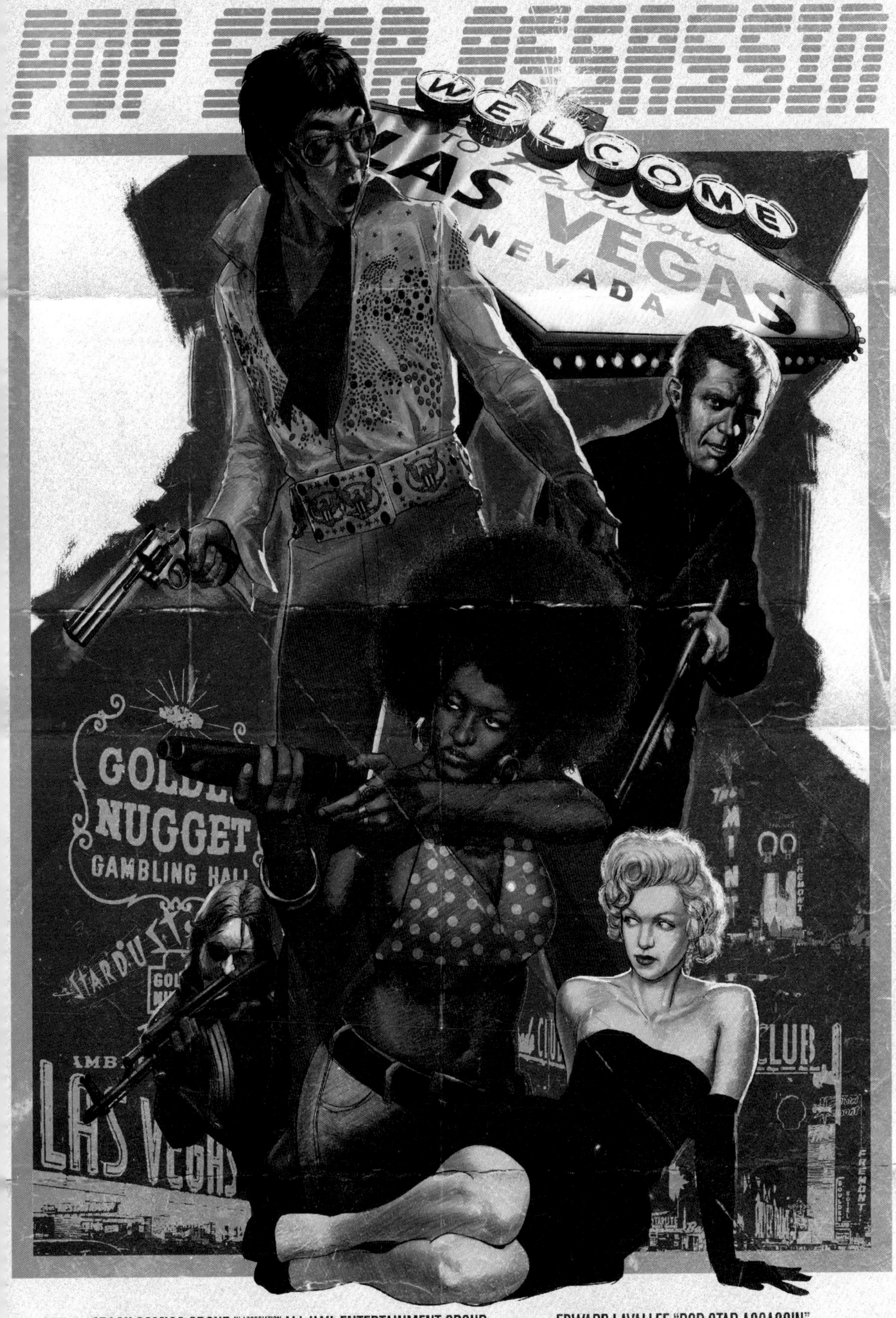
POP STAR ASSASSIN
WELCOME
TO
Fabulous
LAS VEGAS
NEVADA
NUGGET
GAMBLING
CLUB
FREMONT

CRASH COMICS GROUP IN ASSOCIATION WITH ALL HAIL ENTERTAINMENT GROUP PRESENTS A FILM BY EDWARD LAVALLEE "POP STAR ASSASSIN"

WRITTEN AND DIRECTED BY EDWARD LAVALLEE VISUAL EFFECTS BY MARCELO BASILE CO-DIRECTED BY MATT CASHEL EDITED BY TARA CLOUD CLARK

ASSOCIATE PRODUCER NATHAN YOCUM PRODUCED BY RYAN SWANSON PRODUCED BY BEHEMOTH ENTERTAINMENT

BEHEMOTH

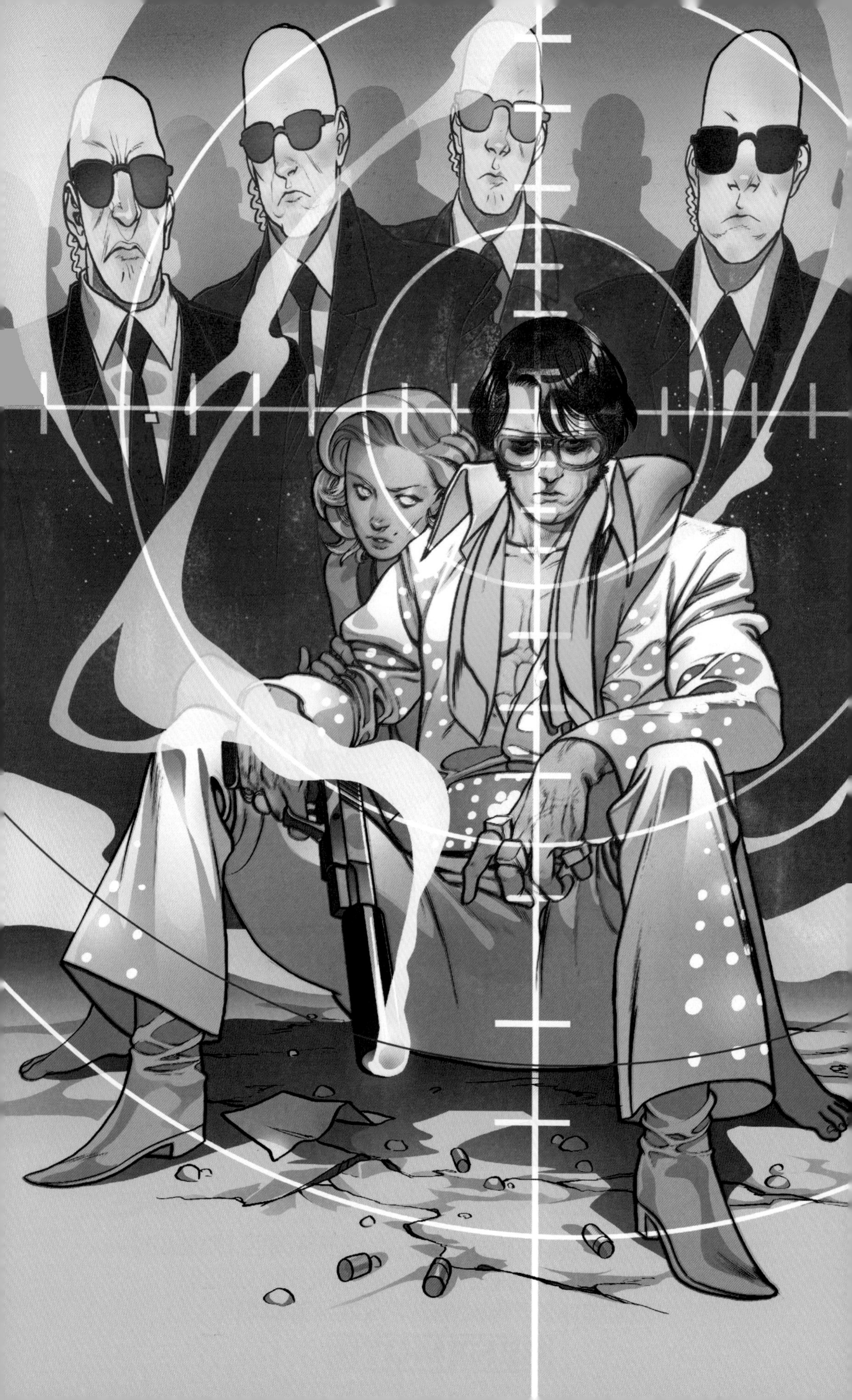

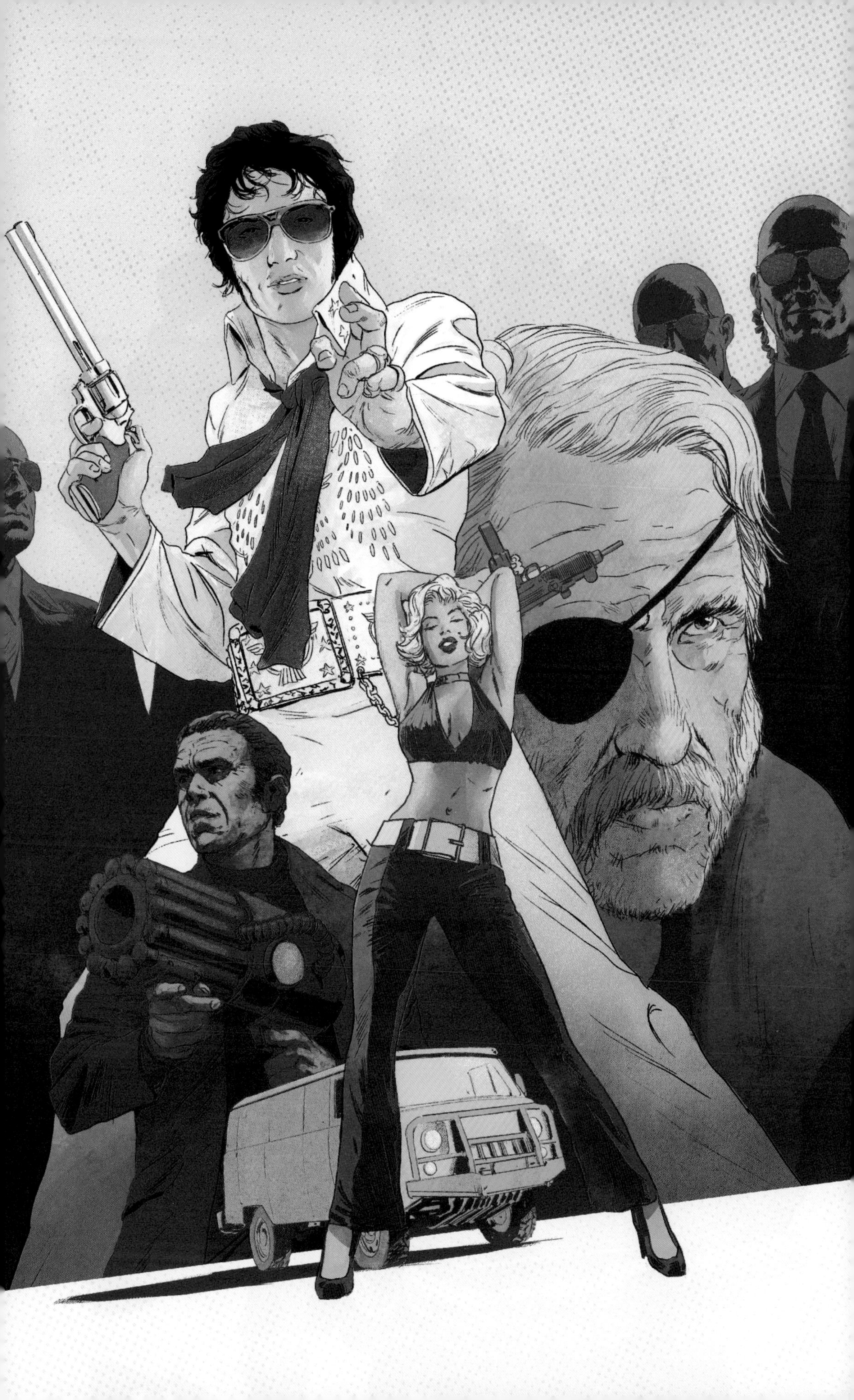

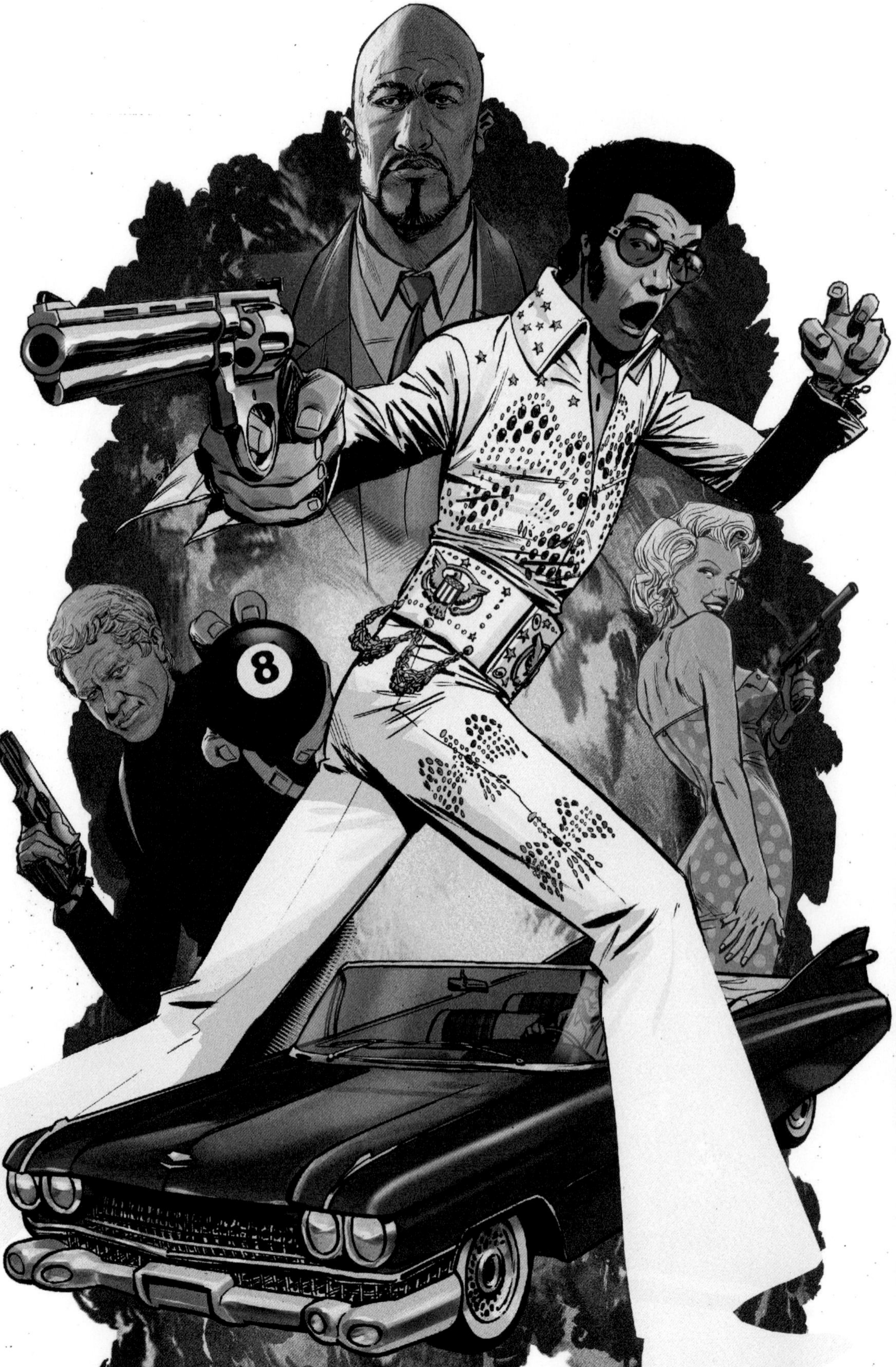

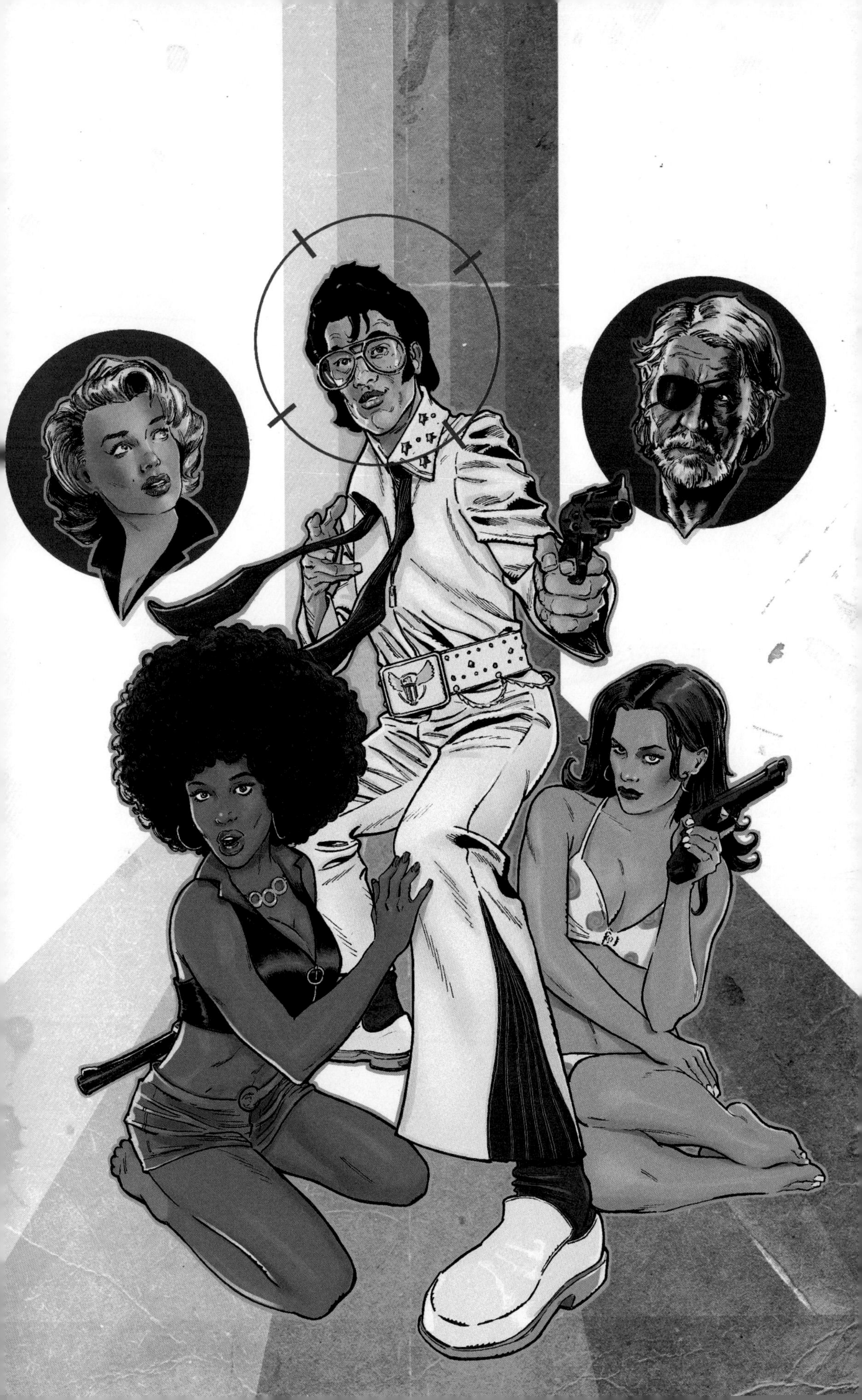

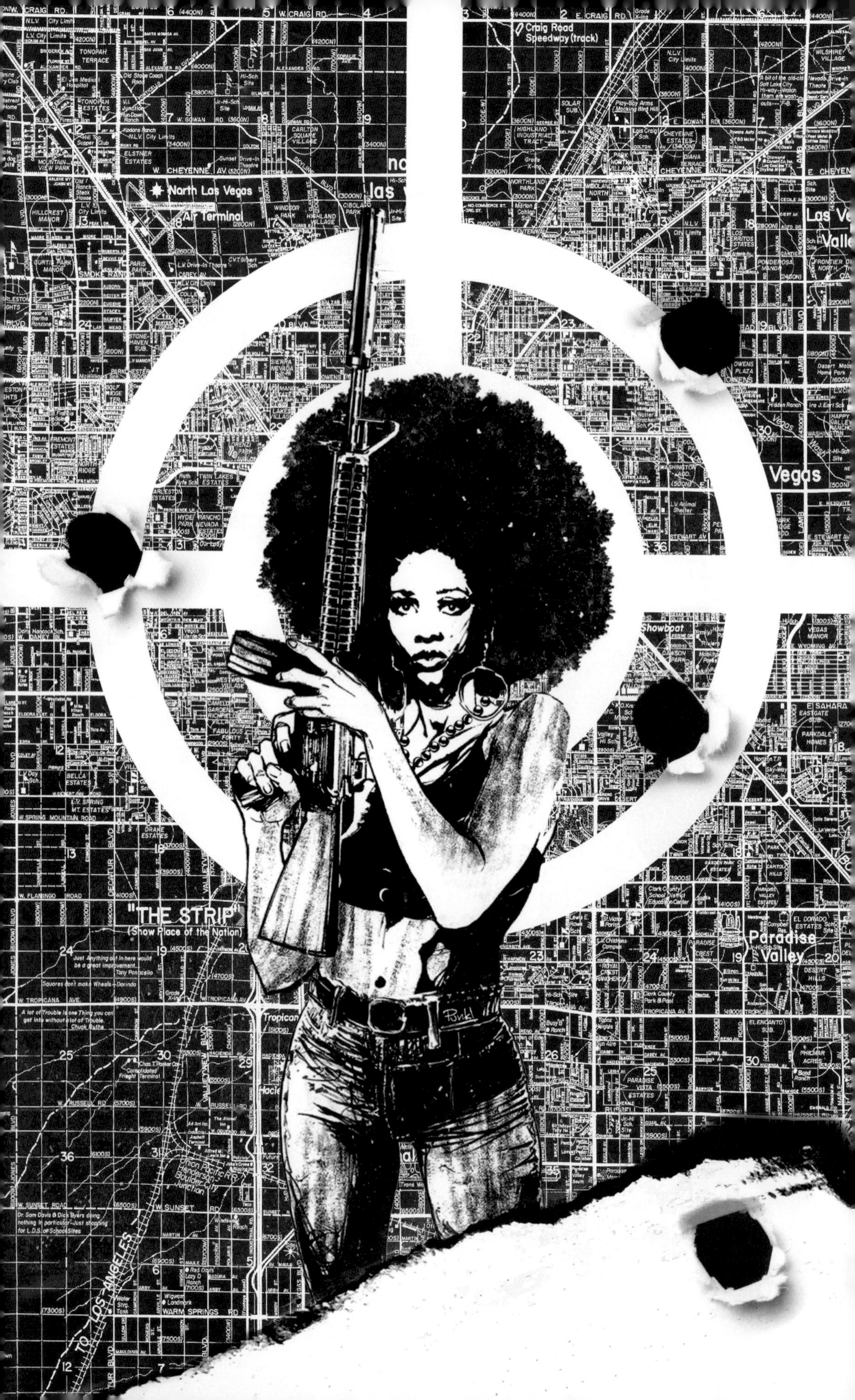

W. CRAIG RD.
Craig Road Speedway (track)
E. CRAIG RD.
N.L.V. City Limits
TONOPAH TERRACE
W. GOWAN RD.
E. GOWAN RD.
CARLTON SQUARE VILLAGE
ELSTNER ESTATES
W. CHEYENNE AV.
CHEYENNE AV.
E. CHEYENNE
North Las Vegas
Air Terminal
Las Vegas
Valley
Vegas
Showboat
E SAHARA
W. SPRING MOUNTAIN ROAD
W. FLAMINGO ROAD
"THE STRIP"
(Show Place of the Nation)
Paradise Valley
W. TROPICANA AVE.
TROPICANA AV.
W. RUSSELL RD.
W. SUNSET ROAD
WARM SPRINGS ROAD
TO LOS ANGELES
Punk!

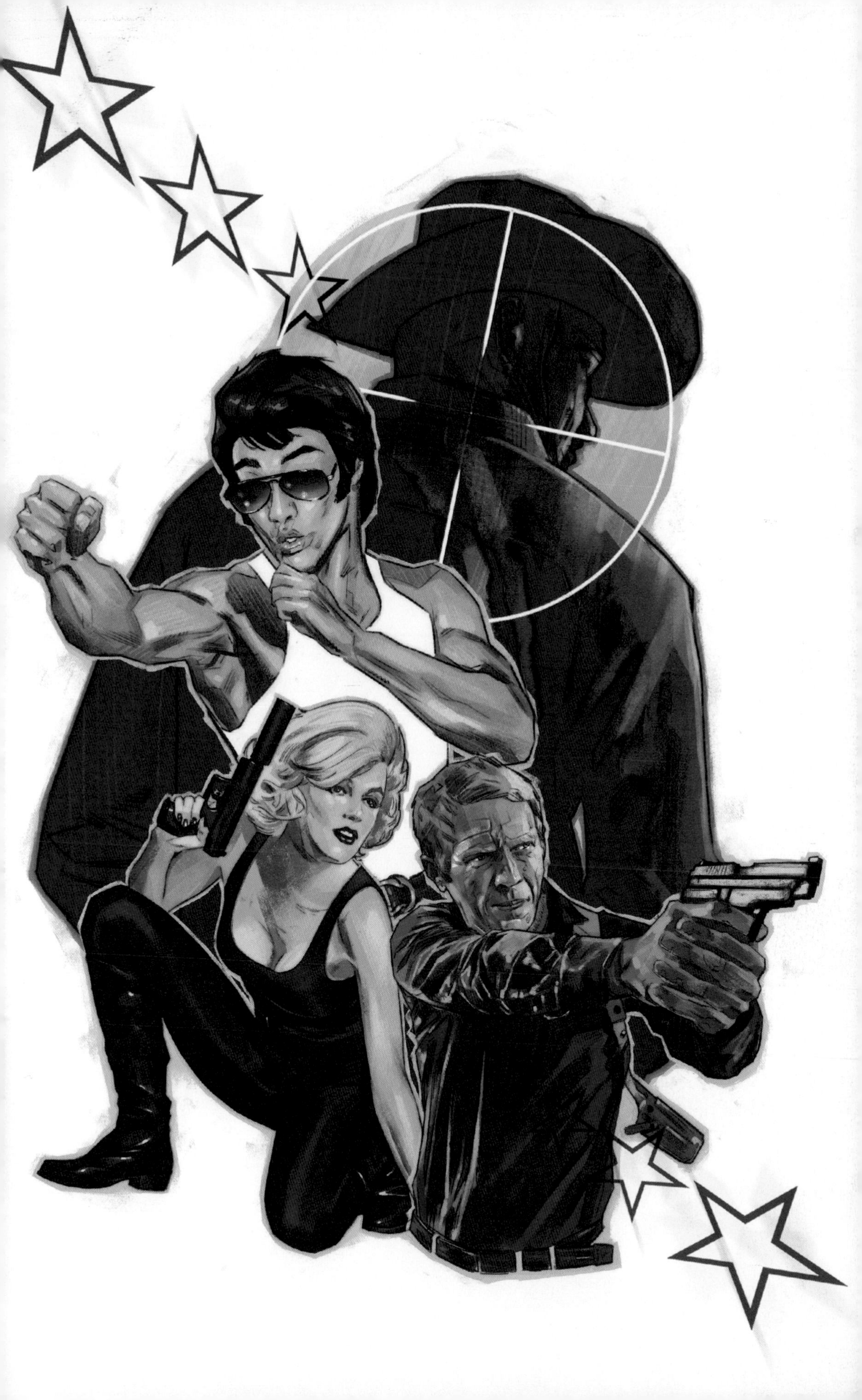

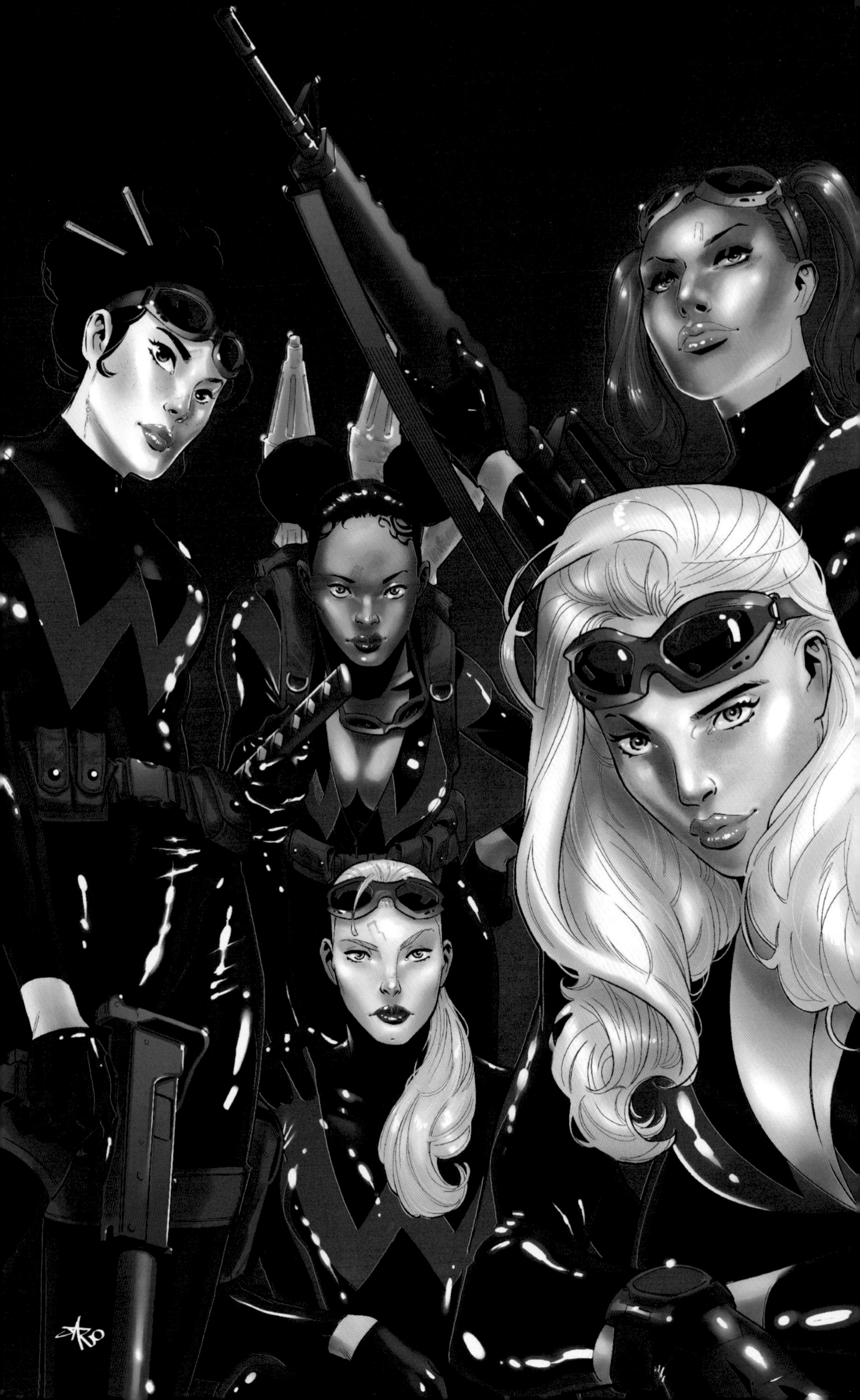

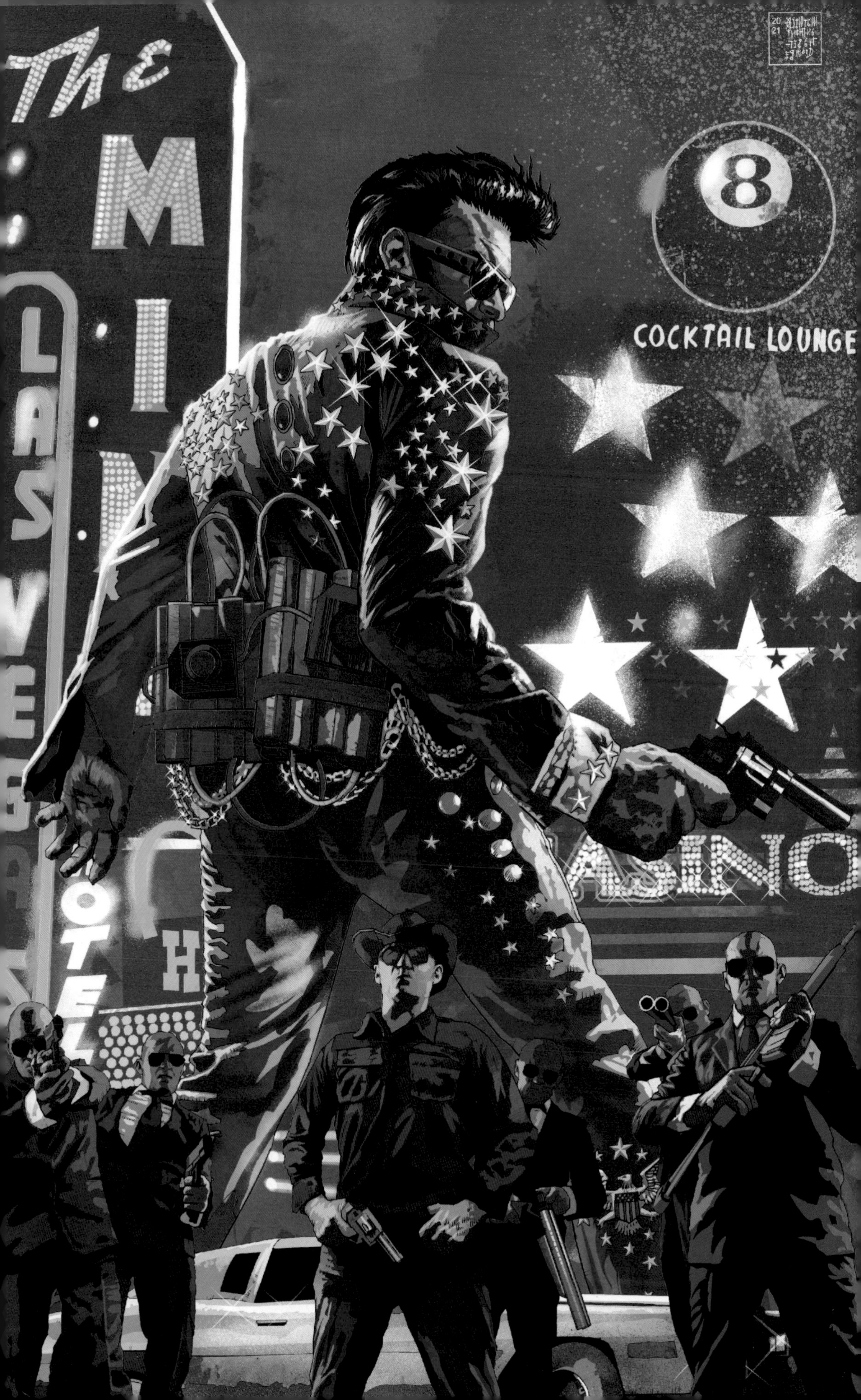
THE
8
COCKTAIL LOUNGE

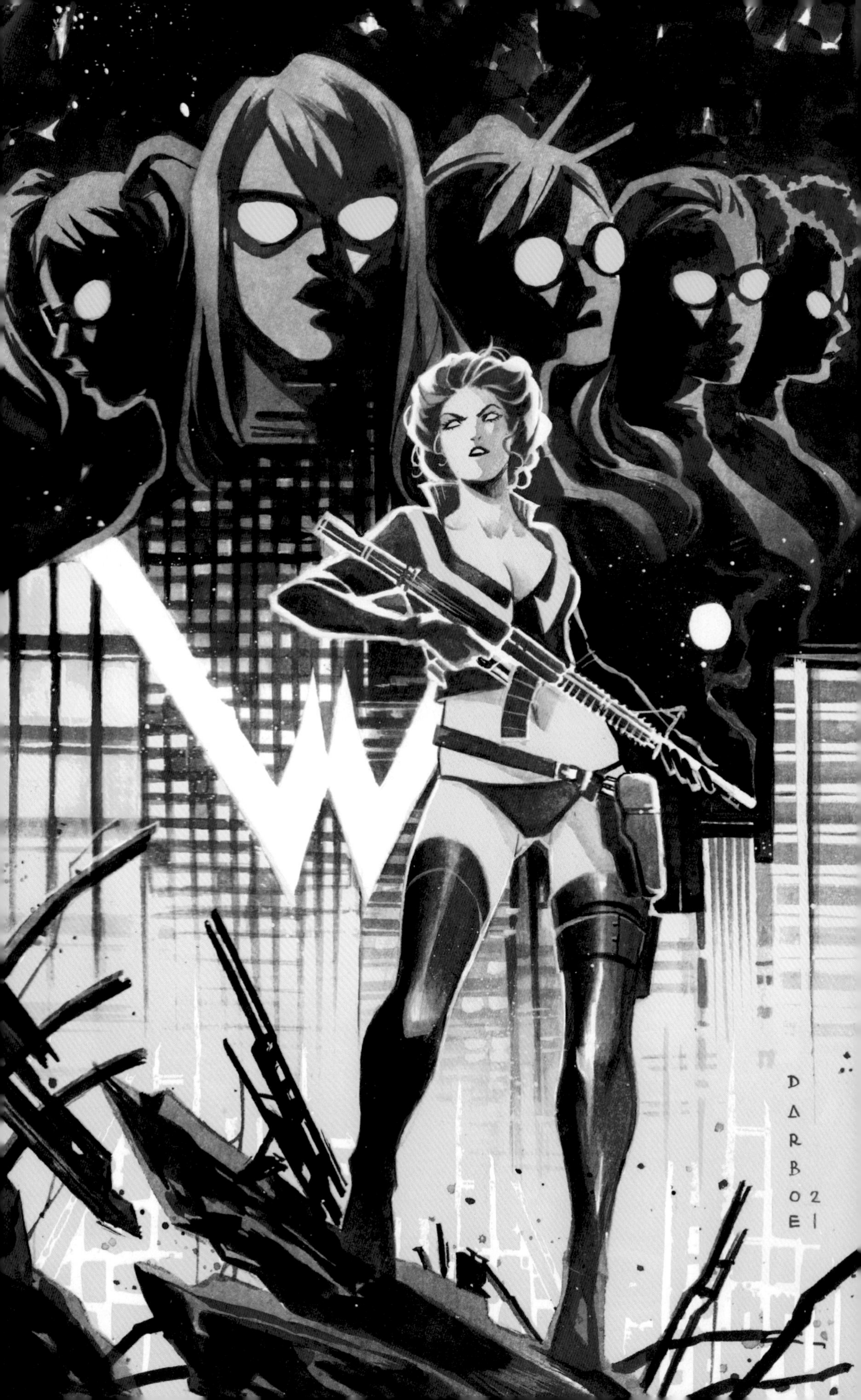
DARBOE 21

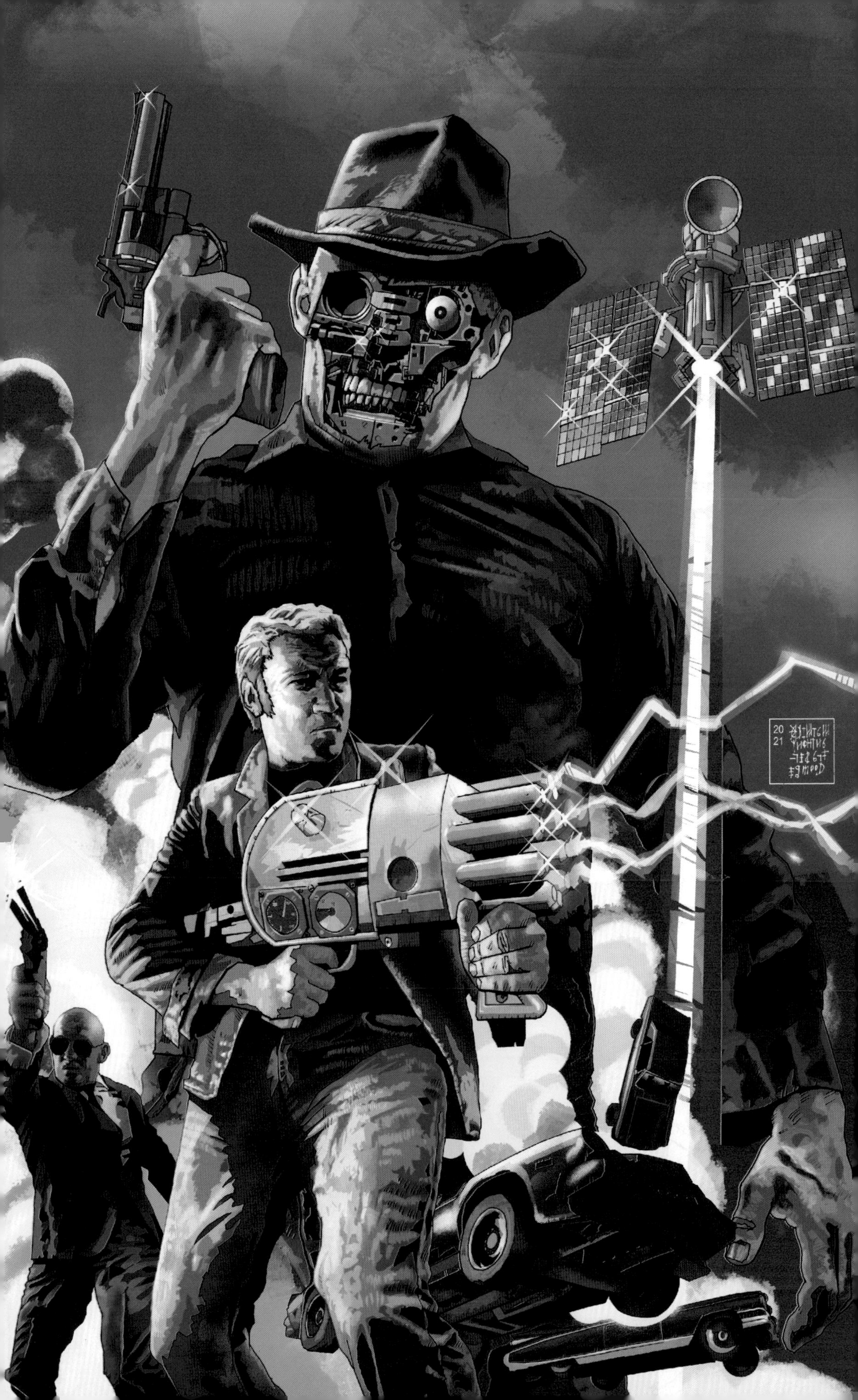

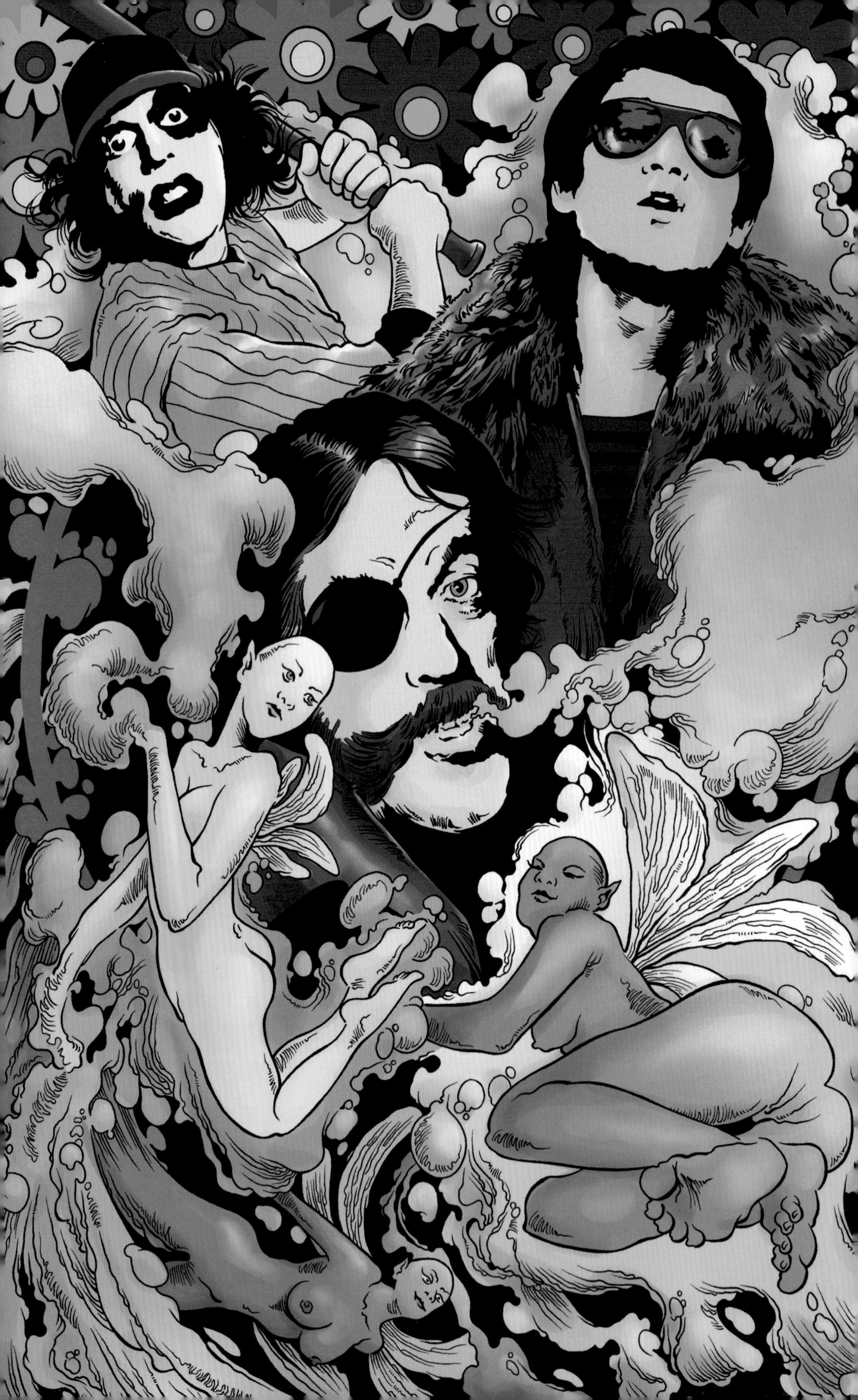